A LOVE OF READING

THE SECOND COLLECTION

A LOVE OF READING

THE SECOND COLLECTION

More Reviews of Contemporary Fiction

ROBERT ADAMS

M&S

National Library of Canada Cataloguing in Publication

Adams, Robert, 1937-
A love of reading, the second collection : more reviews of
contemporary fiction / Robert Adams.

ISBN 0-7710-0662-4

1. English fiction – 20th century – Book reviews. I. Title.

PR881.A322 2003   823'.91409   C2002-905817-1

Published simultaneously in the United States of America by
McClelland & Stewart Ltd., P.O. Box 1030, Plattsburgh, New York 12901

Library of Congress Control Number: 2002116596

Pages 259 and 260 represent a continuation of this copyright page.

We acknowledge the financial support of the Government of Canada
through the Book Publishing Industry Development Program and that of
the Government of Ontario through the Ontario Media Development
Corporation's Ontario Book Initiative. We further acknowledge the support
of the Canada Council for the Arts and the Ontario Arts Council for
our publishing program.

Typeset in Times by M&S, Toronto
Printed and bound in Canada

McClelland & Stewart Ltd.
The Canadian Publishers
481 University Avenue
Toronto, Ontario
M5G 2E9
www.mcclelland.com

1 2 3 4 5   07 06 05 04 03

For Pearl Brownstein Adams

CONTENTS

PREFACE

I was very gratified by the reception accorded to the first collection of my lectures, *A Love of Reading*, but I was given pause for thought by one critic's generous comment that I had "single-handedly defeated the *criteri*, literature's bloodless high priests."

I am as susceptible as the next person to a compliment, perhaps even more so, but I would not have it thought that anything I say on stage or in print is an attack on academics in general. I have taught with and been taught by too many fine teachers to make any such criticism. I have enormous respect for education, which I understand to be at its very heart the process of listening to someone who has spent a lifetime reading and reflecting. Education teaches us how to spell experience.

I am disturbed only when someone suggests there is some mysterious cabalistic body of knowledge that one must master in order to read intelligently and that the secret workings of literature are known only to a priestly caste. It is simply not true.

Everyone can find joy in reading, whatever his or her preparation. It is clear, nevertheless, that the more one reads, the more sophisticated is the joy as one becomes better able to evaluate the skill of the author. If we know how another writer handled the same theme, then it is perfectly reasonable to compare our different levels of satisfaction with the various works. There is undoubtedly an expertise that one can build up over time, and each of us can begin to systematize the criteria by which we judge the craftsmanship demonstrated in what we read. It is also not criminal to borrow from the thought-out opinions of other readers. It is not always necessary to reinvent the wheel. I have never made a secret of my debt to Northrop Frye's *Anatomy of Criticism*. But, while one gains more and more in reading experience, it is vital never to forget that it should be a joyful activity. My own memory of my best teachers is that they clearly loved what they taught and wanted so much to communicate that love.

My best advice to readers (and it is a counsel I give more often than it is asked for) is to read with passion. Give yourself to the book and, as Kafka said, let it free the frozen sea within you. I am thankful that I learned early that it is not unmanly to react to what I read with laughter or with tears.

An older colleague gave me very good direction when I began to teach. He said, "You may be teaching a short story for the hundredth time, but never forget that it is the first time for the students to whom you are speaking. Never forget what that story meant to you the first time you read it. Explain to them why you feel about the work the way you do, and lead them to where they can arrive at their own understanding."

It was an admonition that remained with me for decades in the classroom and lecture hall, and I hear his voice even now when I stand on stage.

All well-written narratives are of interest to me. I love the optimism about the greatness of the human spirit that is inherent in tragedy, and I laugh at the pratfalls of the hapless protagonist in comedy, but, as my perceptive editor has noted, I am drawn most to satire, the record of imperfect human beings making compromises with the fallen world around them. It is the description of our fumblings to survive that most often makes me laugh or cry, and I am content that so many people have laughed and cried with me. They, too, have found resonances in their own lives and marvelled, as I do, at the variety and wonder of our shared humanity.

I am grateful as always to those family members and friends who make it possible and enjoyable for me to give my lecture series. I must also express my appreciation of the dedicated professionalism of my copy editor, Karen Alliston, and my editor at McClelland & Stewart, Alex Schultz, whose gentle persuasiveness as he urges me to work is so compelling that my natural laziness is powerless against him.

Above all, I am keenly aware of what I owe to my beloved wife, Pearl, my manager and partner and editor of first instance, who turned my life around, so much for the better, all those years ago.

Note: All page references in the reviews are to the paperback edition indicated under the title.

ALIAS GRACE

Margaret Atwood
(Toronto: McClelland & Stewart, 1997)

Margaret Atwood's *Alias Grace* is a masterpiece of characterization, with a protagonist so multi-layered as to defy any attempt to pin her down by definition. Character and plot are bound together so artfully in the novel that each movement of the narrative compels its readers to re-examine what we thought we knew about the astonishing Grace Marks. *Alias Grace* is a tour de force in what has been a distinguished career that has included forty-four works of poetry, short stories, plays, and novels.

Born in Ottawa, Margaret Atwood travelled all over Canada and Europe with her mother and scientist father before studying literature at the University of Toronto and at Harvard. In 1966 she won the Governor General's Award for poetry and in 1969 produced her first novel, *The Edible Woman*, an examination of the pain women experience having to live in a male-dominated world. The book was hailed by leaders of the burgeoning women's movement as the great feminist novel, and its theme was one Atwood would explore throughout her work until her sixth novel in 1985, *The Handmaid's Tale*, a dystopian narrative in the tradition of George Orwell's *1984*, set in a future world where a theocratic government has assigned women a subservient role, often as surrogate breeders. The novel won the Governor General's Award for fiction and confirmed Atwood as an icon of the feminist movement, although the Right attacked the work as an extremist's nightmare.

1

In her seventh novel, *Cat's Eye*, her last but one before *Alias Grace*, Atwood shifted her ground. *Cat's Eye* is a cold, hard look at how cruel children can be to each other, particularly girl children, and one passage in particular confounded not her right-wing critics but her many feminist admirers. I am referring to the passage on pages 400–401 of my paperback edition (Toronto: McClelland-Bantam, 1989). Atwood's protagonist, Elaine Risley, trying to create a new life as a single mother while confronting the ghosts of her childhood, is attending a women's meeting:

> A number of these women are lesbians, newly declared or changing over. This is at the same time courageous and demanded. According to some, it's the only equal relationship possible for women. You are not genuine otherwise.
>
> I am ashamed of my own reluctance, my lack of desire; but the truth is that I would be terrified to get into bed with a woman. Women collect grievances, hold grudges and change shape. They pass hard, legitimate judgments, unlike the purblind guesses of men, fogged with romanticism and ignorance and bias and wish. Women know too much, they can neither be deceived nor trusted. I can understand why men are afraid of them, as they are frequently accused of being.

It would be a mistake, I think, to describe *Cat's Eye* as anti-feminist or even post-feminist. By renouncing her beatification by the women's movement, Atwood was rejecting any attempt to label her as anything other than a writer. In the very many interviews she gave after the publication of the novel, Atwood claimed still to be adamant in the belief that women are treated unfairly and that they have an absolute right to control their own bodies. She made it clear, however, that her political attentions had been engaged by larger issues, in particular the importance of the environment and the dangers posed by pollution. She argued, persuasively, that if everyone were dead in a poisoned world, there would be little opportunity to discuss human rights or illiteracy or any other of life's horrible problems.

Alias Grace, Margaret Atwood's ninth novel, is set in nineteenth-century Ontario. A typical patriarchy, it is full of abusive male figures, but Atwood's interest is not in producing another polemic but in what I believe must be the novelist's purest purpose, the creation of a psychologically complex protagonist moving through a believable world. The reader's interest will be in the protagonist's journey and the outcome: defiance of the world will result in Tragedy, compromises will spell out Satire.

Alias Grace won Canada's Giller Prize in 1996, and it should have won the British Booker Prize. In a close contest, the coveted award went to Graham Swift's *Last Orders*. It was not until weeks after the decision that an Australian professor pointed out that Swift's novel was in fact a reworking of William Faulkner's *As I Lay Dying* (1931). Coincidence is impossible: the theme, structure, and even some chapter headings are identical. Swift defended his novel as an act of homage to Faulkner, but one of the Booker judges, the critic and notorious gossip A.N. Wilson, went on record as saying that, if the judges had known how derivative *Last Orders* was, *Alias Grace* would have won.

In an afterword to the novel, Atwood points out that it is based on a real historical incident. The facts are listed. On July 23, 1843, a wealthy Ontario landowner, Thomas Kinnear, was shot to death on his farm at Richmond Hill. A few hours earlier, his pregnant mistress and housekeeper, Nancy Montgomery, had been attacked with an axe and then strangled. Kinnear's stable boy, James McDermott, and Kinnear's maid, Grace Marks, travelling under the alias of Mary Whitney, flee the scene, cross into the United States, and are arrested in Maine. Brought back to Toronto for trial, each of them accuses the other of masterminding the crime and each of them changes his or her version of events several times.

What did not change were their allegations against each other. James McDermott contended that, although only sixteen, Grace Marks was a force of diabolical evil, luring him to murder with the promise of sexual favours. Grace Marks's position, articulated through her lawyer Kenneth MacKenzie, was that she was only sixteen, feeble-witted and possibly mad, and completely under the domination of the twenty-one-year-old.

Both were sentenced to death, but only McDermott went to the gallows, protesting to the end that Grace Marks was the prime mover. Grace's sentence was commuted to life imprisonment, her lawyer pleading the general weakness of her sex in addition to her youth and lack of wit.

Because both Grace and the victim Nancy Montgomery were pretty, the case received a lot of press coverage, and, because it made for more exciting reading, the newspapers took the view that Grace was a sexual temptress and was at least equally responsible for the murders.

Except for an eighteen-month period at the Toronto Lunatic Asylum in 1852-53, Grace served her sentence at Kingston Penitentiary, where she was quite the tourist attraction. Visitors could come and go and Grace would be trotted out for their inspection.

One of the visitors was Susanna Moodie, an English immigrant who wrote about Grace Marks as part of a larger book on Canada, *Life in the Clearings* (1853). Moodie visited her twice, once at the asylum and once at the prison. Influenced by the newspaper reports, she saw what she expected to see and wrote accordingly of a woman of "cunning and cruel expression" and "furtive regard" who was tormented by images of the bloodshot eyes of her victims.

In 1872, after serving twenty-eight years and ten months of her sentence, Grace Marks was freed as a result of petitions by well-wishers, taken to the U.S. border, and released. She was nearly forty-five years old and nothing more was heard of her.

When Margaret Atwood read Susanna Moodie's book decades ago, she accepted Moodie's description of Grace Marks without question. Atwood even wrote a play about the evil servant girl for CBC Radio in 1974. But, over the years, as she reflected on the inaccuracy of most newspaper reporting, she realized that both Grace Marks and the crime must have been more complex than the reports indicated.

Margaret Atwood then became a detective. First, she researched attitudes to women, crime, and class in nineteenth-century Ontario. Then she researched nineteenth-century attitudes to mental illness and its treatment and, finally, the lives of the people involved in the case. She discovered very little about them that she didn't already know. There were really only two new items of information. Thomas Kinnear had come from a wealthy Scottish family, and Grace Marks had been spoken to by the chief doctor at the Toronto Lunatic Asylum, Joseph Workman, who concluded that she was both sane and guilty.

With only this bare framework to begin with, Atwood created a whole nineteenth-century world for her novel, a world of poverty, of immigrant ships, of complicated master-servant relationships, and of an emerging interest in the workings of the human mind. She also had to create a believable, if unknowable, Grace Marks with all the layers and layers and layers that make up the composition of just one human personality.

Atwood had to invent a whole history for Grace before the murders, including the characters of Jeremiah the Peddler and the physician Simon Jordan. Invented, too, therefore, are Simon Jordan's tangled personal relationships and his interaction with Grace Marks at the penitentiary, an interaction that is at the very core of the novel.

And – a disappointment, I know, to many readers – Margaret Atwood invented the whole happy ending, everything that took place after Grace's release in 1872.

The historical Grace Marks was no more than the spark that ignited Atwood's imagination. This novel is not about the real Grace Marks any more than Shakespeare's *Macbeth* is about the Scottish king of the same name. The Grace Marks of the novel exists only in the novel and in the mind of the reader.

The first pages of the book are a patchwork, a kind of literary quilt. There are snippets of poetry, newspaper clippings, lists of prison rules, even haiku. Some, like the prison rules, illustrate the accepted brutality of nineteenth-century life: six lashes with the cat-o'-nine-tails for a convict who laughs or speaks without permission.

Some of the poetry contains the sentimentality of the Victorian period, like Emily Brontë's incredibly idealized portrait of a female prisoner:

The captive raised her face; it was as soft and mild
As sculptured marble saint; or slumbering unweaned child.

Many of the chapters of the novel will begin with fragments of Victorian poetry, chosen to show how the brutality of the period could coexist with the most extreme sentimentality. The Victorians, British or Canadian, could weep over the fate of a child in Dickens but accept that children could be worked to death in chimneys, mines, and factories.

Atwood also uses her quilt of illustrative quotation to remind us of the endless nineteenth-century debate as to whether women were saintly or demonic by nature. In the novel, Grace Marks herself refers to how those competing views applied to her:

I think of all the things that have been written about me – that I am an inhuman female demon, that I am an innocent victim of a blackguard forced against my will . . . that I was too ignorant to know how to act . . . that I am a good girl with a pliable nature . . . that I am cunning and devious, that I am soft in the head and little better than an idiot. And I wonder, how can I be all of these different things at once?

It was my own lawyer, Mr. Kenneth MacKenzie, Esq., who told them I was next door to an idiot. I was angry with him over that, but he said it was by far my best chance and I should not appear to be too intelligent. (pp. 23–24)

When we first meet Grace at the beginning of the novel, the year is 1851 and she has spent eight years in prison. Much of the novel, though not all, will be delivered in her own voice. In her quiet understatement we hear the unbearable strain under which she must be living.

I am a model prisoner, and give no trouble. . . . If I am good enough and quiet enough, perhaps after all they will let me go; but it's not easy being quiet and good, it's like hanging on to the edge of a bridge when you've already fallen over. (p. 5)

It had to have been hell to have been a woman in prison in the 1850s, especially a young, pretty woman. Grace is frequently escorted from place to place between two male warders, each of whom pinches her and fondles her and whispers obscenities to her. Grace has no redress: there is no one to help her. When a doctor at the asylum takes her heartbeat over and over again and puts his hand under her clothes, she complains to the chaplain, whose response is:

And then what did he do? Oh shocking. And then what?
The left hand or the right?
How far up, exactly?
Show me where. (p. 38)

To the extent that Grace Marks suffers under a misogynous patriarchy, *Alias Grace* resembles Margaret Atwood's earlier novels, but Grace Marks is much more than just a symbol of the female as victim.

As one of her strategies for survival and the preservation of her sanity, Grace has invented an alter ego, Mary Whitney. When Grace is abused by the warders, the doctor, or the chaplain, she will make little outward protest – nothing must blemish the mask of model prisoner – but in her mind her other self fights back: "Take your hand off my tit, you filthy bastard, [as] Mary Whitney would have said." (p. 37)

Later, Grace will tell the sympathetic physician Simon Jordan that Mary Whitney was a real person, a maid Grace knew when she entered domestic service at twelve. As related by Grace, Mary's story was a common one, that of a pretty servant who is made pregnant by the son of the house and who dies of a botched abortion. So perfect an example of an abused servant is Mary Whitney that even the gullible Simon Jordan begins to suspect that she never existed. It doesn't really matter: by the time we meet Grace, Mary Whitney, real or imagined, is a part of Grace's internal world and one of the means by which Grace survives.

Simon Jordan is a young American physician, a precursor of Freud, profoundly interested in the workings of the human mind. He gets permission for a series of interviews with Grace Marks in the parlour of the prison governor's wife, a woman Grace serves as a maid.

Doctor Jordan soon realizes that, for all his education and Grace's lack of it, he can never trap her into either a claim of innocence or a clear admission of guilt. There is the most remarkable wordplay between them, and Grace is never the loser.

> "You don't care about my good opinion of you, Grace?"
>
> She gave him a quick sharp look, then continued her stitching. "I have already been judged, Sir. Whatever you may think of me, it's all the same."
>
> "Judged rightly, Grace?" He could not resist asking.
>
> "Rightly or wrongly does not matter," she said. "People want a guilty person. If there has been a crime, they want to know who did it. They don't like not knowing."
>
> "Then you have given up hope?"
>
> "Hope of what, Sir?" she asked mildly.
>
> Simon felt foolish, as if he'd committed a breach of etiquette. "Well – hope of being set free."

"Now why would they want to do that, Sir?" she said. "A murderess is not an everyday thing. As for my hopes, I save that for smaller
matters. I live in hopes of having a better breakfast tomorrow than I
had today." (p. 104)

Rather than deny or confess her guilt, Grace prefers to tell the young
doctor of her early years. The conversations are a pleasant break in the
monotony of prison life, and Simon Jordan has promised that, as long as
Grace will speak to him, there will be no chance of her being sent again to
the asylum. (p. 46)

Grace's version is that she was born in Ireland in the 1830s, one of nine
children of a drunken stonemason and his abused wife, who decide on a
new life in the New World and take ship from Belfast to Canada.

The eight-week voyage is a masterpiece of description. The details are
horrifying and fascinating. The only food was that which the passengers
brought on board. Seasickness was constant, and the buckets of vomit and
human waste were easily spilled. Disease was rampant and Grace's mother
was only one of many who succumbed.

Grace tells the story in a quiet, well-modulated voice – she has used her
first sixteen years in prison to improve her speech – and the evenness of
the tone makes the horror even more unbearable. For the reader who can
stomach them, the most affecting of the details are contained in the four-
teenth chapter. The doctor's reaction is such that Grace comes out with,
"Perhaps you would like to open the window." (p. 134) It is a brilliant sentence. Not only could I see a pale-faced, near-retching Simon Jordan in my
mind's eye, but I realized just how completely Grace Marks was in control
of the conversation. I also thought back to something Vladimir Nabokov
once said about novels: "Caress the details. . . . Style and structure are the
essence of a book; great ideas are hogwash" (*Lectures on Literature*, 1980).
This is a novel of superbly observed and recorded detail. The underlying
criticism of patriarchy is still present, but there is none of the rather obtru-
sive didacticism of Atwood's early feminist works.

Dr. Simon Jordan is no fool. He has travelled, seen prostitution in Paris
and London, even seen children sold by their mothers "to wealthy men who
hope that by raping children they will avoid disease." (p. 100) But he has
not seen what Grace has seen or lived what she has lived. She describes her
life in Toronto with her father. She was at the time not yet twelve.

The older I became, the less I was able to please him, and I myself had lost all of a child's natural faith in a parent. . . . Also his rages had returned, stronger than before my mother died. Already my arms were black and blue, and then one night he threw me against the wall, as he'd sometimes done with my mother, shouting that I was a slut and a whore, and I fainted; and after that I feared that he might someday break my spine, and make a cripple out of me. (p. 148)

At twelve, Grace escapes her father to become a laundry maid in the home of Mrs. Alderman Parkinson. (I loved the "Mrs. Alderman"; it evokes a whole social system in which women derive their social status from their fathers or their husbands.) Atwood records all the harrowing details of servants freezing in attic bedrooms as well as noting the ever-present dangers of employer abuse and a resulting pregnancy.

After the death of Mary Whitney, if indeed she ever existed other than as Grace's alter ego, Grace leaves Mrs. Alderman Parkinson and goes to work for Mr. Dixon, then Mr. McManus, then Mr. Coates, then Mr. Haraghy, and then Mr. Watson. She had six different employers in three years.

Dr. Jordan makes no comment at this point, but the list troubled me. I found it particularly strange that Grace refers to her first employer as Mrs. Alderman Parkinson but mentions only the husbands of the next five married couples she serves. I also did not understand why she had changed jobs so often and how she had found new jobs so easily. Domestic work was not so easy to come by in the 1840s, and Irish girls were plentiful in Toronto. I began to suspect that much more went on in the life of Grace Marks between the ages of twelve and fifteen than she is prepared to tell Simon Jordan.

When Grace is nearly sixteen, the cook at the Watson household is visited by an old friend, the handsome and good-natured Nancy Montgomery, housekeeper for a Mr. Kinnear on a farm in Richmond Hill, sixteen miles up Yonge Street. He needs another servant, and Grace is tempted by the offer of full board and the princely salary of three dollars a month. As Grace considers her misgivings about leaving Toronto, Atwood slips in a lovely description of the great Canadian city in 1843.

I was now used to Toronto life – there was so much to see while walking out on errands, and sometimes there were shows and fairs, although you had to watch for thieves there; and outdoor preachers, and always a boy or a woman singing on the street for pennies. I'd seen a man eat fire, and another that could throw his voice, and a pig that could count, and a dancing bear with a muzzle on. (p. 235)

A pig that could count! Toronto sounds just as exciting then as it is now.

Grace's journey up Yonge Street, a major undertaking at the time, is full of the same kind of well-observed detail of the life of the period. Then she arrives at the fateful farmhouse. It is at this point that Jordan asks her what she understood her duties were going to be, and Grace is taken aback by the question.

He is not making a joke. He really does not know. Men such as him do not have to clean up the messes they make, but we have to clean up our own messes, and theirs into the bargain. In that way they are like children, they do not have to think ahead, or worry about the consequences of what they do. But it is not their fault, it is only how they are brought up. (p. 251)

That is not the response of a feeble-witted person or of an innocent child; rather it is the response of a woman who has learned through bitter experience how to survive.

Grace tells Jordan how she was shown the workings of the household, and Atwood, the scientist's daughter, again provides some superbly chosen detail. I felt as if I had joined Grace and the housekeeper on a tour of the Kinnear home.

Grace continues with a description of the other two members of the staff. Jamie Walsh, the son of Kinnear's estate manager, is the errand boy. Only months younger than Grace, he is years behind her in life experience and soon falls deeply in puppy love with the new maid.

James McDermott, the stable boy, has been with Mr. Kinnear for only a week and is already resentful of Nancy the housekeeper's bossy ways.

It was when Grace is describing to Dr. Jordan the relationship between Mr. Kinnear and Nancy his housekeeper that I became certain that I could not trust Grace's version of events. Grace claims to remember wondering why Nancy's chamber was on the same floor as her employer's and how Nancy could afford such fine gold earrings, but the most striking example of what can only be a pretended naïveté is when she tells of washing one of Nancy's petticoats, soiled after a walk in the country with Mr. Kinnear: "'There were . . . grass stains on a petticoat of Nancy's – I wondered how she had got them, but she had most likely slipped and fallen down.'" (p. 264)

It must therefore be with some reservations that we receive Grace's account of the events of July 23, 1843. According to her, McDermott attacked Nancy Montgomery with an axe and then strangled her out of rage at being given his notice for laziness. In McDermott's testimony at the trial, testimony that Simon Jordan has read, it was Grace, jealous of Nancy, who had proposed murder and robbery, although McDermott admitted that he had lent a ready ear to her discontented pinings. He claimed also that Grace had participated in the strangling.

When Kinnear came home, after Nancy had been killed, he was shot by McDermott. Grace, however, insisted that McDermott also shot at her, whereupon Grace fainted and lay unconscious for a significant part of the day. Of the earlier events, she tells Jordan, she has only the most confused memory.

I found that her confusion – she gave different versions of the story at the inquest, at the trial, and again later – is in sharp contrast to the precise details she provides of every other day of her life. Grace is intelligent, observant, and blessed with an almost photographic memory. As she speaks to Simon Jordan, we are privy to her thoughts, to her own awareness that she was not completely frank even with her lawyer:

> What should I tell Dr. Jordan about this day? Because now we are almost there. I can remember what I said when arrested, and what Mr. MacKenzie the lawyer said I should say, and what I did not say even to him; and what I said at the trial, and what I said afterwards, which was different as well. And what McDermott said I said, and what the others said I must have said. (p. 351)

One fact beyond dispute is that, after the murders, McDermott and Grace flee with all the valuables of the household across the border to the United States. They travel as brother and sister with Grace decked out in Nancy's finery.

In all of Grace's versions of events, there are three constants: McDermott had frightened her into acquiescing; she feared she would be blamed for the murders if she stayed at the house; and she had tried to warn Nancy, who had scoffed at the possibility.

One detail of McDermott and Grace's flight seems to me to support McDermott's claim that he acted in concert with Grace, who had promised him sexual favours. Grace must have been in control as they fled; otherwise surely they would have travelled as husband and wife and slept together openly. If McDermott had dominated Grace as she said he had, he would certainly have availed himself of her favours as soon as possible.

Some of the most telling testimony against Grace at her trial was the evidence offered by the young errand boy Jamie Walsh. He testified that, when he came to the house in the evening, Grace was in good spirits, far from faint, and wearing a pair of Nancy's stockings. In Grace's own words to Jordan,

> "I remember none of this, Sir, but Jamie Walsh gave his testimony in a straightforward manner which it was difficult to doubt.
>
> "But then his emotions overcame him, and he pointed at me, and said, 'She has got on Nancy's dress, the ribbons under her bonnet are also Nancy's, and the tippet she has on, and also the parasol in her hand.'" (p. 433)

Such evidence notwithstanding, a number of influential people took Grace's part, believing her to be mentally defective or under McDermott's control or both. Among them is the wife of the prison governor in whose parlour, sixteen years after the murders, Grace and Dr. Jordan are having their conversations. As the perceptive Grace notes, "[T]he Governor's wife likes to know people who are writing books, books with forward-looking aims, it shows that she is a liberal-minded person with advanced views, and science is making such progress." (p. 29)

Victorian England was in the grip of a crisis of faith. New scientific and pseudo-scientific theories were challenging the certainties of established religion. The governor's wife was only one of many groping for a new truth as they toyed with mesmerism, spiritualism, neurohypnosis, table tapping, head measuring, and the like. The governor's wife exposed Grace to more than one practitioner of the new creeds, and, in Dr. Simon Jordan, she is giving a chance to those who seek to understand the workings of the human mind, would-be psychiatrists attending the infancy of the science.

Simon Jordan, in spite of his best efforts to maintain scientific objectivity, is more than half in love with Grace. As part of his research, he goes to interview Dr. Bannerling, the physician who had seen Grace both at the asylum and at the prison. Jordan is incensed when Bannerling, whom Jordan calls "a conceited little troll," tells him that Grace had found the prison doctor overwhelmingly attractive: "'She was besotted with me, and didn't wish to let me out of her sight.'" (p. 453) Jordan prefers to believe that it is he who has won Grace's heart. He is delighted to receive confirmation from Grace's lawyer, MacKenzie, that "'The poor creature has fallen in love with you.'" (p. 453)

Women in the patriarchal society of the nineteenth century had to learn very early how to manipulate men in order to survive. It does not surprise me that Grace could cause two doctors, each of them in a position to bring about her freedom, to believe that they were the object of her affections.

Simon Jordan even fantasizes about marrying Grace. He examines as scientifically as he can the advantages to himself of such a union. "[S]he has beauty without frivolity, domesticity without dullness, and simplicity of manner, and prudence, and circumspection. . . . And she'd be grateful to him." (pp. 466–67)

What fools men be!

But for all his attempts at objective analysis, it is the thrill of her possible guilt that draws him to her. "*Murderess, murderess*, he whispers to himself. It has an allure, a scent almost. Hothouse gardenias. Lurid, but also furtive. He imagines himself breathing it as he draws Grace towards him, pressing his mouth against her. *Murderess*. He applies it to her throat like a brand." (p. 467) He dismisses the thought immediately as a "madness . . . a perverse fantasy," but the temptation lingers.

Nothing will come of the imagined romance and Grace will not find freedom through the young American. Even while he is falling under Grace's spell, Simon Jordan is seduced by his landlady, Mrs. Humphrey, the disturbed wife of a drunken absentee husband, who even proposes the murder of her spouse so that she might be free to marry Simon.

Panic-stricken, Simon Jordan abandons both the terrible Mrs. Humphrey and his research into the mind of Grace Marks to run to the safe harbour of Massachusetts and his mother.

Mrs. Jordan is a delightful comic creation, easily on a par with Philip Roth's Mrs. Portnoy. For a long time she has been pestering her son by letter to marry a local girl, a certain Miss Cartwright, and, when she finally gets her beloved boy back home, she has no intention of giving him up to a predatory landlady. After receiving innumerable missives from a relentless Mrs. Humphrey, Simon's mother finally writes to inform her that Simon has been wounded in the American Civil War and is being cared for by his new fiancée. She advises Mrs. Humphrey to take up sewing and Bible reading and offers the most glorious parting shot. Her son, she says, could never consider taking up with a woman capable of adultery!

I was struck, as I read, by how many parallels there are between Simon Jordan and Grace Marks. Each of them entered a dangerous, sexually charged situation, and each of them heard murder suggested. For the man, there was a way out; for the poor servant girl, there wasn't.

After the hurried departure of Dr. Jordan, Grace has to spend thirteen more years in prison before her supporters win her release. Almost twenty-nine years after she began her incarceration, Grace is driven by the prison governor and his daughter to the U.S. border, where James Walsh is waiting for her, the same James Walsh who had loved her from afar thirty years earlier on the farm of Thomas Kinnear.

Now a successful American farmer, Walsh has been in touch for some time with the prison authorities and has offered Grace a home with him. He begs Grace's forgiveness for his dramatic testimony at the trial, a forgiveness she accords readily.

No one in Walsh's circle knows of her past. She and James marry and, at the end of the novel, she is forty-five and pregnant. Grace knows why she is so attractive to her husband: "As for Mr. Walsh, after I have told him a few stories of torment and misery he clasps me in his arms and strokes my hair, and begins to unbutton my nightgown, as these scenes often take place at night." (p. 548) It is not only the thought of the abuse that she suffered that excites him; it is the possibility that she might be a murderess, and we remember Dr. Simon Jordan. Grace understands the excitement very well – she understands so much about people very well – it is our fascination with evil and with death. Grace referred to it when she spoke of her prison visitors: " 'The reason they want to see me is that I am a celebrated murderess.' " (p. 23)

As we leave Grace, she is making a quilt, one of the many she has made throughout the novel.

It is a Tree of Paradise; but I am changing the pattern a little to suit my own ideas . . . and I think it will turn out very pretty.

But three of the triangles in my Tree will be different. One will be white, from the petticoat I still have that was Mary Whitney's; one will be faded yellowish, from the prison nightdress I begged as a keepsake when I left there. And the third will be a pale cotton, a pink and white floral, cut from the dress of Nancy's that she had on the first day I was at Mr. Kinnear's, and that I wore on the ferry to Lewiston, when I was running away.

I will embroider around each one of them with red feather-stitching, to blend them in as a part of the pattern.

And so we will all be together. (pp. 551–52)

Thus does Grace Marks draw all the strands of her life together in the quilt under which she will lie with James Walsh. It is tempting, in view of nineteenth-century misogyny, to see the novel as the story of a victim who suffers, who survives, and who finally finds dignity and happiness, but Margaret Atwood has placed too many doubts in our mind. However titillating the pillow talk, if I were James Walsh, I would not lie easily beside Grace Marks.

Grace has drawn together in her quilt some of the chief elements of her life, but I for one am full of unanswered questions. What, for example, am I to make of Jeremiah the Peddler, the handsome stranger who comes in and out of Grace's life both inside and outside the prison? I know that at one level he functions as a *picaro*, the traditional literary figure who visits every level of society during a narrative and thus affords the reader an overview of the society as a whole; Jeremiah is equally at home in servants' kitchens, prison parlours, Toronto theatres, and fashionable drawing rooms. But he is more than just a picaresque character.

We meet him first when he visits the kitchen of Mrs. Alderman Parkinson to sell buttons. He presents the twelve-year-old Grace with a free button and tells her, " 'You're one of us.' " He reappears to chase away a nuisance as Grace travels to the Kinnear farm at Richmond Hill. He comes peddling to the farm just before the murders and tells Grace to leave with him and become a medium. Since he doesn't offer marriage, Grace declines. Sixteen years later, he turns up at the prison as Dr. Jerome du Pont, neurohypnotist, and conducts a séance with Grace, Simon, the governor's wife, and her friends, which is very much to Grace's advantage. He conjures up an evil spirit that professes to have inhabited Grace's body at the time of the murders. Grace, the spirit alleges, was innocent and knew nothing.

As Signor Geraldo Ponti, hypnotist, Jeremiah sends Grace another button, which she takes to be a coded message to button her lip and remain silent. Finally, after her marriage to James Walsh, Grace sees Jeremiah in the street. He is now the celebrated medium Gerald Bridges. They acknowledge each other discreetly and Grace reflects, "I know my secrets are safe with Jeremiah, as his are safe with me." (p. 547)

What does Jeremiah know of Grace that she has chosen not to tell us? After several rereadings of the novel I am no closer to any answer. An explanation of Jeremiah is one of the pieces Grace decided not to sew into the quilt of her narrative.

The quilt is the governing image of the novel, both physically in the quilts that Grace makes and in the sense of the pieces of information she selects from her story to tell Simon Jordan and to tell us, and our perception is so subjective. As Grace points out, one's impression of a quilt depends on whether we focus on the darker or the lighter patches.

There are other recurring images that bind the novel together. There are shirts and sheets that flutter like headless bodies and sometimes like angels. Again, it all depends on one's perspective. There are white flowers that become red, stained with blood. Like the quilts, the shirts, sheets, and flowers are all images drawn from the bedroom, the laundry, or the garden, the places in a household where a nineteenth-century maid would spend the greater part of her day.

It is much easier to examine the imagery of this magnificently challenging novel than it is to decide what is the real character of Grace Marks. She is standing in her cell in a beam of light when Simon Jordan first sees her,

> the timorous hunch of the shoulders; the arms hugged close to the thin body, the long wisps of auburn hair . . . and especially the eyes, enormous in the pale face and dilated with fear. . . . But then Grace stepped forward, out of the light, and the woman he'd seen the instant before was suddenly no longer there. Instead there was a different woman – straighter, taller, more self-possessed. (p. 66)

Which of the two is the real Grace? Or are there more layers to strip away?

We all travel under an alias, a protective facade to shield us from a hostile world. Who is the woman known as Grace? Is she the woman all men fall in love with: McDermott, James Walsh, the Reverend Verringer of the prison committee, Simon Jordan? Or is she the woman who, as a fellow convict Annie Little tells to her face, has " 'such a steady hand, you could murder your own grannie in her bed and never turn a hair' "? (p. 457) I do not know who Grace Marks is, but I know one thing – she scares the hell out of me. To survive all those years in prison, she had to exert iron self-control. Her strength faltered once and she spent eighteen months in the asylum, but, for more than a quarter of a century, she demonstrated an unbreakable will. I cannot know if she was like that when she entered prison or if she developed such self-possession to preserve her sanity and wholeness of self. Did she fashion herself out of steel all the way through or was there always a frightened child in the deepest recesses of her being?

It seems to me that Margaret Atwood agrees with the opinion of the real Dr. Joseph Workman of the Toronto Lunatic Asylum, that the human psyche cannot be dissected. However unsettling it may be for the reader, Atwood's literary creation, Grace Marks, must remain as impenetrable and unknowable as is each and every one of us.

THE HIDING PLACE

Trezza Azzopardi

(Toronto: Key Porter, 2000)

The Hiding Place by Trezza Azzopardi is set in South Wales, in the Welsh capital of Cardiff. Since all the major players in the novel are part of the Maltese expatriate community living in the dockland area of the Welsh seaport, I thought I might spend a few moments on the history of Malta, the Maltese people, and the Maltese language.

The country of Malta is very small, only just over a hundred square miles. It's made up of five islands, only three of which are inhabited. The largest is the island of Malta itself, only fifty-eight miles south of Sicily, about ninety minutes away by ferry. Sustained by tourism, shipping, and agriculture, the population is less than four hundred thousand, with most Maltese living in the capital city of Valletta. Situated as it is in the middle of the Mediterranean, Malta occupied a key position in the commerce of the Ancient and Medieval worlds. It was first settled by Phoenicians in about 1000 BC but was later conquered successively by Greeks, Carthaginians, Romans, Byzantines, Arabs, Normans, and Spaniards.

In 1530, Malta's golden era of architecture began. The island of Malta was given by King Charles V of Spain as a permanent home to the Knights of St. John of Jerusalem. The Knights of St. John were a group of Christian European nobles who had formed their order in 1113 to protect the then-Christian city of Jerusalem. They were driven out of Jerusalem seventy-four years later and wandered Europe for more than four centuries until the King of Spain's gift of Malta. Sworn to chastity, the defence of their Christian religion, and obedience to their Grand Master, the Knights of St. John of Jerusalem, from inheritance, commerce, and the plundering of Arab countries, were wealthy beyond imagination. They compelled the local population to toil in the construction of magnificent churches, castles, and fortresses. All the great buildings of the city of Valletta date from the period of the Knights of St. John of Jerusalem. The knights were required to make a token tribute to the King of Spain of one falcon every year, but they disdained the gift of a mere living bird as unworthy of their debt to their benefactor and chose instead to send a magnificently bejewelled statue of a falcon. This, anyway, is the handed-down story and the inspiration of Dashiell Hammett's novel – and later the Humphrey Bogart movie – *The Maltese Falcon*.

Malta was taken from the Knights of St. John in 1798 by the French general Napoleon Bonaparte on his way to attack Egypt. With the fall of Napoleon, Malta became a British colony in 1814 and remained so until its independence in 1964.

During the Second World War, Malta played a vital role in the Allied war effort. British fighter planes were based on Malta to defend the Mediterranean shipping convoys, but its proximity to Italy made the island vulnerable to Italian and German bombers. Because of their heroic defence against enemy attack, the people of Malta had the unique honour of being awarded, collectively, the George Cross by King George VI in 1942.

The language of Malta, Maltese, is just as fascinating as its history. Most people in the capital, Valletta, speak both Maltese and English, but in the villages of the Maltese countryside, especially fifty years or so ago when our novel begins, an ordinary person like Frankie Gauci when he first enters the narrative, would speak only Maltese. Maltese still has traces of the Phoenician language of three thousand years ago, but it is primarily a form of Arabic, closely akin to the North African Arabic of Algeria and Tunisia, although it is the only form of Arabic to be written in the Roman alphabet. Maltese has also embraced many of the words of its neighbours and conquerors, particularly Italian. I have heard it said in England that the Maltese are Italians who speak Arabic but think they are British. The Maltese are fiercely Roman Catholic and have been for nearly two millennia, ever since, as the Maltese believe, Saint Paul was ship-wrecked on the shores of Malta about 60 AD and converted the island to Christianity. Centuries ago, there was a strong Jewish presence in Malta, descendants of Spanish Jewish merchants, but when Ferdinand and Isabella expelled all Jews from Spain and its possessions in 1492, those who remained in Malta converted, at least publicly, to Catholicism. A few of these Sephardic families continued to practise Judaism in secret, but, over the years, even these *conversos* became fully observant Catholics. It is interesting to note that the author's surname from her Maltese father, Azzopardi, is itself a variant on the word *Sephardi*, from the Hebrew word for Spain.

Trezza Azzopardi has a B.A. in Creative Writing from the British University of East Anglia, the same writers' school that produced Kazuo Ishiguro and Ian McEwan. After working as a teacher of the deaf, she produced her first novel, *The Hiding Place*, in the year 2000.

She was born in Cardiff in 1961, the youngest of six daughters of a Maltese father and a Welsh mother. In a recent interview, she has admitted that "I do have a lot of sisters, so I did have quite a crowded upbringing, and I think unconsciously that was brought to bear in the book." Further, on the subject of Frankie Gauci's gambling, she said, "That partly comes out of the culture I was born into. My father did gamble. He didn't gamble in the way that Frankie gambled; but he did love the idea of luck and if things went well, he'd say, 'That's good luck,' and if things went badly, he'd say, 'That's bad luck.'" There is clearly an autobiographical element in the novel, but far more of it is fiction. Unlike the sad little Dolores, Trezza Azzopardi makes it clear that she was "very spoiled" by her older sisters in an environment that was nothing like the abject poverty of the Gaucis (*Atlantic Unbound*, Interviews, 2001).

Like Zadie Smith in *White Teeth*, Azzopardi is writing of an immigrant world she knows intimately, but the Gauci family is entirely fictitious.

The narrator of the novel is Dolores Gauci, the youngest of six sisters. "I'm the last," she says, "and like Rose and Fran I am shortened in my name: I am Dol. This is so my mother can get us all down for breakfast in one breath." (p. 4) We begin the novel with a memory Dol has of when she was three. Her mother put her at her bedroom window to watch for her father's return while her mother and a woman friend share a bottle of rum. Warned by Dol that Frankie Gauci is coming down the street, the friend, Eva Amil, pockets the bottle and slips out the back door. Mary, her mother, chews on a piece of parsley to mask her breath, and sends the three-year-old back upstairs to her room. As Dol remembers, "I must keep out of my father's way." (p. 6) In the first few pages, Azzopardi creates a family full of tension and concealment and secrecy, a family in which the father, Frankie Gauci, is a figure to be feared.

The memory is followed by an abrupt move to the present: "That was a time before I was four. The house is still here, and now I am here, standing at the window of the bedroom we shared." (p. 6)

Thirty years after the breakup of the family, a breakup that the novel will explore in detail, Dol is standing once again in the pitiful hovel of the family home at Number Two, Hodge's Row, in the squalor of Cardiff's dockland, known to the Welsh and seamen everywhere as Tiger Bay. She has come back from Nottingham to Cardiff for the funeral of her mother, seventy-one-year-old Mary Gauci, and she is waiting for her long-separated sisters to arrive for the ceremony. The time is the recent past, 1995 or a little later.

Once the occasion has been established, we return again to the past, to the year of Dol's birth, 1960, and even earlier to 1948, the year of her parents' marriage. This is a novel of memory, of memories peeled painfully away one by one like bandages from an open wound. The intensity of feeling is heightened by the telling of past horrors in the present tense, and the reader feels the impact on the consciousness of a child who is rarely aware of all the implications of what she sees.

Trezza Azzopardi takes a great risk with her novel. The narrative voice is consistent; it is always that of the youngest daughter, and yet she bears witness to events that took place before her birth. She bears witness to events that took place before her parents married and before her parents met. Dolores Gauci will tell us what was in the mind of each of her parents as they left the home of their births and, later, the most secret feelings of her sisters. In case the careless reader does not catch the challenge to our logic, Azzopardi has her narrator thrust it into our faces: "This is what happens before I am born: it's 1960. My parents, Frankie and Mary, have five beautiful daughters." (p. 8) At one point, her oldest sister, Celesta, challenges Dol, "You *can't* remember. . . . It's only what you've been *told*." (p. 243) On another occasion, we are given two conflicting explanations of the same event. When a disastrous fire breaks out in the Gauci kitchen, the narrator tells us that Dol's sister Fran "sees the smoke leaking out from under our kitchen door, and stands amazed." (p. 31) The implication is surely that some kitchen accident, perhaps a spark from the grate, began the blaze, but, on the next page, the same narrator reports that Mary finds cigarette butts and a box of spent matches in Fran's clothes and that "Her heart turns mad with blackness." Fran is already known to her mother, to the police, and to us as a pyromaniac.

In my view, Trezza Azzopardi's gamble with ambiguity and a child narrator who seems to know more than is possible succeeds wonderfully well. Not only does it add drama and poignancy as the grown-up Dolores journeys through her memories and what she believes are her memories; it also reminds us of how elusive remembered truth can be. Each of us makes up a version of the past that is a mixture of memory, imagination, and informed opinion. In addition, any individual memory of family life must be coloured by the position of that person within the family. My memory of my childhood must be very different from my two brothers' memories of that same period. Even now, I am never sure about which of my childhood memories are untainted by family lore or by accretions borrowed from my parents' accounts of the same time.

The novel seems to me to be largely about the subjectivity of memory and the pain of an adult trying to lay to rest the ghosts of the past as she confronts all the memories she has constructed. It is certain there is little that is not painful in the childhood memories of Dolores Gauci. If there were good days – and there must have been some – she does not share many of them with us. Hers is a story that unfolds with almost unrelenting grimness, with all the calamities stemming from the flawed character of one man, Francesco "Frankie" Gauci, summed up at the end of the novel by Martineau the rent collector as "a superstitious man . . . a stupid man." (p. 264)

The story of our anti-hero Frankie Gauci begins, in the invented memory of his youngest daughter, in a Maltese coastal village near Sliema. Frankie is weak and illiterate, but he wants to escape "the slow turn of his farming life for the glamour of the sea." He hates "the constant mewling of his grandmother, the coins in her pocket clanking her to church three, four times a day." He signs on as a deckhand on a tramp steamer: "His last sight was of Carmel, his little sister, waving madly from the harbour, and behind her, Sliema rippling in a hot mist." (p. 40) This is one of the many foreshadowings in the novel, tragic in its structure though perhaps not in its conclusion. His departure from Sliema will not be the last time Frankie leaves a world of women who have ceased to interest him.

Frankie lands at the Welsh port of Cardiff. His first intention is not to settle but to "register, find a place to stay, then cut another passage on the sea." (p. 40) The village boy, however, did not anticipate the excitement he feels at being in a big city: "He squinted up at the tallest buildings, and down the wide streets to the alleyways off them teeming with people; saw steam from the opened door of a bakery like a giant's breath out; stood amazed at the procession of silent cars gliding through the snow." (p. 40) He is also reassured to hear the familiar "tell-tale rhythm of Sicilian-Maltese," and he remembers what his crew mate had told him: "[T]here's a great clan of Maltese here, with more arriving every day. . . . Tiger Bay – the Valletta of Britain!" (p. 42)

Frankie decides to stay in Cardiff. He shares a basement room with another Maltese, Joe Medora, who has already established himself in Cardiff's Maltese underworld and who introduces the impressionable Frankie to the possibilities of the easy life.

Joe Medora is as strong as Frankie Gauci is weak. He knows that planning and ruthlessness, not luck, are what will bring success. As Dol remembers, Medora will go on to own "nearly everything round here: two boarding-houses on the Terrace, and our home, of course; and four cafes on Bute Street," (p. 23) while Frankie is doomed by his frailties to a life of poverty. It is significant that Joe Medora's first act of friendship towards Frankie is to pierce his ear. Frankie's ear will become infected in what is a very fine little metaphor for the effect Joe Medora has on Frankie's life.

While Frankie is settling down in Cardiff's Tiger Bay, another character is preparing to enter his future daughter's memories.

Mary Jessop is an eighteen-year-old girl living in a village up in the Welsh coal-mining valleys. She hates her village as much as Frankie Gauci hated his, and she plans her escape, to be financed by the little pile of hidden savings she has amassed by slaving at the Miners' Welfare Hall before and after her work as a drudge for an unfeeling father.

Every morning, that walk through the weather to Penderyn and The Miners' Welfare, to that stinking yard behind the hut – chiselling at the ice on the water-butt, plunging her hands in and out of the frozen water until the skin on them gave up and cracked like chickens' claws: all winter, standing in the yard, peeling those potatoes. And the nights! The men with their yeasty breath and glazed stares, watching her as she slopped the beer into their mugs, watching her and saying nothing. The heat of their coal-crusted eyes on her. (p. 70)

Azzopardi conjures up the poverty of life in a village as skilfully as she evokes the squalor of the dockland of a city.

As she makes her bid for freedom and a better life,

> Mary had to walk the two miles from her village to Hirwaun, where Clifford said he would pick her up in his van. She'd planned it well; in her shopping bag she put her purse, her hairbrush, her polkadot dress, her shoes. She clumps along now in her father's old work-boots, the toes stuffed with pages torn from the *Echo*. He'll be mad, she thinks, but he'll be mad anyway, whether I'm there or not. It makes no difference; he's always the same in the morning. (p. 69)

Her lover, Clifford, fails to appear of course, and Mary dismisses him in her mind as "You Idle Bastard" as she hitches a ride to the big city. The reader will realize a little later, if not immediately, that the shortcomings of Mary's father and lover are harbingers of what is to come when she throws in her lot with Frankie Gauci.

Dol remembers that her mother had a lifetime habit of singing brief snatches of popular songs in her sharp, tense voice. One frequently rendered couplet is

> Don't you know, little Fool, you Ne-ver can Win
> Use your Men-talitee, Wake up to Re-alitee . . . (p. 21)

As the reality of Mary's life and the continual failure of her men are revealed to us in fragment by remembered fragment, in a story moving as inexorably as Greek tragedy towards its terrible conclusion, the banal lyrics of the fool who never can win are endowed with a deeper meaning than Cole Porter could ever have imagined. The surprise is not that Mary Gauci, née Jessop, died at seventy-one; it is that she lasted as long as she did.

She meets her white knight when she gets a job as a waitress in a Maltese café where Frankie is a barman. It is fitting and prophetic that he endears himself to her by spitting in the drink of a customer who has been rude to her. She is already entranced by the world of the Maltese immigrant, full of dark men in suits and gold jewellery and fedoras who speak an alien and exotic language, men like Gauci and Medora, "so glamorous and charming" (p. 73) in contrast to the grim miners she has known. It is inevitable that she and Frankie marry in November of 1948. As she whispers into the hair of her fifth daughter years later, "I loved him straight off . . . Stupid Bloody Fool!" (p. 72)

I can understand how Mary is drawn to the world of Frankie Gauci. When I was a boy in my village in South Wales, my greatest thrill was to cycle or hitchhike with a friend the eighteen miles to Cardiff and wander through the streets of Bute Town, the dockland of Tiger Bay. It was a little universe of Chinese and Maltese restaurants and small, snappily dressed men with olive skins and Welsh girls on their arms, girls dressed more flamboyantly than I had ever seen Welsh girls dress before. It was my first taste of exoticism and I loved it. But at the end of the day, I always went, reluctantly, back to my village and my house and my school. Mary Jessop had nothing to go back to, and so she stayed and became Mary Gauci.

Mary Gauci is a fully drawn, complex character, but, if I have one criticism to make of the novel, it is that I hear in Mary's voice none of the Welsh inflections there must have been in the voice of a girl of her background. My mother came from a village not far from Hirwaun, Mary's birthplace, and the manner of speech is very distinctive, full of Welsh expressions and Welsh constructions. It is a very minor fault in an otherwise remarkable novel, but I must admit I was disappointed when I looked for something that I did not find. I suppose that Trezza Azzopardi's own Welsh mother was brought up, not in a village like mine, but in Cardiff itself, a very anglicized city.

Frankie Gauci opens a café, The Port of Call, with an old Maltese friend, Salvatore Capanone. Unlike Frankie, Salvatore is a hard worker and a good and loving man, not only to his wife, Carlotta, but to the whole of humanity. I think Azzopardi's inclusion of Salvatore in the story was a very deliberate move to provide a counterbalance to the anti-social character of Frankie Gauci and Joe Medora as well as to the whole unfair stereotype of Maltese in British fiction and in the British media. Notwithstanding the heroism of the Maltese during the Second World War and the considerable presence of Maltese in the British learned professions, the popular image of the Maltese has long been based on the activities of one family in London in the post-war years. The Messina brothers ran most of the vice in Soho and East End London while I was growing up, and their activities were reported large in the popular newspapers. The Messina brothers did for the Maltese British immigrant what Al Capone had done for the Italian

Americans, and I think Trezza Azzopardi is anxious to give the lie to the unjust generalization, particularly since Frankie and Joe seem to correspond to the stereotype.

As a result of Salvatore Capanone's industry, The Port of Call café makes a reasonable living from its clientele of sailors and prostitutes, but Frankie wastes his share of the profits gambling in an upstairs room. The loss of money is not his only bad luck. Over the next twelve years, Mary gives birth to five daughters and Frankie becomes Frankie Bambina, Frankie Girl-child, to his friends, a constant reproach and mockery in a superstitious Catholic society that values only male children. Mary's life is one of child-bearing drudgery, not much better than the existence she endured with her father. Her only distractions are the popular tunes on the radio, rum on the sly with her friend Eva Amil, and the occasional visits of Joe Medora. We learn the nature of those visits through the memories of our narrator. On one visit, Dolores is hiding in a cupboard and records the following encounter between her mother and Joe the visitor: "They're standing very close and she sighs, a sharp upwards sound like when she pricks her finger. He makes a buried noise, leaning his weight against the cupboard so it goes very dark. He whispers something I can't understand and laughs again." (p. 270) The reader understands what the five-year-old narrator cannot, that she is the witness to an act of sex. But she does understand the offer Joe Medora makes to her mother, "[W]e can leave whenever you like," and her mother's reply, "I can't." On another occasion, hiding this time under the stairs, Dol hears her mother say "Take me with you." (p. 275) Was she overhearing her mother in different moods, at different levels of frustration with the horror of her life, or did Dol not hear correctly on one of the two occasions? We can never be sure. That is part of the fascinating ambiguity of a book made of memory.

Azzopardi is brilliant in her creation of this family in claustrophobic rooms even more unbearable than the squalid world outside. The older Dol, thinking back to her mother's misery, admits that her adult mind cannot really encompass what it must have been like: "My mother had to face us, every day, in this room. I try to imagine the five, then six of us to feed, clothe, take care of. Waiting for Frankie to come back, writing her lists and notes and begging letters for something on tick." (p. 267)

In 1960, Mary enters her sixth pregnancy and Frankie counts absolutely on the child being a boy. He even has a name picked out, Fortuno, "Good

Luck." He is so sure that he will have a son that, when the girl-child is delivered, the midwife, phoning him at his card game with the news, fears to tell him the truth. Frankie is euphoric in his belief that he has a son and calls for one card too many in blackjack and plays for too high a stake, losing as a result

> the cafe, the shoebox under the floorboards full with big money, his own father's ruby ring, and my mother's white lace gown, to Joe Medora.
>
> At least I have a son, he thinks, as he rolls the ring across the worn green felt. (p. 14)

But there is no son, only a daughter who will be named Dolores, "Sorrow," Dol for short. The family will leave the two rooms above the café, now renamed The Moonlight Club, and move into a slum where they will pay rent to Joe Medora. As Medora's rent collector, Martineau, tells Dolores thirty-five years later, "Frankie thought . . . A devil had come into his house" (p. 264) and blamed all his bad luck on the baby he calls "Sinistra." The nickname, with its origin in the evil attributed to the left hand by the seers of Ancient Rome, will seem horribly fitting only a little later in the narrative.

Frankie is not alone in his fear of the baby. Referring to the whole of the Gauci family, Martineau says "They were afraid," (p. 264) and the adult Dolores thinks, "Then I know. Afraid of *me*."

Worse is yet to come. At one month old, Dolores is alone in the kitchen. Frankie has stolen the rent money his wife had hidden, and Mary, outside, is arguing with Martineau the rent collector. Dolores's memory is that Martineau was offering to take Mary inside the house and accept sex in lieu of rent – "Let's go inside, Mary, he says. We'll talk about it" (p. 28) – but that's the memory of a child four weeks old, a memory constructed from later imagination or overheard excuses. At the end of the novel, Martineau as an old man remembers the moment differently: "Mary is desperate. She takes his hands, presses them to her face, moves them down her body. Martineau grips her tight to stop her. He will not take payment this way." (p. 261) Who knows where the truth lies? For "As with all truth," the novel reminds us, "there is another version." (p. 75)

What we do know is that, while Mary and Martineau are arguing in the alley behind the house, a fire breaks out in the kitchen. The baby Dolores is horribly damaged: her face is scarred and she loses the fingers of her left hand. The horror is heightened by the exquisite prose and perfectly chosen similes with which Azzopardi describes the accident and its aftermath, all through the eyes of Dolores:

> I lost the fingers. At one month old, a baby's hand is the tiniest, most perfect thing. It makes a fist, it spreads wide, and when it burns, that soft skin is petrol, those bones are tinder, so small, so easily eaten in a flame.
> But I think of it as a work of art: a closed white tulip standing in the rain; a cut of creamy marble in the shape of a Saint; a church candle with its tears flowing down the bulb of wrist. (p. 33)

It is a measure of Azzopardi's skill that there is a later passage concerning Dol's hand that is even more harrowing. It comes when Dol is a toddler. Her oldest sister is putting on powder and, in a very rare gesture of sisterly affection, Celesta shares the moment:

> Look at this, Dol, she whispers, drawing the powder-puff across my cheek, Close your eyes now.
> She draws it once, twice, down the side of my face. There is a faint scent of lilies. She holds up her compact mirror for me to see: my scar is almost invisible. I hold out my bad hand for mending. (p. 125)

If you have ever loved a little child and loved the innocence of that child, I defy you not to be moved to your depths as the trusting little one holds up her maimed hand for it to be made whole again by her sister's magic powder.

While Dolores is losing the fingers of her left hand to the flames, Frankie Gauci is out gambling away the rent money he has stolen from his wife, money made up of savings, children's allowance, and Mary's meagre wages from the night shift. Even before the fire, there was little left of the marriage. Every time Frankie left the house in his jewellery and smart clothes, Mary felt a greater rage as she coped alone with the five daughters, six after the birth of Dolores.

Mary's rage and the hatred she and Frankie feel for each other is transmitted directly to the children: "My mother mixes up a bowl of something grey for Luca, rapidly beating milk into powder. Her fury travels down the spoon and into Luca's dinner. I am breast-fed: I get rage straight from the source." (p. 22)

It is not surprising that the older sisters, brought up in such an atmosphere, exhibit none of the compassion we might hope for towards their disfigured little sister. They call her Crip, for "cripple," and the first five years of her little life are years of unrelieved horror. She is a naive witness of her mother's adultery with Joe Medora, and a knowing witness of Frankie's brutal beatings of Mary and the sisters. Much of Frankie's violence is reserved for the second oldest, Fran, the pyromaniac. She has also come to indulge in self-mutilation, carving tattoos on her body with a knife. Three times she is brought home by the police for setting fires on waste ground before she is institutionalized for burning down a local grocery store. Frankie's beatings of Fran with his belt are terrible indeed:

> A Liar. Just like your mother.
> Aiming at her head. The sharp claw of the buckle grazes her face, cuts a thin notch of gristle from her ear. A noise like an animal. Frankie catches her up in his hands. Her body bends. So bent . . . she must be broken. He throws her down. His fingers on her neck. (p. 240)

Dol is not only the witness to terrible violence; the terrified child is also the subject of her siblings' cruelty. They delight in tying her up in a sheet and suspending her over the stairwell, chanting, "Liar! Liar! Crip's on fire!" (p. 178) It is a childhood out of hell.

After the birth of Dol and the loss of what little remaining money they had, Frankie solves his short-term financial problems by selling one of his daughters. His plight is desperate; he owes money to the Syndicate, and the organized underworld is a very bad enemy. A local character in Tiger Bay, Len the Bookie, is fond of offering counsel while waving a maimed fist:

> He has only two remaining digits on this hand; forefinger and middle finger. He managed to save his thumb. He used to gamble himself, but now he's found a safer occupation.

Never Bet with the Syndicate, my Friend, is his only piece of
advice. (p. 27)

Dolores is not the only character in *The Hiding Place* with a disfigured
hand as the visible badge of misfortune.

Frankie is able to rescue himself by an ingenious deal with his successful one-time friend Joe Medora. Both Frankie and Joe believe one of
Frankie's daughters, the eight-year-old Marina, to be Joe's child. The deal
is simple:

Frankie gains: the house, enough money to right the damage
caused by the fire; enough money to wipe his slate with the
Syndicate; just that bit extra so that Mary doesn't have to work all
hours to make ends meet. And an offer to manage The Moonlight
when Joe is away.
He loses: Marina. (p. 73)

Unusually in the novel, Marina's leaving is told not in Dol's voice, but in
Mary's, and it is all the more wrenching as Dol relates what her mother
told her.

I don't remember Marina; I was only a month old when she left, and
still in hospital. My mother told me how she went away, listing all
the things she packed into Marina's new brown suitcase:
Two pairs of Clarks' Sandals, what with the weather out there
being so nice; a new dress with little rosebuds running round the
bodice – you know, Dol, like a medieval princess – and three new
blouses; a satin nightie; a proper toilet bag from Marks'; a swimsuit
in emerald green. Oh, she had everything she wanted! We had to sit
on the case to shut it! My mother would tell me this time and again,
her face fixed in a smile. (p. 75)

We remember that we were given a catalogue of Mary's possessions as she
left her father's house, but Marina's leaving is not the free choice of an adult
and we can only try to imagine the frozen horror of her mother's smile.

As Marina is driven away from the house in Joe Medora's car, Frankie
Gauci hurls himself into a frenzy of activity, "anything, to drown out the

emptiness that oozes from the house." (p. 77) He uses scrap wood to build a rabbit hutch, "a thing for his daughter," but it is far too big just for rabbits, it is more like a cage, and the violence of his sawing and hammering until red weals of flesh are raised on his hands suggests more than a simple act of carpentry. Mary sees it as an attack on herself: "What he really wanted was to saw *me* to bits, Dol. Like a magician. He couldn't stand it, you see? Jealousy! That's what jealousy does for you, girl." (p. 77)

Frankie's hatred of his youngest daughter, Dol, increases. Since her birth on the night he lost everything to Joe Medora, he has hated her. Dol remembers,

> I slept in the chest when I was newborn. My mother told me how she wrapped me in a shawl at night and hid me from my father.
> He would've smothered you, she said. (p. 5)

But Mary is not always a protective mother. She is capable of stepping over her daughters, beaten to the floor by Frankie in one of his murderous rages, to reach the water tap in the kitchen to get herself a drink. When Dol is bereft at the death of some baby rabbits, eaten by their mother, Mary does not hesitate to tell Dol that Dol is to blame. She tells her that any mother rabbit will eat her young if the young are contaminated by the smell of a human – in this case Dol – who handled them.

> I had done something terribly wrong by touching her babies.
> You had to interfere, she said.
> I was five; it was the first time I'd heard the word. The way she said it made it sound like murder. (p. 78)

When Fran, so abused by her father, draws "angry pictures of bonfires using three crayons at a time," (p. 9) Mary pays no attention to a warning sign that would not escape even the least perceptive of parents. Given a childhood like Mary's, with a father whose only comment on her leaving home was "Good riddance," it is no surprise that she became both victim and victimizer. Given the parental role models of Frankie and Mary, it is understandable that Dol's older sisters are cruel and unfeeling towards each other, forming temporary alliances among themselves only to create a defence against the world outside, including their parents.

There are few moments of happiness for any of the children. In between setting fires, Fran collects shards of glass from the nearby waste ground; they are the only objects of beauty in her life. Her finest piece is "a single marble with a twisted turquoise eye." (p. 20) She collects cigarette butts, too, in her secret hiding place: these and the shards of glass form a metaphor for her young psyche, fragmented beyond hope of repair by a hundred blows.

This seems to be a family without hope of healing, and Mary begins a retreat into insanity, interrupted by ineffectual gestures towards suicide.

On at least one occasion Dol is with her mother when Mary considers death as an alternative. Dol already knows that her family and neighbours regard her as the embodiment of bad fortune. She knows from an overheard conversation that the husband of her mother's friend will not allow her into his house because of what she represents – "[H]e's superstitious about my bad hand" (p. 186) – and her sister drives the point home. Rose tells Dol that their mother has kept Dol home from school "because I'm bad luck and I mustn't be seen." (p. 79) It is a burden that no child should have to bear.

Mary is confined to a mental hospital but is allowed out in one of her lucid periods to take her youngest daughter for a walk. The walk is to the railroad track in a storm that mirrors the turmoil in the Gauci family. In one of Azzopardi's wonderfully evocative passages, Dol remembers the event, and again, just as when Mary prepared Marina to leave forever with Joe Medora, Mary will smile her terrible smile, a smile that is not described and that we can only imagine, the smile of someone whose emotions have been distorted by suffering into something no longer recognizable.

> She bends again, crouching, and I can see beyond her, to the rain in sheets and the blackberry bushes shuddering in the wind. She lays her head down sideways on the track. People choose to die this way, but I don't know this yet, at five years old. I know about dinosaurs and pop music and harvest festival, and about the Virgin Mary and how Christ suffered for us, but I don't know about suicide or what the weight of a passenger train can do to the bones in the skull. She smiles up at me from the track, and her hair slicks across her cheek like pond grass. She rises, flays the water from her face with her hand.
>
> No trains coming, she says. (p. 196)

But Mary can still summon up the strength to attend the wedding of her oldest daughter, Celesta, seventeen years old. Fran will be released from her institution for the event, but she has been damaged beyond repair, and "her eyes are dead as stones." (p. 144)

Celesta's wedding is to a local soft-drink merchant, thirty years older than she is. Pippo Seguna has nursed an invalid wife for years and now wants the comfort of young flesh. He is so obese that the neighbourhood children run after him calling out "Pippo the Hippo." Celesta is as beautiful as her mother had been, but there are few options available, and Frankie is aware of what happens to beautiful girls in Tiger Bay. The daughter of his neighbours, the Jacksons, is only one of many who call out to passersby, offering their bodies from the darkness of doorways. Even Frankie is revolted by the match between his daughter and Pippo the Hippo – he vomits – but it is less objectionable than the alternatives. Celesta is being courted by Marcus, the manager of the shop where she works, but he is not an attractive option, even compared with Pippo.

> She can have Markus with his creepy hands and his greasy parcels of bacon; or she can have big soft Pippo and all the fizz she can drink. It helps that Pippo has lots of money and a nice house. It helps that he's kind. But more than anything, it is my father who helps Celesta choose. She thinks about the thick sting of his rage, his hands on her, his breath hot on her hair. It happens as quickly as blinking: she will have Pippo. (p. 133)

It is under cover of the wedding celebration that Frankie Gauci will abandon his family and make his break for freedom, stealing all the money from the safe at The Moonlight Club, thereby robbing both Joe Medora and his lifelong friend Salvatore Capanone. Salvatore will fall into the mud at the bottom of a dry dock in a vain attempt to prevent Frankie's flight and his body will not be found for thirty years. Thus does the one embodiment of goodness disappear from the novel, just as Frankie disappears forever from the life of his wife and daughters. This is not a novel in which there is any sense of justice, divine or otherwise.

Mary descends into total insanity; Marina is somewhere with Joe Medora; Celesta is making what new life she can with Pippo; and Fran the pyromaniac is returned to her institution. The remaining three children, Rose, Luca, and Dolores, will be allocated to separate foster homes by the welfare authorities, but not before one of the rare moments of humour in the novel. Their mother's friend Eva and the social workers escort the girls to have their photographs taken so that they can be listed in the catalogue of children on offer. The children, with a resilience that can only make the reader gasp, decide to enjoy the occasion. Dol remembers:

> The image of me is nervous, shifty, scowling over my shoulder like a fugitive on the run. Any second now, the sniffer dogs will leap up behind me and tear me to ribbons. The pictures of the others are even worse. Rose holds her chin high, her nostrils flared like a hippo emerging from the swamp; Luca has her eyes crossed like one of the Keystone Cops. Our group photograph makes Eva laugh out loud.
>
> The Bash Street Kids and no mistake, she says, bending double in the middle of the pavement. Lizzie Preece doesn't think it's funny.
>
> The Agency won't use these, she says, We'll never place them!
> (p. 190)

But the Agency does manage to place them, and they will not be together again for three decades.

The reunion, at Mary's funeral, will take place in a scene of desolation. Once again in the novel, the exterior world will mirror the misery in the minds of our characters. Much of the area has been bulldozed and those buildings that remain have been boarded up. There are only a few exceptions, and the Gauci house is one of them. Dol stands in the grime, looking at the chest in which her mother hid her from her father's rage, and the memories flood back, memories that form the story we have read.

> Under the window sits the chest. I wait for my eyes to adjust, for the outline of the wood to separate from wall and shadow and become itself; long, low, oblong. It belonged to my father, and now it will be mine: I'm claiming it back. I will take what I can. Darkness has come down. While the waiting happens, I go through it all again. (p. 199)

And then her sisters arrive.

Rose was forbidden by her husband to attend the funeral, but she had money for the journey hidden under the stair carpet. There are so many hiding places in the novel: almost every character has something to hide, either in a physical place or in the recesses of the mind. In only a few sentences, Rose reveals the whole picture of her life with her two children and soldier husband:

> I've left him to fend for himself for a bit. . . . It'll do him good – That's the last time *anyone* hits me.
> The phrase comes too easily; she's used it before. (p. 212)

Rose is as unfeeling towards her sister at the funeral as she had been thirty years earlier. At first, Dol thinks Rose may be moved by their meeting, but Rose is unchanged: "Well, I never, she says, dispelling my illusion, Little Crip's come back." (p. 211) Dol realizes that the pain and neglect of their shared childhood has created not a bridge but a chasm between them:

> She was making herself perfectly clear; her past wasn't mine, and I couldn't be part of it. Her likes and dislikes were written in the slant of her eyes: she despised Celesta and my mother; she admired Luca. Marina, my father, Fran, they were dismissed with a flick of the head. And me – I was still Crip. (p. 223)

Luca is apparently prosperous, with a new home in a Vancouver suburb and a Korean housekeeper. But she does not want to share Dol's memories – "Bad dreams, she says quietly, That's all they are" (p. 219) – and there is talk of her recent divorce. As her head scarf slips, Dol sees that Luca is bald.

> It'll grow back, she says, smiling faintly.
> I used to think my hand would grow back too. I'd watch for signs. At night, I'd will the fingers to sprout, eating up the vacant space like a bloom captured on a time-lapse camera. So I know what will and won't grow back, and I know now when Luca is lying. (p. 278)

Luca's body will be eaten away by cancer as surely as the bad dreams have eaten away at her inner peace for thirty years.

Celesta has also prospered materially. As Rose tells Dol,

> All I know is Celesta's doing alright. Family business, two sons to
> look after her. She's rich now old Pippo's gone to that big pop factory
> in the sky. Very posh, our Cel.
> Rose breaks into a sudden, bitter laugh. Just like my mother's.
>   She doesn't want to know *me*, that's for certain, she says, looking
> me up and down, So – no offence, Crip – I can't imagine she'll be
> glad to see *you*. (p. 213)

Celesta has tried to distance herself from the other Gaucis. Her sons
have heard nothing from her of the family, only wildly exaggerated
neighbourhood stories, "gilt-edged stories – of a vice ring, a murderous
feud, a child sold into prostitution." (p. 244) But Celesta still has the
bitterness of her childhood within her. We are made privy to the inner
workings of her family life: when her boys are late for supper, she throws
their food into the garbage and, as one of them calls to his mother for
his dinner,

> Celesta lies back on the bed and stares at the ceiling.
>   It's in the bin, she says to the room. (p. 216)

Dol sees Celesta, for all her prosperity, as a reincarnation of Mary:
"Celesta is like an older version of the mother I remembered, right down
to the way she stands, with one foot out at an angle and the other tapping
madly on the pavement – as if there's a beat thrumming in her head that
no one else can hear." (p. 236)

The funeral takes place, and there is another moment of humour that
reminds us of the taking of the group photograph thirty years earlier. When
the girls were little and had to pray before the meal served at Sunday
school, the priest would address the Almighty Father,

> Dear God in Heaven,
>   Yes? a little voice would cry, as if it came from the ceiling. And
> he would look up, amazed. It was Rose's trick. He always fell for it.
> (p. 253)

Rose repeats the trick at the funeral, pretending to be Mary and crying "Ouch" and moaning as the dirt hits the coffin. "And suddenly we are all laughing, embarrassed and raucous under the cold eyes of the priest, the dank air, the drops of mist falling from the sky." (p. 253) But the moment is brief, and the laughter derives from a ventriloquist's trick, not from shared affection.

The mist at Mary's funeral reminds us of the mist over Sliema when Frankie left Malta and the story began. But the story is over for Mary, and Frankie never came back. Her friend Eva, addled and befuddled in an old folks' home, tells Dol that Mary had always hoped Frankie would return.

Even Fran makes an appearance. Whether it is for devilment or from a well-meant desire to reunite the sisters we can never be sure, but Celesta's son Louis finds Fran from Dol's description of her tattoos. Dol, about to leave for Nottingham, sees a bag lady approaching in the street, preceded by Louis "looking pleased and sheepish." "Did I do the right thing, Aunty Dol?" he asks. "Her arms are bruised and liverish, but in the tint of the street-light, I see upon the dirty skin a faded blue crucifix, an inky stain spelling FRAN." Fran, the most visibly damaged of the sisters, has "her arms held straight out in front of her, as if she expects to be handcuffed," (p. 282) and we cannot fail to see how she was imprisoned by her childhood.

The sisters, the walking wounded, are thus reunited.

What has Dol learned through the reunion and the reliving and retelling of confused, imagined, and ambiguous memory? She has learned even more than her mind permitted her to remember. She had a recollection of her sisters locking her up in the great rabbit hutch in the backyard, but Luca disabuses her – "Dol, we were *letting you out*, she says" (p. 274) – and both Dol and the reader comprehend a truth so terrible Dol had put it away in the hiding place of her mind. Her father had built the cage to confine, not rabbits, but his baby daughter. He wanted to imprison the evil spirit he believed had wreaked such havoc in his life. I thought back to the violence of Frankie's carpentry and the immensity of the cage, and I had a sudden vision of a modern Ahab attributing all evil to Moby-Dick.

We are not told how this horror or seeing the wreck of her sister Fran will further mark Dol as she returns to her life as a librarian in Nottingham, a life of which we know almost nothing. Azzopardi is wise, I think, to leave it to us to decide how it will be for Dolores, Dol for short. Our imaginings are always more terrible than anything an author can tell us.

I have heard readers compare this novel to *Angela's Ashes*, but I don't believe the comparison holds true. Both are accounts of childhood poverty, but Frank McCourt's book is a memoir, and we know that he came out of his childhood whole, with a thirst for knowledge and with a memory of a loving mother.

This novel, *The Hiding Place*, is a fiction of children brought up in a climate of hatred who carry that hatred within them forever, and their memory is of a father governed by his weakness and obsessions and of a mother too damaged to help them.

Trezza Azzopardi has gone all the way back to Greek tragedy, to the very roots of drama, for her narrative. She is writing of humanity as the playthings of amoral gods, human beings condemned undeservedly because of their own weaknesses, the weaknesses of those around them, and the randomness of events. It is a bleak vision of the universe and one entirely without hope, redeemed only by the observation that the individual is capable of surviving almost unbelievable hardship.

If it is so grim, why has this novel found so large an audience? The terrible beauty of the language is one reason, of course, and so is the skill with which a truly dysfunctional family is dissected, but there is another reason. We read this novel for the same reason that we watch *Oedipus* or *Electra* or *Medea*, dramas that hold audiences two and a half thousand years after they were written. Our feelings of pity and compassion are pushed to the very edge as we wonder how much more horror the moment can hold. When the narrative comes to its inevitable conclusion, we experience a catharsis, a purging of violent emotion, which in turn gives way to a great sense of relief. Dolores Gauci has survived, and so have we.

DISGRACE

J.M. Coetzee

(London: Vintage, 2000)

Because *Disgrace* deals in part with contemporary relationships between black and white South Africans, it might be useful to consider how the phenomenon of the white South African came into being.

The first white settlement in South Africa was at the southern tip of the continent, the Cape of Good Hope. In 1652 the Dutchman Jan van Riebeeck established the little colony as a stopping-off place for Dutch ships on their way to the Far East and the Spice Islands. Over the next one hundred and fifty years, Dutch farmers, *boers* in Dutch, arrived, and Cape Colony expanded inland and farther along the coast, fighting all the while against the indigenous black tribes, enslaving many of the defeated for use as farm labour and confining the rest to reservations.

In 1806 the British seized the Dutch colony in order to protect their trade route to India. The Dutch-speaking Boers were profoundly unhappy under British rule, particularly when the government encouraged British immigration to the newly acquired colony. The last straw came when Britain abolished slavery throughout the Empire in 1833. Determined to live outside British rule and its anti-slavery laws, the Boers decided to move farther inland. In 1836 they began what they call the Great Trek. Over the next sixteen years, the Boers moved inland from Cape Colony and crossed the great Drakensberg Mountains. On the other side of the Orange River they founded their own republic, the Orange Free State. Some of the

41

voortrekkers went even farther north, across the Vaal River, and founded the South African Republic, later known as the Transvaal. The British took advantage of the Boers' departure to annex the second Dutch colony on the coast, little Natal, adjoining Cape Colony to the east.

Relations between the two British colonies on the coast and the two Boer republics inland frequently erupted into war, particularly after the discovery of diamonds in the Orange Free State in 1866 and gold in the Transvaal in 1886. In 1899 the deciding conflict began.

During the Boer War, British troops were unable to defeat the Dutch farmers who moved so quickly in their small units, called *kommandos*, mounted on little ponies. Only in 1901 did Lord Kitchener, the British commander, hit on a solution with the invention of the concentration camp. After a year of seeing their farms burned and their families imprisoned, the Boers surrendered. The experience of losing twenty to thirty thousand of their women and children to starvation and disease in the dreadful camps was too much for them, and in 1902 the Orange Free State and the Transvaal became British colonies. In 1910 they were combined with Cape Colony and Natal into the Union of South Africa. The new entity had two official languages, English and Dutch. There was no official recognition of any black language like Zulu or Xhosa. (In 1925, Cape Dutch, which had evolved differently from the Dutch of the mother country, would be declared a separate language, known as Afrikaans.)

The constitution of the new country gave some small representation to the South Africans of mixed race and of Asian descent, called "Coloureds," but none whatsoever to black South Africans. For most of the twentieth century, they would be the hewers of wood and drawers of water for the white minority, and their situation grew even worse after the Second World War.

In 1948, the Nationalist Party, which was dominated by the Afrikaners, as the Boers were now known, won federal power for the first time. Its victory coincided with demands for independence by non-white peoples all over the world. The Afrikaner Nationalists decided on a pre-emptive strike. The racial segregation that already existed *de facto* was formalized in law into a system called *apartheid*, "separate growth." The Afrikaner Dutch Reformed Church gave apartheid religious legitimacy by teaching that blacks are descended from Noah's rebellious son Ham (Genesis 12:25) and are thus cursed by God to be servants forever.

In 1959 the Bantu Self-Government Act created ten black "homelands" within South Africa, four of them technically independent countries, the other six semi-autonomous regions. No country outside South Africa recognized the legitimacy of these so-called ten black nations. The Nationalist government declared that every South African black was a citizen of one or other of these "homelands," all situated in desolate areas, and was therefore a foreigner in South Africa with no civil rights.

In 1961, angered by criticism of apartheid from all over the world, South Africa declared itself a republic, withdrew from the British Commonwealth, and entered a period of thirty years of relative isolation from the international community.

Not all the criticism of the South African government came from outside the country. Non-white South Africans formed the African National Congress, the ANC, but it was proscribed by the government as a Communist organization, and its leader, Nelson Mandela, was jailed for life in 1964.

By 1990 the situation had become untenable for everyone except the most extreme of the Afrikaner Nationalists. The English speakers of the coastal cities like Cape Town and Durban had always advocated a more liberal racial policy. Morality apart, the demographics of the country demanded a change. Of a population of about thirty million people, 72 percent were black, 9 percent were of mixed race, and 3 percent were of Asian descent. The 16 percent white minority could no longer hold them back. The laws forbidding racial intermarriage and requiring blacks to carry passes at all times were allowed to fall into abeyance, the African National Congress was declared a legal organization, and Nelson Mandela was freed after twenty-six years of imprisonment.

After lengthy negotiations between South Africa's president de Klerk and the ANC, the country's first free elections were held on the basis of one person, one vote, and on May 10, 1994, Nelson Mandela became president of the republic with de Klerk as vice-president.

There was, of course, some violence. The black community was divided into the Zulu-dominated Inkatha Party and the Xhosa-dominated ANC. Afrikaner extremists organized private armies. But whatever their efforts, the die was cast. In 1994, a new South Africa was born.

No longer a police state, South Africa faced a huge crime wave, the same phenomenon that follows the end of any dictatorship, be it in Spain or Russia or South Africa. Freedom is always initially intoxicating, especially with a police force bound for the first time by the rule of law.

But there was a problem even greater than the crime wave. Blacks and whites had to redefine their relationship to one another. The new South Africa came with a huge amount of baggage. To take just one example: for every thirty dollars spent on the education of a white child, *one* was spent on the education of a black child.

For decades, black South Africans had been treated as unwelcome foreign workers in their own country. For decades, even centuries, white South Africans, particularly the Afrikaners, had seen themselves as God's anointed. After the installation of democracy in 1994, and the installation of a black South African president, all those attitudes had to change, and the change was, of necessity, painful.

That painful change is the context of *Disgrace*, which won an unprecedented second Booker Prize in 1999 for its author J.M. Coetzee.

Coetzee was born in Cape Town in 1940, the child of Afrikaner parents who were supporters of the English-dominated, racially moderate United Party. Out of their anglophilia came Coetzee's first names, John Michael. He grew up in rural Cape Province, about ninety miles north of Cape Town, in the Karoo, the dry uplands of Cape Province, where his alcoholic father scratched out a relatively poor living as a lawyer.

Now, Coetzee is an established author of international reputation. He has degrees in English Literature and Mathematics and a Ph.D. in Linguistics from the University of Texas. He was a computer analyst for IBM in London for three years in the sixties and taught at New York State University at Syracuse from 1970 to 1971. Since 1972 he has been a professor of English at Cape Town University. He is divorced with one surviving child, a daughter. He is a confirmed vegetarian, exceptionally shy, and dislikes both interviews and wasted words.

Coetzee wrote about his childhood very objectively, in the third person, in a 1997 memoir, *Boyhood: Scenes from a Provincial Life*. Four of the memories struck me as very significant: the ongoing struggle between his weak father and his fiercely protective mother; the physical punishment meted out to the non-white servants; the bullying Coetzee, a sickly boy, endured at the hands of his schoolmates; and the castration of sheep he witnessed on his grandfather's farm. One does not have to be a Freudian not to be surprised by the themes of the eight novels he would later come to write.

Above all, his novels examine the nature of power as it is exercised in all its forms – in racism, in imperialism, in the relationship between the sexes, and in the relationship between the human and the animal world. Coetzee examines the effects of power on those who exercise it and on those upon whom it is exercised. At the same time, his novels consider the universal nature of humankind and the profound problems of existing in what he sees as an indifferent universe, a universe without God.

Because he is concerned with universality, Coetzee has, until this novel, resolutely refused to anchor any of his work in a particular place or time. Unlike other South African novelists, notably Nadine Gordimer, he has refused to adopt any political stance on South Africa or its politics in his novels. Only in *Age of Iron* (1990) did he set the action in a recognizable South Africa, but even there the focus is not on politics but on the protagonist's preparation for death.

Coetzee's preference has often been for the fable, a little reminiscent of Kafka, although without the magic realism. His first Booker Prize winner, *Life and Times of Michael K* (1983), was typical in that it followed the movement of a simple-minded outcast trying to find a home during a vaguely defined civil war.

But it's impossible to label Coetzee as a successor to Kafka. Indeed, he resents the suggestion: "I don't believe that Kafka has an exclusive right to the letter K. Nor is Prague the centre of the universe." (Interview with Tony Morphet, "Two Interviews with J.M. Coetzee, 1983 and 1987," in *Tri-Quarterly*, No. 69, 1987)

Coetzee's virtuosity is incredible. His first novel, *Dusklands* (1974), consists of two fables, both written in Afrikaans. In his second novel, *In the Heart of the Country* (1977), he not only switched permanently to English but experimented with a stream-of-consciousness narrative. Twice he has dipped deep into postmodernism and rewritten history, reworking episodes in the lives of Daniel Defoe in *Foe* (1986) and Feodor Dostoevsky in *The Master of Petersburg* (1994). Coetzee is preoccupied with the concept of authorship, with the idea that the writer of history controls history.

He has also written a great deal of non-fiction, particularly essays. In one superb semi-fictional work, *The Lives of Animals* (1998), Coetzee put together three lectures he had just given at Princeton University, creating an alter ego, Elizabeth Costello, a professor engaged in a debate with her university audience about her empathy with the animal world. Elizabeth

Costello, a.k.a. J.M. Coetzee, sees in the eyes of all animals in zoos and laboratories and slaughterhouses the same haunting, beautifully formulated question that we human beings each ask ourselves: "Where is home and how do I get there?" It was the question that Michael K asked himself in Coetzee's first Booker Prize-winning novel, and it is the same question that we see in the eyes of the unwanted animals in Bev Shaw's clinic in *Disgrace*. Coetzee is profoundly concerned with both the human and the animal worlds. The animals in *Disgrace* are not a metaphor for some oppressed segment of human society. When Coetzee is writing about goats and dogs, he is writing about goats and dogs.

Disgrace is the first of Coetzee's eight novels to deal directly with South Africa's socio-political upheaval in the 1990s. Appropriately, it is also the most realistic of all his novels, and yet as multi-layered as any of his early fables.

The plot of *Disgrace* is simple – deceptively simple. David Lurie is a fifty-two-year-old, twice-divorced professor at Cape Technical University in Cape Town. He has a brief affair with a twenty-year-old student; it becomes known; he is censured and chooses to resign. He goes to live with his grown-up daughter, Lucy, who lives on a little farm in the rural east of Cape Province. She has lived alone since her female lover left her. Helped by her black neighbour Petrus, who has just bought one of her five hectares of land with a government grant, she makes a subsistence living by boarding dogs and selling flowers and farm produce at a local market.

Professor Lurie finds work by helping his daughter at the Saturday market, digging foundation trenches for Petrus's new house, and helping at an animal euthanasia clinic run by another of his daughter's neighbours, Bev Shaw.

It would seem that he has immersed himself in the back-to-nature life advocated by the nineteenth-century English Romantic poets like Wordsworth whose work he has been teaching. The idyll is shattered, however, when he is attacked and his daughter is raped by three black strangers, at least one of whom is related to Petrus. The novel ends with Professor Lurie living alone and doing menial work at the animal clinic. His daughter, pregnant as a result of the rape, has to forge a new life for herself and a new relationship with her black neighbour.

After my first reading of the novel, I saw it clearly as an allegory, with a symbolic role for each main character. The professor's seduction of his

student has its parallel in the rape of his daughter. At one level, David
Lurie and the three black men represent patriarchy, men imposing their
will on women. At another level, especially after the rape, David and his
daughter Lucy represent white South Africa going through the pain of
transition into a new set of attitudes towards their black compatriots. The
old world they knew has vanished, the old world in which Petrus could
have been forced to explain his absence during the rape and in which the
young Pollux, one of the three participants in the rape, could have been
tortured by the white police to reveal the identity of his accomplices.
These two symbols of white South Africa have to face a new world where
none of the old certainties exist. That, I repeat, was my first reading of the
novel, and I was comfortable with it until I started to think about it with
reference to something Coetzee has asserted in every one of the few interviews he has given over the years. He has always denied that he writes
allegories. He says that his characters are individuals, not symbols. I
thought particularly about the interview he gave Tony Morphet in 1983.
They were discussing the doctor in *Life and Times of Michael K*, and
Morphet kept calling the doctor "the liberal." Coetzee's response was that
"first of all he seems to me a person." (op. cit.)

With that exchange in mind, I decided to reread *Disgrace*, this time
focusing on the characters as unique individuals, not allegorical, symbolic
figures. It was then that I discovered how simplistic my first reading was. I
had uncovered only the first of many layers of this multi-layered masterpiece, and I had misunderstood even that first layer.

Let us return to the novel and look very closely at Professor David Lurie.
His world at the university, formerly Cape Town University College and
now renamed Cape Technical University, has changed dramatically, but
not because of the coming to power of Nelson Mandela in 1994. His colleagues have names like Manas Mathabane, Aram Hakim, Desmond
Swarts, and Farodia Rassool. These are the names of Zulus, Asians, and
Afrikaners, and some of them have clearly been his colleagues for some
time. Cape Town, with its English, liberal, United Party traditions, was
always more moderate in its application of the race laws than the
Afrikaner-dominated cities. The change that has affected David Lurie far
more profoundly is "the great rationalization" that swept across the world
of education, particularly the English-speaking world of education, in the
last decades of the twentieth century. "Rationalizing" education meant, to

a large extent, throwing overboard the past, the classical languages of Latin and Greek, even the study of history. Consider how little time our children or grandchildren spend on such studies, how little they know of bygone events or the questions of the philosophers and the dreams of the poets, "the glory that was Greece and the grandeur that was Rome." In the movement over the last twenty or thirty years of "rationalization," "relevance" has become the watchword. All subject matter must be "relevant" to the student's contemporary needs. Science, mathematics, marketing, the computer – all these are "relevant." Above all, the study of "communications" is relevant.

The critics of the new "rationalization" of education would call it a dumbing down of the curriculum. What, after all, is being communicated if we have abandoned the study of what humankind has thought and dreamed and aspired to over the centuries? Supporters of "rationalization" call the critics' attitude elitist and it is certain that David Lurie, reduced from teaching Classics and Modern Languages to being a professor of Communications I and Communications II, feels himself a part of an emasculated elite. He has contempt for his post-literate students and, I quote the omniscient narrator, he "has no respect for the material he teaches. . . . He continues to teach because it provides him with a livelihood." (pp. 4–5) Cape Technical University has offered a sop to David and his "rationalized" colleagues. Each of them is permitted to offer one course a year of his or her own choosing. David offers a course on the early nineteenth-century Romantic poets. Of the three books he has published, one was on vision as Eros, one was on opera, and one was on Wordsworth. Blake, Byron, and Wordsworth: these are the Romantic poets he teaches. He despises his other courses, Communications I and Communications II, with their banal definition of language as the means by which "we may communicate our thoughts, feelings, and intentions to each other." (p. 4) Rather, David thinks, the origins of speech and language "lie in song, and the origins of song in the need to fill out with sound the overlarge and rather empty human soul." (p. 4)

Consider for a moment that last phrase, the "rather empty human soul." That is a fair description of David Lurie's own soul when we meet him. He admires the Romantics so much for the fullness of their passion, but there is none of that fullness in his own life. There is a void at his centre. He is not, however, without self-knowledge. Our narrator gives us David's own view of himself:

> He is in good health, his mind is clear. By profession he is, or has been, a scholar, and scholarship still engages, intermittently, the core of him. He lives within his income, within his temperament, within his emotional means. Is he happy? By most measurements, yes, he believes he is. However, he has not forgotten the last chorus of *Oedipus:* Call no man happy until he is dead. (p. 2)

This is a man careful to avoid the extremes of emotion. Extreme emotion can lead to ecstasy or misery, and he would rather avoid both until death brings peace. He reflects upon Flaubert's great Romantic heroine, Emma Bovary, sated after "an afternoon of reckless fucking. *So this is bliss!* says Emma. . . . *So this is the bliss the poets speak of!* . . . [he would] show her what bliss can be: a moderate bliss, a moderated bliss." (pp. 5–6)

I found David Lurie an absolutely brilliant creation by Coetzee. This is a protagonist whose scholarly life is entirely concerned with the Romantics who gave themselves to passion and action without thought of consequence, and yet in his own life he is as careful and measured as T.S. Eliot's Prufrock or any of Anita Brookner's characters.

David certainly acknowledges and acts to satisfy his sexual needs. We are made privy to that in the wonderful opening line of the novel: "For a man of his age, fifty-two, divorced, he has, to his mind, solved the problem of sex rather well."

The *problem* of sex! No true Romantic could ever have used such a phrase! How has he solved the problem? When he was younger, with his Byronic good looks and flowing hair, women flocked to him. As he grew a little older, "his powers fled." Now, after two failed marriages and a relative loss of vigour, he contents himself with Thursday afternoons with the Discreet Escort Agency's exotic Soraya, an Asian housewife working while her two children are at school, and the occasional affair with a student. As the narrator says of Lurie, "barely a term passes when he does not fall for one or other of his charges." (pp. 11–12)

Now, at fifty-two, his sexual needs have become rather a nuisance. In one idle moment, he actually considers castration: "Might one approach a doctor and ask for it? A simple enough operation, surely: they do it to animals every day, and animals survive well enough, if one ignores a certain residue of sadness." (p. 9)

He is a very long way from the passion of the Romantics he admires, who bit the universe off in chunks. Thinking of Soraya, he imagines that his affection for her "is reciprocated. Affection may not be love, but it is at least its cousin." (p. 2)

When Soraya cancels their appointment because he has become too familiar, David turns to one of his students, dark-haired Melanie Isaacs, whom he calls Meláni, "the dark one." One may see in these two relationships, with a dark prostitute and a dark-haired girl, some echo, some faint echo, of the old exploitive white-black situation in South Africa, but I think it might be more productive to focus on the individual, David Lurie, exploiting the power of the teacher's function. He does it brilliantly in the first seduction scene.

"You're very lovely," he says. "I'm going to invite you to do something reckless." He touches her again. "Stay. Spend the night with me."

Across the rim of the cup she regards him steadily. "Why?"

"Because you ought to."

"Why ought I to?"

"Why? Because a woman's beauty does not belong to her alone. It is part of the bounty she brings into the world. She has a duty to share it."

His hand still rests against her cheek. She does not withdraw, but does not yield either.

"And what if I already share it?" In her voice there is a hint of breathlessness. Exciting, always, to be courted: exciting, pleasurable.

"Then you should share it more widely."

Smooth words, as old as seduction itself. Yet at this moment he believes in them. She does not own herself. Beauty does not own itself. (p. 16)

That passage is Coetzee at his best. David is not only persuading Melanie, he is persuading himself. In those smooth words, he is using two axioms of the Romantic poets. First, one has a duty to oneself to act "recklessly," literally to act without thought of consequence, and the reader harks back to David's reference to Emma Bovary. Second, beauty is a value in and of itself; beauty is owned by no one, it is an independent truth that we must all serve. As Keats put it, " 'Beauty is truth, truth beauty' – that is all / Ye know on earth, and all ye need to know."

As David serves up the Romantic lines, "at this moment he believes in them." This careful man has adopted the Romantic stance. It is a false step, false to his nature, and it will prove his undoing. Melanie will become frightened by the affair, her boyfriend will find out, and, worse, her father will find out and take the matter to the authorities. David has to face the University Sexual Harassment Committee. In his arrogance, he stands firm: " 'I was not myself. I was no longer a fifty-year-old divorcé at a loose end. I became a servant of Eros.' " (p. 52)

The women on the committee want him crucified, but the men, the majority, urge him to go beyond merely admitting the affair to a proclamation of his repentance. This, they promise, would result in suspension rather than outright dismissal. In his pride, the deadliest of the Deadly Sins, Lurie will not retreat from the Romantic high road. He will not admit wrong. He claims to his student hecklers that it was "an enriching experience" and later tells his daughter, quoting William Blake, that he would " 'sooner murder an infant in its cradle than nurse unacted desires.' " (p. 69)

Speaking of the committee to his daughter, David says, " 'It reminds me too much of Mao's China. Recantation, self-criticism, public apology.' " (p. 66) I thought that, for all his Romantic posing, David has a point. And so does Coetzee, his creator. He puts the reference to Mao's China into his character's mouth, but I am convinced that he intends us to compare the University Harassment Committee to South Africa's Truth and Reconciliation Committees set up under Archbishop Desmond Tutu after Mandela came to power in 1994. All those who had done wrong to their compatriots, black or white, during the apartheid years were to come forward, confess their sin, offer their apology, and receive absolution. It seems to me that Coetzee is suggesting that truth, repentance, and reconciliation are much more complex than words in front of a committee, even a committee as well-intentioned as that of Archbishop Tutu. I think we are also meant to note that Desmond Swarts, speaking for the male majority on the university committee, intimates very strongly to David Lurie that it is not actually necessary to repent; it is necessary only to *express* repentance in an acceptable form. (pp. 53–54) David, trapped in the image he has embraced, refuses any compromise, resigns from the faculty, closes his Cape Town house, and goes to join his daughter, Lucy, far away in the rural east of the province.

At first sight, Lucy, barefoot and comfortable, appears to embody the ideal preached by Wordsworth and Jean-Jacques Rousseau. She is living in a state of nature, where the true noble heart of humankind will manifest itself.

Six years earlier, she had come to the little commune near Salem to join with the others in growing marijuana and selling their own pottery and leather goods at the market in nearby Grahamstown. When the commune broke up, Lucy had stayed on with her friend and lover Helen. Her father had helped her to buy the five hectares of land. Now Helen, too, has left, and Lucy is alone on the farm.

At the market on Saturdays, there she is, with the neighbouring stalls run by black African women and a delightful old Afrikaner couple known to everyone as Oom and Tante, "Uncle" and "Auntie." The multi-racial fellowship of the market seems to confirm the Romantic claim that, in a life lived as close as possible to nature, all the hatreds will fall away.

Now that David Lurie has embraced the Romantic-pastoral ideal that he taught for so long, he should fit in wonderfully well. His daughter has long rejected such bourgeois conventions as the capitalist imperative to get rich as well as the traditional female road to marriage and motherhood. She tried living in Holland after David and his Dutch first wife ended their marriage, but she found that she wanted neither Holland nor any part of David's life in Cape Town. The farm is now home. She feels a oneness with the land and, even more so, a oneness with the animal world. This latter she has achieved through her closeness to the dogs she boards in her kennels and through the animal clinic run by her friend Bev Shaw. Bev conducts an amateur secular ministry to the animal world, a kind of cross between St. Francis of Assisi and Mother Teresa, in which she gives comfortable last days and a peaceful, dignified death to unwanted and tormented animals. Lucy tries to explain to her father:

> "They [the animals] are not going to lead me to a higher life, and
> the reason is, there is no higher life. This is the only life there is.
> Which we share with animals. That's the example that people like

Bev try to set. That's the example I try to follow. To share some of our human privilege with the beasts. I don't want to come back in another existence as a dog or a pig and have to live as dogs or pigs live under us." (p. 74)

Her father cannot understand her point of view, which, as evidenced by his earlier work on *The Lives of Animals*, is also that of J.M. Coetzee. He argues, gently:

"Lucy, my dearest, don't be cross. Yes, I agree, this is the only life there is. As for animals, by all means let us be kind to them. But let us not lose perspective. We are of a different order of creation from the animals. Not higher, necessarily, just different. So if we are going to be kind, let it be out of simple generosity, not because we feel guilty or fear retribution." (p. 74)

One notices that he says one should be kind to animals out of "simple generosity," not out of empathy, not out of love.

Certainly, David Lurie loves his daughter. We are told that "From the day his daughter was born he has felt for her nothing but the most spontaneous, most unstinting love." (p. 76) We have no reason not to believe that. Yet Coetzee, in spite of the exquisite simplicity of his prose, is never content with simple relationships. We are meant to remember that David's sexual preference is for much younger, subordinate women. We are meant to remember what he said so much earlier to his frightened student, Melanie: "'Tell me what is wrong.' Almost he says, 'Tell Daddy what is wrong.'" (p. 26)

I am not suggesting that, from those two references, we should deduce any unnatural relationship. What I am suggesting is that nothing in Coetzee's work is as simple as it first appears.

What I do know is that David Lurie has tremendous difficulty in accepting the full autonomy of his child's existence. Perhaps all parents do. David and Lucy have great difficulty communicating. Lucy is an intelligent woman and she knows her father much better than he knows her. The subordinate in any relationship always has to know the dominant partner better. When David tells her he will not back down at the university from his High Romantic stand – " 'I am not prepared to be reformed' " – Lucy counters with a gentle " 'So you are determined to go on being bad. Mad, bad, and dangerous to know.' " (p. 77)

Lucy is repeating Lady Caroline Lamb's description of David's beloved Byron, and she knows her father will appreciate the reference. Much of the verbal exchange between father and daughter is composed of that kind of elegant discourse. It rarely goes deeper.

I found it one of Coetzee's great ironies in the novel that the professor who so despised the teaching of "Communications" should have such a problem communicating with his daughter.

The novel is full of irony. Sometimes it is we, the readers, who detect it. Sometimes it is the characters themselves.

When David first arrives at the small holding, Lucy suggests that he fill his time by helping Bev Shaw at the clinic with the dying animals and by working for her neighbour Petrus, formerly her assistant. " 'Ask him to pay you,' Lucy suggests. At that, David smiles, 'Give Petrus a hand. I like that. I like the historical piquancy.' " (p. 77)

Then comes the rape. Two black strangers and a black boy turn up at the farm, lock David in the lavatory, take turns raping Lucy, pour methylated spirits on David and set him alight, strip the house of possessions, steal David's car, and, in one final gratuitous act of cruelty, shoot the six dogs in the kennels.

We are never given the details of Lucy's rape. It's a brilliant decision by Coetzee: the horror of the event is heightened because it is left to the imaginings of her father and the reader. For Lucy it is a private matter for which she will find a private solution. When her father calls the police, she refuses to let him report the rape. " 'You tell what happened to you, I tell what happened to me.' " (p. 99)

Lucy decides that she must take no official action against the men and the boy, even though she admits to her father that she fears their return. Her house is the only home she knows; South Africa is the only home she knows. She has answered the question "Where is home?" and she has got there. Now she believes her only way to stay there is to accept what has happened and move into the future without seeking revenge. Speaking to her father about her fear, she says

   "[W]hat if *that* is the price one has to pay for staying on? Perhaps
that is how they look at it; perhaps that is how I should look at it too.
They see me as owing something. They see themselves as debt collectors, tax collectors. Why should I be allowed to live here without
paying? Perhaps that is what they tell themselves." (p. 158)

Petrus, her neighbour, clearly knew about the impending attack. He was
conveniently absent and, after the rape, the third participant, the boy
Pollux, a relative of some kind, becomes a part of Petrus's household and
all David can do is challenge him verbally. Petrus agrees that the rape was
wrong. Of the boy, Petrus says, "'He is not guilty. He is too young. It is
just a big mistake.'" Petrus has decided that "'now it is all right . . . I will
protect her.'" (pp. 138–39)
   When I read of Lucy's acquiescence and Petrus's calm acceptance of
the rape, my first reaction was incredulity. But then I realized that their
solution, to accept the past with all its wrongs without any call for revenge,
is precisely the one advocated for South Africa by its white community and
even well-meaning members of the black community like Archbishop
Tutu. We may find Lucy's solution incomprehensible, but there is no doubt
that it is exactly what black South Africa is asked to do.
   David has immense difficulty respecting Lucy's position, particularly
when she agrees to sign over her remaining land to Petrus and to hold the
titular position of his third wife in return for the right to live in her house
alone but under his protection: "'Lucy, Lucy, I plead with you! You want
to make up for the wrongs of the past, but this is not the way to do it. If
you fail to stand up for yourself at this moment, you will never be able to
hold your head up again. You may as well pack your bags and leave.'"
(p. 133) But Lucy is adamant. One part of her refusal to listen is her desire
for autonomy from her father. As she says, "'What happened to me is my
business, mine alone, not yours, and if there is one right I have it is the
right not to be put on trial like this, not to have to justify myself – not to
you, not to anyone else.'" (p. 133) She further points out to David, "'You
don't know what happened,'" an assertion echoed by her friend Bev Shaw,
"'[Y]ou weren't there, David. She told me. You weren't.'" (p. 140)
   There is a clear implication that no man can understand the full meaning
of rape for a woman. That leads us to another of Coetzee's themes in this

novel, the sense of power over women that patriarchal societies give to men. David has had two failed marriages. We meet his second wife, Rosalind – they have an amicable enough relationship – and it is clear from her insights about him that she is his intellectual equal. We begin to suspect that it was his inability to accept her as his equal that may have ended their marriage. Certainly, in David's relationships with other women, the prostitute Soraya and the student Melanie, he exercised power. In his last sexual encounter with Melanie, Lurie realized himself that, in her passivity, there was something of the victim: "Not rape, not quite that, but undesired nevertheless, undesired to the core. As though she had decided to go slack, die within herself for the duration, like a rabbit when the jaws of the fox close on its neck. So that everything done to her might be done, as it were, far away." (p. 25)

The difference between what he did to Melanie and what the three rapists did to Lucy is only a matter of degree in the exercise of power. His daughter challenges David on the point: "'Maybe, for men, hating the woman makes sex more exciting. You are a man, you ought to know.'" (p. 158)

I have never felt the chasm between the sexes as acutely as I did at that point in the novel. The great irony of course is that, while asserting her independence from her father in placing herself under the protection of Petrus, Lucy is substituting one patriarchy for another. She will be lucky if all Petrus wants is her land. That is certainly what she hopes: "'[I]t is not me he is after, he is after the farm.'" (p. 203)

If she is to stay in the house she has decided is home, there is no choice but Petrus. His name is a nice play on Christ's words in Matthew 16:18, "Thou art Peter [Petros], and upon this rock I will build my church." (I have always found it strange, by the way, that a Nazarene carpenter should make a Greek pun to a Jewish disciple, but faith has no limitations.)

Petrus is part of the 84 percent non-white majority, the rock on which the future of South Africa will be built, but he is a man we do not come to know very well. I think it was a very considered decision by Coetzee not to give us abundant individual details of Petrus because, if any one character in this novel represents something more than himself, it is Petrus. He is the South Africa to whom Lucy is entrusting her future. He is the master now.

I found Lucy a fascinating mixture of wisdom and innocence. She is wise in her recognition of her father's need to direct her life, but she is innocent, even naive, in her belief in nature as a source of grace. When she discovers that she is pregnant as a result of the rape, she tells her father that she intends to bear the child. David startles himself by asking, " 'Do you love him yet?' " to which Lucy replies, " 'The child? No. How could I? But I will. Love will grow – one can trust Mother Nature for that.' " (p. 216)

I would have thought that one of the lessons of the novel is that nature is not as full of grace as Rousseau and the nineteenth-century English Romantics believed. Living on the land may have produced an interracial market on Saturdays, but it also produced a competition to own the land. Living close to the land did nothing to moderate the violence of the rapists. I found it touching that Lucy, in her innocence, could not understand their hatred of her – she sees them, like herself, as part of the idyllic pastoral community. Nor did living in nature, close to the soil, do anything to moderate the acquisitiveness of Petrus. As for the animal world that so inspired Wordsworth, it is here manifested in the pack of dogs that comes night after night to gnaw at the testicles of a poor, wretched, living goat. The Romantic poets who so glorified nature didn't actually live in it, did not see the truth, as Tennyson later put it, that nature is "red in tooth and claw."

It is a mark of David Lurie's growth during the novel that, when Lucy finally proclaims her faith in nature and her innocent desire to be a good mother and a good person, he no longer challenges her.

Like her father, I fear for Lucy's future as the novel comes to a close. Her solution, I believe, is based on a misguided perception of nature, but she has responded to the question of what "home" might mean to her with her own answer, and neither her father nor I have the right to gainsay her.

The David Lurie at the end of the novel is not the David Lurie of the beginning, the arrogant academic who espoused the Romantic ideals of action without conscience, of the supremacy of beauty, of nature as the source of grace. By the end of the novel, he has given up everything: his lechery, his role of father-counsellor, his Romantic pose, his faith in beauty, even his name – he is now Lourie instead of Lurie, taking advantage of a newspaper article's misprint. He has even given up much of his ethnocentricity: the black languages of Zulu, Xhosa, and Sotho, he now reflects, are more appropriate to express the truth of South Africa.

Once the teacher, David has become the student. He learns so much from Bev Shaw and her loving euthanasia at the animal clinic. When he first meets her, he is flippant. " 'Do I like animals?' " he says, repeating her question. " 'I eat them, so I suppose I must like them, some parts of them.' "

(p. 81) He asks Bev if she minds putting down the unwanted animals she loves, and she says, " 'I do mind. I mind deeply. I wouldn't want someone doing it for me who didn't mind. Would you?' " (p. 85) At that, David Lurie is silent, but something clearly begins to work within him. He can't explain to his daughter why he is reluctant to go to Petrus's land-acquisition party with its attendant slaughter of two sheep:

> "Yes. No. I haven't changed my ideas, if that is what you mean. I still don't believe that animals have properly individual lives. Which among them get to live, which get to die, is not, as far as I am concerned, worth agonizing over. Nevertheless . . ."
> "Nevertheless?"
> "Nevertheless, in this case I am disturbed. I can't say why."
> (pp. 126–27)

The process continues.

> The more killings he assists in, the more jittery he gets. One Sunday evening, driving home in Lucy's kombi, he actually has to stop at the roadside to recover himself. Tears flow down his face that he cannot stop; his hands shake.
> He does not understand what is happening to him. Until now he has been more or less indifferent to animals. (pp. 142–43)

After Bev injects the animals, it is David who takes them to the hospital incinerator. He is no longer prepared to leave them on the hospital dump for incineration by someone else. "He is not prepared to inflict such dishonour upon them." (p. 144)

As David Lurie loses his anthropocentric view of the world, other of his views begin to change. Just as he finally accepts his daughter's autonomy, her right to her own solution to her problem, so he goes to Melanie's father and, for the first time, expresses repentance: " 'I am sorry for what I took your daughter through. You have a wonderful family. I apologize for the grief I have caused you and Mrs. Isaacs. I ask for your pardon.' " (p. 171)

Mr. Isaacs, a religious man, tells David that he is following a path ordained by God. Implicit in that is the possibility of God's forgiveness. But David understands that, as a non-believer, he cannot seek refuge in the consolation that God has a plan for him. If he is to find grace it must be by his own action, and the path will be difficult: "'I am sunk into a state of disgrace from which it will not be easy to lift myself.'" (p. 172)

After a brief return to Cape Town to find his house stripped and vandalized, David realizes that his answer to the question "Where is home and how do I get there?" lies back at Bev Shaw's animal clinic. To that clinic he returns, renting a little room in the nearby town.

He has already lost all the personal vanity that so marked his earlier life. When Bev first offered him sexual congress, this one-time devotee of Beauty accepted her offer without reflecting that he had once found her unattractive. Why she offered her body, neither David nor we know. Coetzee is not one to clarify the complexity of human motivation. The best explanation, I think, is that Bev was reaching out to succour one more wounded animal.

As the novel comes to its end, David describes himself as "a mad old man." (p. 212) He appears to have lost everything, just as he sees his daughter stripped of everything. It's how she describes herself:

> "Perhaps that is what I must learn to accept. To start at ground level. With nothing. Not with nothing but. With nothing. No cards, no weapons, no property, no rights, no dignity."
> "Like a dog."
> "Yes, like a dog." (p. 205)

Some readers have seen in that "like a dog" an echo of Kafka. It is indeed the last line of Kafka's novel *The Trial*. Perhaps the simile is true of Lucy, as dependent on Petrus as is an animal on the goodwill of human beings, as helpless a victim of the forces of history as any of Kafka's protagonists. But when I think of David Lurie, stripped to his essence, "a mad old man," I think, not of Kafka, but of Lear, and I realize that "Lurie," the name, is not too far from "Lear."

Consider the story of David's planned opera on the poet Byron and his mistress Countess Teresa Guiccioli. Originally conceived in David's Romantic heyday as a chamber opera with lush orchestration, a meditation on Romantic passion, he has stripped it of all affectation by the end of the novel. Now he conceives it as a lament, sung by the fat, middle-aged countess to the dead lover who had finally so cruelly mocked and abandoned her; a lament sung to the simple accompaniment of a tune picked out on a humble banjo. At the end, David lives a life stripped of pose and pretence, imagining a musical work equally stripped of pose and pretence. No longer does David Lurie identify with the poet Byron or even the Countess Teresa, voluptuous when Byron met her at nineteen, nor does he identify with their initial passion. Now, at last, he finds himself just in the music, the simplest of tunes picked out on a seven-string banjo.

Just as Lear found redemption in his love for his once-rejected daughter, so David will find his redemption in a love for the most afflicted of creatures. In the last pages of the novel, he works side by side with Bev at the euthanasia clinic. "He and Bev do not speak. He has learned by now, from her, to concentrate all his attention on the animal they are killing, giving it what he no longer has difficulty in calling by its proper name: love." (p. 219)

The novel is called *Disgrace*, and there is much disgrace within it. David Lurie disgraced himself as a teacher, the rapists disgraced themselves as human beings, white South Africa disgraced itself as a nation with its policy of apartheid, Petrus disgraced himself as a patriarch exploiting the vulnerability of a rape victim, and at the end of the narrative David Lurie and his daughter have accepted menial situations that would have been considered a disgrace only ten years earlier.

All of that is true, yet I would argue that the novel could as well have been called *Grace*, because that is the state David Lurie achieves. Consider the final lines of the novel. David has developed a particular love for an unwanted young male dog with a dragging, withered leg:

> He opens the cage door. "Come," he says, bends, opens his arms. The dog wags its crippled rear, sniffs his face, licks his cheeks, his lips, his ears. He does nothing to stop it. "Come."
>
> Bearing him in his arms like a lamb, he re-enters the surgery. "I thought you would save him for another week," says Bev Shaw. "Are you giving him up?"
>
> "Yes, I am giving him up."

This is not the hateful David Lurie we met back in Cape Town. This is a new man, stripped to his essential self and full of love. He carries the dog "like a lamb," Coetzee tells us, and I was moved to a vision of David offering up the dog, and his love for the dog, like a Pascal sacrifice to a God in whom he does not believe. It is perhaps the supreme irony of this brilliant novel.

Despite the bleakness of much of the narrative and the uncertainty of Lucy's future in what promises to be an acquisitive, patriarchal culture, the novel leaves me with a vision of an individual who has found his home and who lives in a state of grace. David Lurie is finally a man greatly to be envied.

COLD MOUNTAIN

Charles Frazier
(Toronto: Viking, 1998)

There really is a Cold Mountain. It lies in the Blue Ridge Mountains, a part of the Southern Appalachian chain, in North Carolina near its border with Tennessee. It's an area of small communities like Asheville and Franklin, communities that still lament the defeat of the South in the American Civil War.

Ostensibly fought on the issue of slavery, the war was in fact about power – about who would control the American economy and thus the American government, the factory owners of the North or the plantation owners of the South. The issues were not clear even at the time: the slave-owning states of Maryland and Delaware, for example, fought with Abraham Lincoln, while the majority of the Confederate troops fought simply to protect their farms from Northern invaders. One of the great successes of Charles Frazier's *Cold Mountain* is that it shows so clearly the confusion of motives during the war. When Lincoln introduced conscription in the North in 1863, riots broke out as Northern workers blamed the black population for the struggle. During the whole period of the war from 1861 to 1865 there were more lynchings in the draft riots of the North than there were on the plantations of the South.

Two million men fought in the Civil War, and one-third of them died. But not many rich people died. In North or South, one could buy one's way out of military service either by paying an indemnity to the government or by paying a proxy to fight. By the time Inman, the protagonist of *Cold Mountain*, deserts from the Confederate forces, the soldiers on both sides were calling it a rich man's war but a poor man's fight.

The fact is that slavery was already on its way out when the conflict began. Morality apart, more and more Southern farmers were realizing that a paid hand produced much more than a slave who could expect no reward. The "peculiar institution" of the South was dying simply because it wasn't economically sound. But the war over power was fought anyway, and the myth of Southern nobility and the superior Southern way of life would persist long after Lee surrendered in 1865.

Charles Frazier himself commented on the myth in an interview with *The New York Times* (August 27, 1997):

> "When you grow up in the South, you get this concept of the war as this noble, tragic thing, and when I think about my own family's experience, it doesn't seem so noble in any direction. To go off and fight for a cause they had not much relation to, that's the part I see as tragic."

The Frazier family has lived in the Blue Ridge Mountains for more than two centuries. But they aren't hillbillies. Charles Frazier's father was a high school principal and his mother a librarian. Together, they brought up their two sons and a daughter to love history, literature, and, above all, the land they lived on.

Born in 1951, Charles Frazier has a Ph.D. in American Literature and taught for a while at the University of Colorado, but, when his daughter was born in 1986, he and his wife decided to move back to the mountains of their beloved North Carolina. There is something in his decision to abandon academia and go home that has a lot to do with the theme of *Cold Mountain*. Also, Frazier was becoming increasingly interested in the history of his part of the Southern Appalachian chain. His father had sparked the interest by researching the life of a great-great-uncle, W.P. Inman, who had fought for the Confederacy but who, after he had had his fill of the horror and misery, had deserted and walked home to the Blue Ridge Mountains. Frazier's father had been unable to find out any more than the bare outline of the journey – the results of the years of research could be summarized on one page – but Charles Frazier realized that a novel based on that journey would permit him to examine both the confusion of the Civil War and the ideal of home to which Inman was escaping.

Writing the novel became an obsession, but Frazier was fortunate in the understanding of his wife, Katherine, by now teaching at North Carolina State, who told him to stay home and write. *Cold Mountain* took its author eight years of daily effort, but now, as a result of the enormous success the novel has enjoyed, including winning the National Book Award, the Fraziers spend their days raising show horses on their eleven-acre ranch. They are safely home.

In its engrossing description of flora and fauna, *Cold Mountain* owes a great debt to an eighteenth-century travel book, William Bartram's *Travels*. Our protagonist, Inman, picks up a copy at the military hospital where he is recuperating and carries it with him on his journey. He reads from it frequently to himself and to us. Through a combination of Bartram's observations and Frazier's masterful storytelling, every twig, every flower, every tree, every hollow is invested with meaning, and we gasp with Bartram and Inman at the beauty and the mystery of creation.

The debt owed by Charles Frazier to his father's research and to Bartram's book is evident, but there is another debt to acknowledge, to the Western world's first great storyteller. There are so many parallels between Frazier's *Cold Mountain* and Homer's *Odyssey* that it is worth recalling a little about Homer and his works. Homer lived nearly three millennia ago on one of the Ionian islands off the coast of Greece, and tradition has it that he was blind. He composed two great epic poems about events that were supposed to have taken place some three centuries earlier. The first of the two poems, *The Iliad*, is set in the city state of Troy on the Turkish coast. According to Homer, one of the Trojan princes, Paris, had kidnapped Helen, the wife of the king of one of the Greek city states. A party of Greeks, including Odysseus, King of Ithaca, besieged Troy for ten years, achieving victory and the destruction of Troy by the trick of the wooden horse.

For the Greeks to whom he sang his poems Homer created a mythic past, full of great and noble ancestors. He gave them a past that never happened, a glorious explanation of their beginnings. It is a phenomenon true of most cultures, including the people of the postbellum South nearly three thousand years later, who would dream of a graceful, magnolia-blossom way of life before the Civil War that had never been a reality for most Southerners.

Exulting in their victory, the triumphant Greeks failed to give proper tribute to the gods, who, in revenge, made Odysseus's journey home to Ithaca a ten-year nightmare of obstacles to overcome. This is the subject of Homer's second poem, *The Odyssey*. On his way back to Ithaca and his wife, Penelope, Odysseus is often saved from disaster by the goddess Athena, who admires his courage, his fertile intelligence, his thirst for knowledge, his cunning, and, above all, his will to go on. Odysseus, in spite of all his human frailties, is the ultimate survivor.

Frazier gives the reader clear clues that we are meant to see a modern *Odyssey* in *Cold Mountain*. Both Homer himself and *The Odyssey* make what amount to guest appearances in Frazier's novel. At the beginning of *Cold Mountain*, one of Inman's fellow patients is translating a Greek classic, and there is a wise, blind old storyteller outside the hospital window. Inman's neighbour back at Cold Mountain, Esco Swanger, follows the practice of the Ancient Greeks in reading the future in the entrails of animals. Ada, Inman's fiancée, the parallel figure to Odysseus's Penelope, reads to her friend Ruby out of *The Odyssey* itself. At the end of the novel, as a reunited Inman and Ada plan their future, Inman makes a promise to learn Greek and study the wisdom of the Ancients.

Both Inman and Odysseus face great tribulations and are often tempted to abandon the struggle, but both are able to summon up from within themselves the strength to continue. It might be helpful to note briefly the major events of Odysseus's ten-year journey.

Odysseus's men will be disobedient and want to lie in the land of the Lotus-Eaters forever, a disobedience that will later bring about their deaths.

Odysseus will incur the dangerous enmity of Poseidon, King of the Sea, when he kills Poseidon's son, the one-eyed Cyclops Polyphemus.

He will meet cannibals and he will pass by Scylla, the man-eating, cave-dwelling monster; Charybdis, the deadly whirlpool; and the Sirens, those terrible women who call sailors to their doom.

Twice he will dwell with witches, one year with the enchantress Circe and seven years with the beautiful Calypso. It is the first, Circe, who turns Odysseus's men into swine for behaving like swine. (At another point in the narrative, Odysseus nearly becomes an animal himself.) It is Circe, too, who will send Odysseus to visit the land of the dead, where he meets the prophet Tiresias and the dead Greek hero Achilles at whose side Odysseus had fought at Troy. In a passage that is central to Homer's poem, Achilles tells Odysseus that he would rather be a slave on earth than King of the Dead. The message is clear: life is infinitely preferable to death. Whatever the cost, go on living. Odysseus's visit to the land of the dead is often seen as a metaphor for the journey he makes within himself to the centre of his being, a journey common to the myths of the beginning of cultures. It is the journey of Moses to the mountaintop, Christ's journeys to another mountaintop and to the desert, and Mohammed's journey to the cave near Mecca, and the message received is always the same, to go on, to go forward, and never to abandon the struggle.

After his rescue by the princess Nausicaa, Odysseus arrives in Ithaca only to be warned by an old swineherd of the danger he must still face.

Penelope, Odysseus's faithful wife, has been alone in a man's world for twenty years. Her struggles to survive form the content of the first five books of Homer's poem and the reader of *Cold Mountain* must surely think of Ada's effort to live alone in the absence of Inman and after the death of her preacher father.

The young men of Ithaca will have no more of Penelope's tricks and prevarications and demand that she choose a new husband. Desperate, Penelope devises a test of strength that only Odysseus could win: she will marry the man who can bend his great bow. Disguised as a beggar, Odysseus wins the contest, slays all the rival suitors with the help of his son Telemachus, and, for the rest of *The Odyssey*, immerses himself in the happy trivia of daily life until his death from old age.

And there you have it, all the beauty and excitement of the twenty-four books of *The Odyssey* reduced to a few inadequate paragraphs. But it's enough to show how much in *Cold Mountain* has been borrowed and how much has been transmuted and how much of the novel comes out of Frazier's own imagination.

As we meet our protagonist, called, simply, Inman, he is recuperating from a neck wound in a military hospital in his home state of North Carolina. The year is 1864, and we know that the war has one more year to run, but Inman is sick of the slaughter. As he says to the blind storyteller who is selling newspapers, "There's plenty I wish I'd never seen." (p. 9) Chief among the images of torn bodies that haunt his memory are those of the Battle of Fredericksburg two years earlier, when the troops of the Confederacy, hidden safely behind a long stone wall, had massacred twelve thousand Union soldiers as their incompetent commander, General Burnside, sent them on impossible charges up a steep, exposed slope. Inman can still hear "the slap of balls into meat." (p. 11) (The horror affected not only Inman. Lincoln, who had appointed the inept Burnside, said, after he received the news, "If there is a worse place than hell, I am in it.") Frazier is heart-rending in his evocation of the hellishness of the scene and of its aftermath, when Confederate soldiers go out among the wounded to steal their boots, finishing them off with a hammer in order to conserve ammunition. The battle scene is worthy of comparison with those of Sebastian Faulks's *Birdsong*, in which soldiers rising out of the trenches of the First World War charged machine guns and barbed wire and fell in the hundreds of thousands. Charles Frazier sings as effectively as Sebastian Faulks of arms and the man, and I can think of no higher compliment.

Inman has lost all faith in the South and the Cause. Much later in the novel, he will confess to a wise old goatherd that he felt shame "to think of his zeal in sixty-one to go off and fight the downtrodden mill workers of the Federal army." He knows, too, that the soldiers against whom he fights are as confused in their motives as he is: "anyone thinking the Federals are willing to die to set loose slaves has got an overly merciful view of mankind." (p. 275)

Inman is a profoundly thoughtful man. If anyone has ever led an examined life it is Inman, and he understands that, whereas General Lee "looked on war as an instrument for clarifying God's obscure will," (p. 12) in fact the war had an awful fascination for those who fought – "the more terrible it is the better." He knows that the war is robbing all its participants of their humanity: "[A]t the rate we're going we'll be eating each other raw." He is frightened by the void he sees approaching, a fear revealed to us in a passage where the beauty of the language emphasizes by contrast the bleakness of his prophecy: "[H]e had seen the metal face of the age and had been so stunned by it that when he thought into the future, all he could vision was a world from which everything he counted important had been banished or had willingly fled." (p. 4) When he looks at the Northern enemy, all he sees are the faces of young men and his soul shrieks out to them and to himself to go home.

The word "home" and the idea of home become endowed with mystical meaning. Inman thinks back to the wisdom of Swimmer, a Cherokee friend of his youth, who had told him that their home, Cold Mountain, was so tall that it jutted up into the heavens into a celestial place where the spirit could be reborn. As Inman reflects on his memories, the mountain "soared in his mind as a place where all his scattered forces might gather." (p. 23) In a world "so frequently foul," home becomes a magical refuge, a place untouched by war. Inman marries that ideal to his love of nature, a nature made even more real to him by the beauty of the descriptions in Bartram's travel book.

As Inman writes to Ada, the girl back home, he tries at one point to describe the horror he has seen. The images are compelling, as is the incremental repetition of the word "blood": "The ground was awash with blood and we could see where the blood had flown onto the rocks and the marks of bloody hands on tree trunks." (p. 24) But those who have lived such horror know that no one can be made to comprehend it, and he wads up the letter and writes instead what Ada will understand: "I am coming home. . . ."

Inman had loved Ada before the war with a delicate, inarticulate love, exquisitely handled in the novel. Ada was the gently nurtured daughter of Monroe the preacher, whose sermons have been a great comfort to Inman. He often thinks back to one in particular, the sermon Monroe delivered on the day Inman first saw Ada.

Whenever Inman is at the point of despair, he is sustained by Monroe's promise that each of us moves towards goodness in a way that is godlike, and that each of us has a God-given mission, although Inman does not yet know what his mission is. All he can think of is his pure image of home with his gentle Ada waiting. His only concern is that he has been so changed by war – "his spirit, it seemed, had been about burned out of him" (p. 22) – that she might no longer want him. But the vision of home triumphs over his fears. It is a vision enhanced by his readings from Bartram, who had visited Cold Mountain and revelled in its beauty, and Inman sees the place as even more intensely lovely than he remembered it: "The peaks now stood higher, the vales deeper than they did in truth." (p. 349) So often do we all make of our remembered beginnings something more beautiful and more untouched by time than they could ever have been.

Inman decides to resign from the war and walk the five hundred kilometres or so across the whole state of North Carolina back to Cold Mountain, to his little settlement of Black Cove, back to Ada and to home.

The reader might wonder what this deserter has in common with Odysseus, a king and one of the victors at Troy. They have much in common. Each is heartily sick of war. Each is going home, and to a home they have idealized, imagining it to be immutable. Each is returning to a woman who, they will find, has been made strong by courage and loneliness and hostile circumstances.

As Inman begins his long journey, he is attacked by three men and escapes across the river only through the help of a girl and her canoe, and we remember how often Odysseus is helped by a woman. Circe, Calypso, Nausicaa, and Athena herself are more than nurturers; they are strong and capable and confident, just as Penelope and Ada are revealed finally to be. Both *The Odyssey* and *Cold Mountain* are testimonies to women as powerful characters.

First among the difficulties Inman faces as he travels towards his goal is the Home Guard. Led by the evil Teague, its members are Southern deserters – "outliers," as the Guard calls them – and it represents many of the forces that so plagued Odysseus.

As he wanders, Inman meets other troubled souls, including the one-time preacher Solomon Veasey, the vehicle for much of the humour in the novel. When Inman first sees him, Veasey is about to throw his pregnant girlfriend off a cliff to get rid of all evidence of his adulterous affair. If the scandal should come out, it would destroy his career as a preacher in his little community, although Veasey confesses to Inman, "I now believe that when I took to preaching I answered a false call," a comment that elicits Inman's delicious understatement, "Yes . . . I'd say you're ill suited for that business." (p. 118)

After Inman returns the girl to her home and permits Veasey to get a well-deserved beating from his neighbours, Veasey throws in his lot with Inman and, in so doing, assumes the role of Odysseus's men. Like them, Veasey is disobedient and self-indulgent and Inman has to club him when he tries to rob a country store. After Veasey unwisely spends the night with the prostitute Big Tildy, who cuts him badly in an argument over price, he admits to Inman, "I am a man overly charmed by the peculiarities of the female anatomy." (p. 174) Veasey will meet his death on the journey, but, unlike Odysseus's men, he will redeem himself in his final moments. Caught by Teague's Home Guard, Veasey is shot while crying out, not for mercy, but for the salvation of the souls of his executioners. He walks towards them with exhortations to put away their evil (p. 228) and in so doing becomes an example of the depths to which man may sink and of the heights to which he may rise.

As he travels, Inman meets kindness surprisingly often from those whom life has treated most miserably. A male slave gives him food and a map and good advice, and a female slave gives him safe directions. He falls in with gypsies and comes to admire their rejection of the rest of humankind, their enjoyment of every moment, and, above all, their sense of oneness with the land. Inman turns again to Bartram's *Travels* and fills his mind and ours with the detail and the wonder of creation.

Not all of the episodes of Inman's journey owe something to Homer's epic. There are marvellous and meaningful adventures that have no parallel in the Greek original. There is one heartbreaking little digression when Inman meets Odell, the son of a Georgian plantation owner who had fallen in love with one of his father's slaves. His father mocked him coarsely and then sold the girl "down river," into the deeper South, into Mississippi. Now Odell is searching for his lost love and tells Inman of the horrors of slavery he has witnessed, the maimings and the cagings and the lynchings, and one could weep for the purity of his love and for the fallen world that keeps Odell and the girl apart.

It is indeed a fallen world through which Inman moves. At one point he comes to the house of a man and his three sisters who live at the level of animals, in a coarse combination of the Sirens who tempted Odysseus and the swine into which Circe turned Odysseus's sailors. The sisters stare at Inman with open, bestial lust:

> One of the sisters gazed at Inman and said, I wish he'd hug me till I grunt.
> Lila said, This is mine. All that's left for you is just to look at him and then to go to wishing in one hand and shitting in the other and see which one gets full first. (p. 219)

Even Inman himself is later reduced to a near-animal state: "He found himself one afternoon crawling on the mossy ground of the creekside, grazing at the water edge like a beast of the wild, his head wet to the ears, the sharp taste of cress in his mouth and no idea whatsoever in his mind." (p. 299) Frazier is particularly adept at showing to what dramatic lows the human being can sink.

Twice during the novel, Inman is tempted to give up his journey. The first occasion is when he meets the widow Sara, whose husband died fighting in Virginia. Inman labours with her on her farm to the point that each night, both physically exhausted, they lie together and do no more than hold hands. It is a delicate and loving human relationship, and Inman knows that he could end his journey there and become a part of Sara's life. But still he dreams of Ada and he dreams of home, and the same indomitable will that Athena admired in Odysseus will cause him to go on.

More serious is the second temptation, in the person of an old slavery-hating woman who has lived alone with her goats for twenty-six years. In her wisdom, she is an elaboration of the goatherd Odysseus meets on his return to Ithaca. Inman's friend is more fully drawn than her Greek counterpart, and she tells Inman a story worthy of a novel in itself. Many years before, she had been the fourth wife of an old man, and she wanted no more of that world. "You've seen these old men – sixty-five, seventy – and they've gone through about five wives. Killed them from work and babies and meanness." (p. 272)

The world she knew was a very small place. She had travelled, as she puts it, "all over the world. As far north as Richmond and all the way south, nearly to Charleston." She had looked upon what she saw and found it wanting and had made a new home for herself in nature. In that haven she had discovered a truth that satisfied her. Plants supply all her needs and she records every moment of her life in her journals and her life is full. The woman needs no one and, when Inman tells her of Ada's beauty, she comes out with an oddly compelling piece of folk wisdom: "Marrying a woman for her beauty makes no more sense than eating a bird for its singing. But it's a common mistake nonetheless." (p. 279)

We will remember the goat-woman's words when Inman finally reunites with Ada. Matured by his journey, he will love her not for her beauty but for her strength and the fullness of being she has achieved through her suffering.

Inman is briefly tempted to join the goat-woman in her retreat from the madding crowd: "This would be one way to live, Inman thought, a hermit among the clouds. The contentious world but a fading memory." (p. 282) But he knows he would eventually be overcome by a longing for home, and he has gained a new understanding that home involves a relationship with other people. He now knows that only in communion with other human beings can we achieve a completion of self. To withdraw from the world would be to die. Isolation may suit the old woman, but it is not the answer for Inman. For him, to be alive is to live *in* the world with other people in a shared humanity, and we remember Achilles' advice to Odysseus that it is better to live as a slave than to be King of the Dead, however comfortable death might be. Life is precious, and Inman finds within himself the will to go on.

As he nears home and Cold Mountain, Inman begins to recite the names of the geographical features like a litany. But he is concerned. He longs to see again the girl with whom he had exchanged only one chaste kiss before going off to a war he had not really understood, but he fears he has changed. In a letter to Ada he spoke of a photograph he had given her: "Should you still possess the likeness I sent four years ago, I ask you, please, do not look at it. I currently bear it no resemblance in either form or spirit." (p. 246) Inman believes that the misery of war and the killing he has been forced into to survive during the long journey home may have rendered him unfit to live among people. At different times during his odyssey, he has felt an affinity with the bear, with its simple routine of survival, and with the crow, with its ability to fly free, but he is still not sure that his experiences have not disrupted his relationship with the natural world whose mystical nature his friend Swimmer had so patiently explained to him. He has come to doubt Swimmer's romantic view of nature just as he has abandoned any political affiliation – the insanity of the war has seen to that. Organized religion offers him no comfort: as he told the girl whom he saved from Veasey, "That preacher does not speak for God. No man does." (p. 121)

All Inman has left is his inner strength, the self-reliance he has learned during his ordeals, and a belief in the healing power of "home." The only certainties he sees outside himself are Ada and Cold Mountain.

We have learned much about Ada in chapters alternating with those that chronicle Inman's progress. Ada is a sheltered child and her skills are those of a city girl, ". . . French and Latin. A hint of Greek. A passable hand at fine needlework. A competency at the piano, though no brilliance. The ability to render landscape and still life. . . . And she was well read." (p. 30)

Ada had shown some independence when she rejected myriad suitors, to the horror of the local matrons who believed that the first duty of a married woman was submission to her husband's will. Her cousin Lily had taught her the techniques of masturbation, so she was self-sufficient in that regard, but, with the death of her father, she was alone in what she knew to be a man's world. All the accomplishments of a cultivated young woman, all the pleasure she finds in the classics, are of little practical use on Cold

Mountain, and she is tempted to return to the safety of the city. But she
refuses to turn the clock back twenty years. Just as Inman refused the non-
life of the goat-woman's seclusion, so Ada finds something within her that
impels her to move forward. She will make a journey as fraught with
difficulty as Inman's.

Initially Ada is helpless and as dependent as Inman on the kindness of
others. A neighbour's gift of strawberry jam she gobbles up with her
fingers, and she has no idea how to look after a house and barn and three
hundred acres. There seem to be for her, as for Inman, no certainties
outside herself. Nature itself seems hostile, and she is attacked by one of
her own roosters. The Federalist liberators steal, and Confederates like
Teague and the Home Guard are as bad or worse. Ada is as disillusioned
with either cause as is the long-absent Inman. Her late father's Platonic
version of Christianity, that this life is a mere shadow of some other beautiful reality, offers little comfort to a young woman faced with the very real
problem of starvation.

Salvation comes to Ada in the form not of a belief but of another human
being. Ruby is a local girl who has survived a hard and neglected childhood with Stobrod, her ne'er-do-well and often absent father. Illiterate but
hard-headed, Ruby teaches Ada how to farm in harmony with nature and
the seasons. Ada comes to realize that all Ruby's talk of signs and portents is
no more than a sound, practical, empirical observation of natural processes.
Frazier spent years in meticulous research into the daily lives of those who
stayed home and survived the Civil War, and I found the details of Ada and
Ruby's struggle fascinating. Just as every twig and leaf is infused with
meaning during Inman's journey, so every object on Ada's farm is given its
full measure of texture and solidity. I could feel every turnip and every
carrot. I could even feel salt!

Life is harsh, and Ada, like Inman, is reduced at times to grubbing in
the dirt like an animal, but there is a superb counterbalance in the delicacy
of the growing relationship between Ruby and Ada as they do each other's
hair and exchange confidences about their so-different childhoods. Each
learns from the other. From Ada, Ruby acquires an appetite for literature
and perhaps a little more compassion than her hard life has permitted her
to exercise. From Ruby, Ada gains some of the girl's immense store of practical knowledge. Ruby calls it "grandmother knowledge," but we know it

as the oral tradition of women who have been left so often to cope as men run off to war.

Ruby brings a refreshingly harsh and realistic perspective to Ada's book learning. When Ada reads to her of Odysseus carousing with his men, Ruby comments caustically that it took him one hell of a long time to get home, what with all the women, all the drinking, and all the adventures.

By the last year of the war, we have a very different Ada. Like Inman, she has thought of renouncing the world for the life alone. Like Inman, she has watched the birds, in particular the blue heron, "the solitary pilgrim," and envied their free and solitary majesty. But, like Inman, she has put temptation behind her and chosen human communion.

When Ruby's long-gone father, Stobrod, turns up and tells the story of how his soul was revolted by the waste after he was asked to play his fiddle for a girl dying of her burns, it is Ada who believes in his repentance. As she says, "[N]o matter what a waste one has made of one's life, it is ever possible to find some path to redemption, however partial." (p. 297) War and the agony of survival have not brutalized Ada Monroe.

It is striking how often in the novel music is associated with the higher reaches of human nature. When Stobrod and the half-wit Pangle are faced with execution by Teague's Home Guard and are playing their last music, one of Teague's men says, "Good God, these is holy men. Their mind turns on matters kept secret from the likes of you and me." (p. 368) Teague's reaction is to look off into the distance "as if trying to remember something." What he has forgotten is his humanity, and he orders the men shot anyway. Stobrod will survive, but as a cripple dependent on the goodness of his daughter and Ada.

Like love, nature, and humankind's potential for goodness and will to survive, music is a redemptive element in a novel so full of brutality and the trying of souls.

As we near Inman's reunion with Ada, she writes him a letter as she has written so many before, although none have reached him. But in this letter there are no literary references and no dreamy digressions. Ada still loves the beauty of books, but they are no longer replacements for life itself. Like Inman, like Odysseus, she has cut through all the inessentials. "She inked her pen and then sat and stared at the paper until her nib dried out. Every phrase she thought of seemed nothing but pose and irony. She wiped the pen clean on a blotter and dipped again and wrote, Come back to me is my request." (p. 344)

When they finally meet, the scene is unbearably poignant, with all convention and pretension gone. Inman calls out to her, "Ada Monroe," and Ada, seeing a wild man, answers, "I do not know you." But then she sees him more closely. "He was blasted and ravaged, worn ragged and weary and thin, but he was nevertheless Inman." (p. 405) The word "blasted" took me back to Lear's heath, and I understood that Inman and Ada have both been stripped to their essence as surely as was Lear. Inman fears that he is beyond repair, but Ada in her new wisdom knows that people can be mended. She takes Inman to a nearby abandoned Cherokee village and they lie together in a perfect loving communion. Neither speaks much of the past; each has learned that we all make our own odyssey and impose our own meaning on it. Inman dismisses all his adventures with a single sentence whose magnificent understatement made me laugh out loud. "I met a number of folks on the way." (p. 432) There is nothing important to say; all that was needed was "the easement of a companion voice." (p. 406)

What they speak of is the future. In a lovely balance of learning and practicality, they plan to farm, to play music, and to read. Inman will study Greek, and they will live by the seasons. The immediate step to take is for Inman to cross the mountains into Federalist territory and wait out the war. The only alternatives are to return to fight or to await capture by the Home Guard. Flight is not the perfect solution, but, like Odysseus's choice between Scylla and Charybdis, it is the least of the available evils.

Then comes the supreme irony of the novel. They are discovered by Teague and the Home Guard. A desperate Inman charges and kills them all. Almost all. Inman falls victim to his own humanity when a wounded boy, whom Inman is reluctant to kill, puts an end to Inman's life. He dies cradled in Ada's arms, dreaming "a bright dream of home." (p. 445)

Odysseus lived happily ever after with his Penelope, but our world is not as beautiful as Homer's poem.

The novel, however, has an epilogue, set in 1874, nine years after the end of the war. Ruby has married a deserter from Georgia whom she had found "not particularly worse than the general order of men, which is to say that he would greatly benefit from having someone's foot in his back every waking minute." (pp. 378–79) Ada has a daughter, the legacy of her one perfect embrace with Inman, and there is poor, wounded Stobrod to play his fiddle for them. Ada tells them all stories from Greek mythology, including the favourite of Baucis and Philemon, the lovers who were never separated, even in death. Ada and Ruby and the others have a home full of love and music and literature and a life in harmony with nature. It is the home of which Inman dreamed.

It has been a wonderful journey in which we have lived the courage of the soldier coming home and the courage of those who stayed behind.

We have seen how necessary human beings are to each other and of what goodness people are capable. Inman was helped by many, and Ada and Ruby helped each other. Even the indomitable Ruby owes much to the woman who first sent her to Ada. Few of us can make our journey alone.

As we come to the last lines of the novel, as the women make their warm home secure for the night, we understand how much they have achieved. May we all strip away the illusions and find our true selves, and may we all find our way home.

THE DRESS LODGER

Sheri Holman
(New York: Ballantine, 2000)

Sheri Holman's novel *The Dress Lodger* is set in Sunderland, a port on the northeast coast of England, in the year 1831. England is the first country in the world to industrialize, to switch from an agricultural to a factory-based economy, and England is rich. It destroyed the threat of Napoleon in 1815 and its empire is growing day by day. British textile factories have already begun to clothe the world, and in six years Victoria will come to the throne of the greatest empire the world has ever seen. Yet the great majority of the population lives in a poverty and under working conditions that are hard for us now to imagine.

Many believed that the misery of the poor was inevitable and indeed necessary. A 1798 essay by Dr. Thomas Robert Malthus had obtained a wide following. In "On the Principle of Population," Malthus argued that poverty was the inescapable lot of humankind. He believed that, since population will always grow more quickly than food production, government should not intervene to prevent death by famine, war, or sickness. Such forces must be allowed to diminish population growth, else we will all starve. You will remember Scrooge in Dickens's *A Christmas Carol*, who refused to give money to relieve the suffering poor at Christmas by invoking Malthus. They should die, said Scrooge, and so decrease the dangerous surplus population.

There were social reformers in England, like the seventh Earl of Shaftesbury, but they were relatively few. The teachings of Malthus were embraced by most industrialists since they justified working the poor to death in the factories and coal mines that generated British wealth. The investigative commissions of the 1830s and 1840s organized by Lord Shaftesbury revealed that children as young as four years old were working in coal mines and cotton mills and that the average age of death in great industrial cities like Liverpool and Manchester was twenty-one. The rich controlled Parliament and the political process. Women and the poor were not allowed to vote, and it would not be until 1918 that the last property qualification was removed and universal suffrage granted. It was only with great difficulty and by using his immense wealth and influence that Lord Shaftesbury was able to force two reform bills through Parliament in 1842 and 1847, prohibiting the labour of children under ten years old in mines and limiting the work in textile mills to ten hours a day, six days a week.

In 1831, the year of *The Dress Lodger*, Shaftesbury's reforms had not yet come to pass, and the poor were being allowed to die in accordance with Malthusian theory, a theory summarized in *The Dress Lodger* on page 140. Women were still employed to make matches by painting phosphorus onto little wooden splinters. Over the years, the splatters of phosphorus would eat away the face of the worker in a condition known as Fossie-Jaw, and it is small wonder that characters like Fos in the novel should seek drunken oblivion to forget how their hands and faces glow in the dark and the "freakish mess" that is their face. (p. 4)

Even those of the poor fortunate enough to find employment had to supplement their miserably low earnings. Their children could always be put to labour, and Whilky Robinson, the pimp of *The Dress Lodger*, is bitterly resentful that his six-year-old daughter, feeble-witted Pink, is "too daft to be sent out to work." (p. 53) For women, and for children of both sexes in sophisticated centres like London, prostitution was an available occupation. As Gustine, the young whore of *The Dress Lodger*, tells us, "Half the girls in Sunderland have sold their bodies at some point to put food on the table or to keep their families from the workhouse." (p. 89)

There was one other avenue of profit that the poor might explore. Parliament had not yet passed the Anatomy Act of 1832, permitting doctors to obtain bodies by legal means for study and dissection, and would-be surgeons and teaching doctors were desperate for cadavers. An enterprising person with a spade, a strong back, and a nearby graveyard could make quite a handsome income as a "Resurrection Man," as a grave robber was known in the gallows humour of the time. Jerry Cruncher was a Resurrection Man in Dickens's *A Tale of Two Cities*. For those lucky enough to find an unburied body, there was little risk and great reward. All that was necessary was a barrow and a short journey to the nearest interested medical man.

In 1827, William Hare, the owner of an Edinburgh boarding house, had one such piece of luck. After one of his boarders died of old age, Hare, with the help of another of his tenants, carried the corpse to Dr. Robert Knox, a well-known surgeon and teacher. William Hare and William Burke were paid seven pounds and ten shillings for the corpse, a staggering sum for those days, equivalent to many months' wages for a day labourer. It was easy money, and Burke and Hare decided to accelerate the natural process. In twelve months, beginning in late 1827, they suffocated between fifteen and eighteen people, selling the bodies to Dr. Knox for the purpose of teaching anatomy. (*The Dress Lodger* suggests sixteen victims, p. 31.) The murdered included a boy known as Daft Jamie and a prostitute, Mary Paterson, by all accounts very beautiful. (p. 127) After the murderers were caught, Hare went free after turning King's Evidence against Burke, but Burke was hanged and a new word entered the English language. "To burke" meant to murder to obtain a saleable corpse. The activity was "burking" and a practitioner a "burker." All three forms are used extensively throughout *The Dress Lodger* by the poorer classes, terrified of losing their own lives to burkers or the remains of their loved ones to the Resurrection Men. Although their fears were often fuelled by wild rumours, they were not without foundation. In *The Dress Lodger*, a panicked mob crying "Resurrection" digs into the graves of Trinity Pit, the local paupers' cemetery, only to find empty coffins and bags of sand where their loved ones used to be. (p. 259)

The poor had other, even more pressing terrors. There had been a terrible cholera epidemic in 1817, brought to Europe by British soldiers originally exposed to the disease in India, where it was endemic, and in 1831 cholera was for a second time ravaging Europe and threatening again to cross the Channel to visit the British population. As *The Dress Lodger* begins, the port of Sunderland is already under a fifteen-day quarantine. No ships may put in at the harbour, and business is at a standstill. When a second period of quarantine is proposed at a meeting of Sunderland's leading citizens and medical men, all hell breaks loose. One businessman shouts, "'My doctor told me if everyone would just stay away from oysters and cucumbers we wouldn't number a case among us.'" (p. 188) The chairman of the meeting is an honest doctor who summarizes the confusion about cholera: "'Our medical community is split on whether it was imported or generated on local soil. Some believe it can be transmitted from person to person and thus we need the Quarantine; others that we take it straight from the atmosphere, and no Quarantine can help.'" (p. 188) Feelings run high and the Marquis of Londonderry makes a powerful point:

> "Exactly how long do you think we can keep the East End idle before it rises in revolt?" demands Londonderry, for the first time this afternoon losing his composure. "You think the cholera is killing them? Starvation will kill them quicker; and the hungrier they get, the more they'll cry for our flesh. Fully employed, they barely survive from day to day. Two weeks out of work is death to them!" (p. 189)

Economic considerations win out, as they often do, and every businessman and fifteen out of twenty doctors vote that there is as yet no cholera in Sunderland, that if it comes it is not contagious, and that there is no need to prolong the quarantine. As one cynical doctor points out, "'The physicians don't receive their fees from the poor.'" (p. 191)

Meanwhile, many of the poor agree with Whilky Robinson, our pimp and boarding-house keeper, who sees the coming of cholera as part of a Malthusian conspiracy by the rich to get rid of the excess population, "'the Grand Plot that began with this summer's "census" . . . will culminate in this so-called cholera morbus they've imported to eliminate us all. Did they honestly think we wouldn't catch on?'" (p. 55)

It is against this background of the greed of the industrialists, the misery and fear of the poor, and the resulting class suspicion and hatred that Sheri Holman has set her novel. Many readers have told me they were amazed that a young American woman born in rural Virginia and now living in Brooklyn with her husband, an academic, could present so compelling a portrait of another age and another country. The explanation is simple: Sheri Holman does her homework.

Her first novel, *A Stolen Tongue* (1997), was an intellectual mystery set in the fifteenth century. It followed a Dominican friar from Germany to the Sinai Desert as he tries to recover the stolen relics of his favourite saint. Immense research, including Holman duplicating every step of the friar's journey, resulted in a novel absolutely convincing in its historical detail, a triumph she repeats in *The Dress Lodger*.

The inspiration for *The Dress Lodger* came when Holman was working as a secretary at the Penguin publishing house in New York. She had trained as a Shakespearean actress but had to supplement her income with more menial work. To relieve the monotony, she read voraciously under her desk and one passage in particular caught her eye. It was in Henry Mayhew's *London Labour and the London Poor*. It mentioned the nineteenth-century phenomenon of the dress lodger. The pimp of Sheri Holman's novel, Whilky Robinson, explains the practice:

> [N]othing swells Whilky's chest more than the knowledge that he alone was responsible for the importation of dress lodging into Sunderland. Obvious in its simplicity, yet strangely unknown outside of London, dress lodging works on this basic principle: a cheap whore is given a fancy dress to pass as a higher class of prostitute. The higher the class of prostitute, the higher the station of the clientele; the higher the station, the higher the price. In return, the girl is given a roof over her head and a few hours of make-believe. Everyone is happy. (p. 58)

Every entrepreneur faces initial difficulties, and Whilky's first dress lodger ran off with the dress. He solved the problem by finding "the Eye," a terrible and frighteningly strong old woman with one eye who trails the dress lodger everywhere, protecting both her and Whilky's property.

Sheri Holman read not only Mayhew on the poor, but countless nineteenth-century volumes on medicine, cholera, pottery, street lighting, and grave robbery. She went to England to study old documents on cholera at the University of Newcastle and the specimens at the Hunterian Anatomical Museum in London. She spent much time in the city of Sunderland itself, walking its streets, studying old maps, and delving into local history at the city library. Her research caused her a well-publicized problem with the Sunderland City Council when *The Dress Lodger* finally came out in the year 2000.

Chief among Sunderland's real-life heroes was a young seaman, Jack Crawford. In one of England's naval battles during the Napoleonic Wars, Crawford climbed up the broken mast of his ship to reaffix the fallen

British colours, a dangerous feat at the best of times and incredibly so during the heat of a sea battle. The hero of the Battle of Camperdown became a local legend. The first corpse we meet in *The Dress Lodger* is tattooed with the scene of the triumph, and we meet the aged Crawford himself during the course of the novel. The problem was that Sheri Holman describes Crawford, a cholera victim, as drink-sodden, with a memory not of volunteering but of being ordered to climb the mast under penalty of being shot. He had not even volunteered to join the navy in the first place, but had been seized by a press gang on his way to a pub, an abduction sanctioned by the British authorities in time of war. He remembers how he was whipped and sodomized and then exploited shamelessly as "a shill for George's government, a working-class hero to gain sympathy among the poor for a most unpopular war." (p. 113)

The destruction of the Crawford myth, a destruction supported by all of Holman's research among original documents, may have earned her the enmity of Sunderland's mayor and council, but in the novel it is far from a digression. It is a particularly fine illustration of the chasm between the rich and the poor, worlds so far apart that Prime Minister Benjamin Disraeli would later describe them as two nations.

The upper class will supply us with one of our two protagonists; the poor and exploited will supply us with the other.

Henry Chiver is a relatively new doctor in Sunderland. He has been taken under the wing of his uncle, Dr. Clanny, a real historical figure whose book on cholera, *Hyperanthraxis*, was a part of Sheri Holman's research. I cannot do better than the introduction afforded Dr. Chiver by the narrator of the novel:

> Little is known of the new Dr. Chiver beyond what the town gossips could collect, and we can tell you very little more. He studied at St. Thomas's in London with one of the nation's most acclaimed surgeons, Sir Astley Cooper. He graduated top in his class, and was handpicked by the even more famous Dr. Knox to teach anatomy at his extramural school at 10 Surgeons' Square, Edinburgh. About two years ago, Henry left under a cloud, which for all the town's expert seeding has not been made to precipitate the truth. . . . Though it does seem odd his exit coincided exactly with his mentor Dr. Knox's implication in the Burke and Hare murders. (p. 17)

Henry Chiver now has four would-be doctors studying anatomy with him, but in the absence of corpses they have had to make do with animals. They yearn for cadavers, and Henry, in particular, is obsessed with the study of the human heart. It began with the picture of Christ's Sacred Heart over Henry's childhood bed, and he has become convinced that the essential secrets of the human body can be found in "the most ancient symbol of Man's very Self, his passionate heart." (p. 19) In spite of the disgrace he so narrowly escaped, desperate for a body, he tries to rob a grave. He flees in terror, however, not from the putrefaction in the grave but from the imagined presence of Burke and Hare's victims. It is a powerful passage:

> Just behind him he hears a stampede of stumbling, heavy footsteps, he feels the heat of breath against the back of his neck, reeking of filthy rags, sweet drugged-gin, yellow-tongue, headachy anger. It overpowers the putrescence of the graveyard, coming closer and closer; the fetid breath that hid in the mouths of all sixteen corpses delivered to Dr. Knox's school. (p. 31)

Dr. Henry Chiver is not a monster – "Back in Edinburgh, Henry was the only instructor willing to dig a pit for the gristle and scraps of the school's dissected corpses" (p. 127) – and he is tormented by the memory of Burke and Hare bringing to Knox the body of Mary Paterson, the prostitute with whom Henry had been only the night before, "giddy and beautiful and very much alive." (p. 32) When Henry confesses later to one of his students his involvement with Dr. Knox and Burke and Hare, the student tries to comfort his teacher, "You were not to blame," but Henry, to his credit, refuses to shrug off his moral if not legal culpability: "They would never have murdered had we not provided the market." (p. 195)

Henry is engaged to the seventeen-year-old Miss Audrey Place, a tender-hearted but naive social reformer concerned by both the plight of the poor and the enforced absence of her father, a ship's captain stuck in the Baltic, forbidden by Sunderland's quarantine to return to his home port. But Henry has a taste for alcohol and a little rough trade in sex, and we remember how he was tempted by the prostitute Mary Paterson the night before her murder. One night, while drinking at a pub aptly called Labour in Vain, for such was the condition of the poorer classes, he pours out his soul to a young prostitute, telling her of his desperate need for bodies. (p. 24)

We have already met the girl. She is the dress lodger for whom her pimp Whilky Robinson procured the fine blue gown and who is followed everywhere through the streets by the Eye, the garment's implacable guardian. Gustine is fifteen years old, has been prostituting herself for two years, and has a four-month-old baby. Gustine and her baby and the Eye and Whilky Robinson and his slow-witted daughter, Pink, share Whilky's boarding house with all his other tenants. Although Gustine frequents the Labour in Vain pub, owned by Whilky's brother John, in an effort to find clients, she doesn't drink. As she refuses the offer of alcohol, she says of her mother, also a prostitute, that she "'died of drink when I was twelve. I have no desire to follow her.'" (p. 176) Temperance was an unusual practice for a young prostitute in 1831, but Gustine is a remarkable young woman. Although underfed, she is not unattractive, "with delicate arching brows, a reasonably straight nose and large, dark, almost navy blue eyes." Her face and limbs "possess the sort of pallor that scatters light, the sort of luminescence that great ladies, it is rumored, take small tastes of arsenic to achieve. Hers is the skin of a girl who never sees the light of day." (p. 6) In her fine blue dress, Gustine is "a walking confection. A tasty morsel." (p. 7)

Streetwise Gustine knows what will titillate her clients. Pushed against the wall under a bridge, she plays the virgin, begging the customer not to take her innocence, "'Please don't, I never have.'" (p. 13) As the man attends to his business, "Gustine turns her head to watch the river lazily carry downstream a bloated sheep. . . ." (p. 13) It is one of Sheri Holman's many superb sentences. The juxtaposition of the dead sheep with the act of copulation suggests that both Gustine and the animal are, during those few moments, simply meat. I have never, ever, been able to understand men who go to prostitutes. In that one marvellous sentence, Holman manages to convey the total lack of interest of a prostitute in what is being done to one part of her body. Whatever some prostitutes may pretend to experience, how do men get past the awareness that the woman they are paying must surely be feeling either contempt or boredom or both?

For all her nightly efforts, Gustine receives four shillings a week pocket money from Whilky Robinson, plus a roof overhead for herself and her baby. She also has the services of Whilky's six-year-old, Pink, to mind her infant. Babysitting is essential, because Gustine has two jobs. At night she sells her ravaged little body; in the day she has work as a potter's assistant. For nine years, since she was six years old, Gustine has worked at the potting house, carrying sixty-pound slabs of clay and cutting them into twenty-four wedges ready to be worked by the potter, who is himself paid only for what he produces. Holman honours the traditionally didactic function of the novel by treating the reader to lengthy and fascinating digressions on the whole process of pottery making. Gustine's potter pays her out of what he receives, and if the clay is poor because the slappers have not rid it of all the air, and if the production is low, Gustine will receive nothing. The greatest disaster for Gustine would be if the potter were to fall ill. She needs all the money from both her jobs for her child.

I found it strange at first that a child so loved should, after four months, have no name, and then I remembered that the urban poor in the crowded slums of Britain's Industrial Revolution were slow to name their children as they were so likely to be taken from them in infancy by malnutrition or disease. Rats, too, were a constant threat to the life of a baby. Many an unattended child became food for the ubiquitous vermin. One of the great advantages to Gustine of living at Whilky Robinson's is that the boarding house, although filthy, is rat-free. Whilky keeps a pet ferret, Mike, and Mike is a champion rat catcher, one of whose triumphs we are privileged to attend.

It is clear that Whilky loves his ferret much more than he does Pink, who frequently imitates the "eek-eek" noise of a ferret in order to attract her father's attention and perhaps a little of his love. She is not, I think, nearly as slow-witted as we might first have supposed but rather the victim of cruel neglect.

Whilky is the embodiment of the belief, widely held outside the British Isles, that the British prefer their animals to their children, and there may be some truth to the old canard. Certainly, Queen Victoria always donated much more to animal charities than to those for children, and I cannot imagine Britons then or now sending their animals off to boarding school for ten years.

Gustine, however, adores her child and is even tempted to give him a name, but fails to do so for a reason peculiar to herself.

I will call him William after our most beloved king, a man who certainly finds favour in Your sight; but even as Gustine thinks the name William, unbidden comes the image of William Marion, vestryman, who left a xylophone of bruises down her spine when he took her on the table of the Corn Exchange. No, William is not the right name. Let it be George then, she thinks, our previous king. But a George forced her to her knees in front of his friends, a Harold, a Buck, a Tim, and a Jerry. No, all of those names are out. Closed too are all Bobs and Bills and Bruces, all Franks, Andrews, and Charleses; and certainly not a Henry. To every name, she can fix a leering, brutal, pitiless face; hands of Dicks and dicks of Thomases. (p. 220)

And so the baby remains unnamed.

No mother has ever loved a baby more than Gustine loves hers. It is, indeed, a special baby, a rare case of *ectopia cordis*, a condition in which the heart, totally exposed and covered only by a thin layer of skin, beats on the outside of the chest.

If Gustine has a dream it is this: that her baby will live. There is nothing complex or especially overweening about her dream: she does not wish for her child to become an altar boy or a businessman; she cares not whether he learns to read or write or play a sport. She is elementary in her singular desire. Life for her child. (pp. 141–42)

When Gustine sees a dead body floating under Sunderland's Iron Bridge, she remembers the drunken young doctor she met a month earlier at the Labour in Vain and her promise to find him bodies if "'in return you will let me ask you a favour.'" (p. 33) Gustine hurries to find Henry Chiver and together they go to the body. But the body has disappeared. Gustine knows well the mean streets of her city and leads the doctor to the pawnshop of Mag Scurr (the name of a real pawnbroker taken by Holman from the census of 1828). All found bodies end up at Mag Scurr's. She is paid one shilling per corpse by the council to prepare the body for the death certificate and burial, but ekes out her income by selling the deceased's clothes and displaying the corpse, decked out with appropriate indications of what might have been his or her trade, an oar, perhaps, or a piece of lace. The backroom exhibition lures the curious public, who will also browse among the items for sale in the front of the shop, full at the moment of items pledged by desperate sailors trapped in Sunderland by the quarantine. Creative and inventive, Mag Scurr, a wonderfully Dickensian minor character, is described by Holman as "Sunderland's East End Renaissance woman," who "brings her myriad talents together under one roof." (p. 40)

Gustine claims the body as her father, citing the corpse's Crawford tattoo as positive identification. She and Henry Chiver make off with the body only minutes before the dead man's wife arrives.

Thus, a relationship is forged between Gustine and Henry, and she further insinuates herself into the doctor's good graces by providing a second corpse, that of Fos, hideously disfigured by phosphorus, whose body is extracted from Whilky Robinson's lodging house. Gustine is determined to tie herself closely to the doctor. She knows that he has already seen her special child, although he does not yet know that it is hers. Henry's fiancée, Audrey Place, had seen the baby on a chance charity visit to Whilky's hovel and had told Henry of her remarkable discovery. At one of their meetings at the Labour in Vain, Henry tells Gustine of the incredible baby and of an earlier case of *ectopia cordis* he has read about in which the patient, with proper medical care, lived into his seventies: " 'I know I could preserve this child's life, too, if I could only get to it.' " (p. 135)

It is just after Henry makes that claim that Gustine binds him yet more closely to her. Even when he is with his fiancée, the omniscient narrator has let us know that Henry is drawn in thought many times a day to the child prostitute and "the feel of her tiny cat ribs." (p. 96) Alone with her in an upper room of the Labour in Vain, the temptation overcomes him in one of the many surprisingly funny moments in this generally grim narrative.

> "Gustine," Henry says, embarrassed, watching her fit the key into the lock. "Do you have to go so soon? Downstairs they'll think we – they'll think I couldn't – of course, we wouldn't –"
>
> Gustine turns back in surprise. With a few words, the stern surgeon of moments before has been transformed into a blushing schoolboy. She smiles at him from the doorway . . .
>
> "Will ten minutes do?" she asks with a grin. "Most don't even last that long." (p. 136)

When Henry invites her to go for a Sunday picnic, Gustine brings her baby and makes the offer to Henry that she has considered so carefully. The picnic is a superb piece of narrative construction. In a scene that might deceive the reader into believing that the novel is a bleaker version of *Pygmalion*, Henry takes Gustine and the baby into the countryside. They will visit the grounds of Hylton Castle. It is the first time Gustine has crossed over the Iron Bridge that leads out of Sunderland, a bridge under which she has so many times sold herself. It is the first time she has seen a cow other than in city streets on its way to the abattoir: "'How foreign and beautiful the white creatures seem in this habitat.'" (p. 171) It is the first time she has seen fields and green grass, and the castle itself is a glory to her beyond imagination. She peeks through the windows and gasps in excited disbelief at the magnificence of the interior. It is a perfect rendition by Sheri Holman of the chasm between the two solitudes of rich and poor: "'I'm just so happy to have had a chance to see it. . . . I never knew there were such homes in the world.'" (p. 175)

Aware more than ever of what the world has to offer, Gustine asks Henry for fair exchange for the services she has provided, "'Life for my son.'" (p. 177)

Henry, momentarily at a loss for words, realizes that "with a single visible beat, his [the child's] heart can teach me more than all the cadavers in Sunderland." (p. 180) But he needs the boy to be with him, not with Gustine, and he makes a forceful argument.

"How do you expect him to survive growing up in the East End?" Henry feels he must speak directly. "Suppose he's not killed by the next fever that sweeps through – how long do you think it will be before he is brutalized by one of the other children there? Can you protect him every hour of the day? Especially when you are working two jobs? He's not a normal child. He is special." (p. 179)

Gustine is not ready to give up the child, and the afternoon ends without resolution. But when, back in Sunderland, Gustine finds that her potter and all the others have succumbed to cholera and she has lost her daytime work, she has to reconsider Henry's suggestion. She runs to Henry to make him an offer.

"I want no money from you, only an exchange of services," Gustine starts, and almost immediately falters. "I have come to make you an offer, Dr. Chiver. You may take my baby and keep him, but let me be close by, to watch over him and soothe him when he is frightened.

Take me as a maid in your house. I will cook for you; I will clean and sew. I have worked a long time in the factory, so I have not mastered all the household skills, but I am a hard worker and I will learn. My potter collapsed today –" Her voice breaks with emotion, but she cannot stop before she's gotten everything out . . . "– I know you are to be married, and I swear to make a diligent and obedient maid to your new wife." (p. 214)

Astonishingly, at least to me, Henry refuses: "To even consider having her in the same house with Audrey – a street prostitute who has made her life picking through coffins for him – no, no, it is too much." (p. 214) He offers her a pound, in full payment for all her services, and a threat to seek legal custody of the child. "[Gustine] reaches out and takes his money. At last she sees the hollow in his chest for what it really is." (p. 218)

I could have forgiven Henry for the terrible hypocrisy and overlooked that it was he who had made her a body snatcher and that it was he and his like who had compelled her into prostitution. But I could not forgive his threat to take her baby from her. With justification, Gustine saw the law as the weapon of the rich, and she knows the threat is not empty.

Inevitably, Gustine's child dies of cholera, and the distraught mother goes to the river with thoughts of suicide. She is interrupted by a young sailor who slips ashore in a skiff. He has evaded the quarantine to bring to Audrey Place the clothes and personal effects of her ship's-captain father, dead of the cholera. It is ironic that such an act of kindness should help to further the disease, just as it is ironic that the travelling players who had brought such joy to the town should take, with their "curling blue feathers, blue gloves, blue boots," the blue disease of cholera to all the cities and countries they will go on to tour. In an exquisite play on the word "tragedy," the narrator tells us that "Before they retire their show, there won't be a country in the world that has escaped their little tragedy." (p. 280)

The ever-present Eye witnesses the meeting of Gustine and the young seaman, and she knows what the bundle is made up of. She strikes the young man down and gives the contaminated clothes to Gustine: "You desired a weapon she seems to say; I present you with one." (p. 268)

Gustine takes the clothes to Audrey Place. Henry's fiancée will pay for what Henry did. At the last moment Gustine turns away from her revenge, but it is too late. Audrey has already seen and seized the fateful legacy, and we leave her to a death by cholera after she clutches her father's clothes to her "to inhale her certain fate." (p. 277)

I was sorry when the foolish but well-intentioned Audrey died, but I was glad of the pain her death caused Henry. I was glad when his fiancée's ill-advised petition drew attention to him – a petition, signed by Audrey herself and by the four young men known to be Henry's students, asking people to donate their bodies for medical research. I was glad when the rioting mob broke into Henry's house and discovered the corpses of Fos, the tattooed man, and Gustine's baby. I was glad when the crowd led by Whilky Robinson compelled Henry to dissect the body of his fiancée, newly dead from cholera. He had cut up bodies before with little thought that each had a history and was as important in his or her world as Audrey had been in hers. I was glad when the disgraced Henry fled to his mother's house in London, spending his remaining time on earth ministering to the poor in the slums of Stepney. He was no doubt seeking an absolution that I, for one, would not have granted him. When he threatened to take Gustine's baby he damned himself, and I wish that the mob, finding an empty graveyard and the corpses in Henry's house, had hanged him in fact and not in effigy. (I remember my perceptive mother telling me when I was young, "Rob, you are a good hater.")

Just as I came to loathe Henry in the last chapters of the novel, so I had to rethink my opinion of the Eye. When she gives Gustine the contaminated bundle, it is a moment for Gustine – and for me – of blinding revelation:

Gustine sees in her enemy's face everything she never thought to find there: compassion, pity, sadness, regret. . . .

Why? wonders Gustine. Why [would the Eye] help her now, when the Eye's whole life has been set in opposition to hers? But then, as if sleep has been wiped from her eyes and she is suddenly, for the first time in two years, fully awake, the dress lodger sees and understands.

"You loved him, too? Didn't you?" Gustine asks. "You loved my child."

And in acknowledgment, the shadow, of her own free will, disengages forever, turns, and walks away. (p. 268)

The Eye has been a fearsome presence throughout the novel. One local theory is that she had sold her missing eye to the devil for a bottle of gin, (p. 11) and there certainly is great power in her one remaining visual organ, "a single gray carbuncle that has, over the years, siphoned from her other four senses every bit of potency. . . . No one may steal an apple but the Eye sees it." (p. 10) As she trails Gustine in the blue dress beneath the chimneys of Sunderland's factories, the "red flames of the furnaces hellishly light her face." (p. 14) Although the Eye is mute, the narrator allows us into her mind, and we know that she sees humanity as rats. But this is no agent of the devil; the truth of the Eye is more mundane.

When the Eye was nine years old she was employed in the coal mines of Durham. It was her duty to watch the chain that pulled the miners' cage up from deep within the bowels of the earth.

> You have to watch carefully, for sometimes the engine catches and then you have to shut it off quick or the cageful of miners will fall to their deaths. . . . It is important to watch the chain and never take your eyes off it. But it is hard to watch a chain in a hole in almost total darkness, in silence, thirteen hours a day, when you are only nine years old. (p. 202)

On one occasion she is distracted by a rat. She does not see the engine malfunction and thirty miners meet their fate. The beating she receives causes her to lose one of her eyes, and from that moment on she sees nothing but rats all around her. When Gustine's baby dies and the body disappears, the Eye sees it in terms of a rat victory: "[T]he rat snuck in and stole away the baby." (p. 278)

Rats are frequent in the novel, as they were frequent in the homes of the poor. Before cholera came to Sunderland, the town was beset not only by rats but also by a plague of frogs. When Whilky Robinson's little girl, Pink, skitters about the house on all fours, imitating the ferret that brings such joy to her father, she catches a frog in her teeth and looks up at her father "with her glittering black, pink-rimmed eyes, reptilian-scaly from years of infection, her pink-tipped nose twitching over the flailing frog in her mouth." (p. 53) The description is not that of a child; it is of a rat, or perhaps a ferret, and we realize that the persistent rat imagery is not only a means to show the mental condition of the Eye, or to illustrate the filth and poverty of the time, or a device to bind the novel together; it is a potent reminder of the animal state to which the poor of the Industrial Revolution were reduced.

Gustine had always believed the Eye was responsible for her baby's heart condition; that, as Gustine was giving birth, the devil-woman had tried "to draw out from her baby's body its very heart . . . but Gustine's miraculous child was too strong for the old woman. He survived . . . and wore his heart as a badge that good shall always triumph over evil." (p. 143) Gustine had misread the Eye's attention to her baby as a threat to his safety, as had I, and only when the Eye gives her the means of revenge against Henry does Gustine finally see that, in the Eye's love for her child, she had experienced a rebirth of her own heart, her own humanity, "as close to motherhood as the Eye was destined to come." (p. 282)

When Gustine and the Eye are both stricken with cholera and tended to by Dr. Clanny, (p. 288) only Gustine will recover and help the good doctor in nursing the old woman through her last days. I grieved when the Eye died, and it brought home to me how successfully Sheri Holman had manipulated my sympathies. At the beginning of the novel, I had admired Henry Chiver and his obsession with the advancement of knowledge, and I had feared the terrible guardian of the blue dress. At the end of the novel I reviled the doctor for his lack of humanity and I ached for the suffering the old woman had endured.

Sheri Holman is a great lover of the nineteenth-century novel, and she respects its tradition by tying up all the loose ends in the final chapters. Whilky will sell Gustine's ripped, stained blue dress to Mag Scurr for a few shillings. Other Whilky gowns will take the place of the blue dress in the marketplace of young flesh – white gowns, gowns of jade green, gowns of lavender silk – but they will all disappear with their absconding wearers, and it will not be Gustine who wears them. After the Eye's death, Gustine left Whilky's hell at 9 Mill Street to work as a nurse at Dr. Clanny's fever clinic. She crept out of Whilky's house in the dead of night with the six-year-old Pink, the little girl in the patched pink dress who slipped her hand into Gustine's and begged to be brought along. Poor little Pink, who had dreamed of being taken into the paradise home of Miss Audrey Place after Audrey's marriage to Henry Chiver, a dream actually promised to the child by the tender-hearted Audrey, a dream never to be realized.

The narrator takes us two weeks into the future and across the town to Dr. Clanny's clinic.

Do you see a tidy adolescent girl in an indigo frock, her hair smoothed back into a demure knot at the nape of her neck, her white nurse's apron tied in a perfect bow in the back? She stands on a wooden box, applying whitewash to the new fever hospital's walls, handing her brush off to the younger girl in her own simple blue pinafore, who splashes the stuff all over herself and drips it across the floor. They work in earnest, these two, as if their lives depended on a job well done. They wouldn't want Dr. Clanny's faith in them to be misplaced, nor would they want to lose the room they share with the other women who work at the hospital. (p. 288)

Remarkably, Gustine has found a safe haven. From the blue dress to the nurse's apron: it is a wonder how successfully Sheri Holman endows clothing with significance. The blue dress, with her pathetic workboots peeping out from under, defined Gustine at the beginning, just as her white nurse's apron defines her at the end. It is a writer's device that began in English literature with Chaucer's description of his fourteenth-century pilgrims and has been used by great writers ever since, including Sheri Holman's idol, Charles Dickens. Miss Havisham's ruined wedding dress spoke to the reader as eloquently as Pip's foppish London styles.

There are many debts to Dickens in *The Dress Lodger*. Just as Dickens sought to temper the bitterness of his message with humour, so does Holman know how to lighten the moment. The pimp Whilky Robinson is often the vehicle of that humour. When Audrey promises to take Pink into her future married home, the conscientious six-year-old wonders who will mind Gustine's baby. I found the exchange that follows to be blasphemous but very, very funny.

"I have a feeling that by the time I am married, Jesus will be minding that sweet babe, dear."

"Da says Jesus is a bloody git who won't take care of no one." Pink smiles, getting her father's words exactly. "I must be better than him." (p. 166)

I like Whilky the pimp much more than I think I was supposed to. A man who sees himself as tender-hearted when he bricks up windows so that his tenants do not overlook the slaughterhouse is, at least, interesting. When he is trying to make the connection between Audrey Place, the name on the petition, and Henry Chiver, he remembers an engagement announcement in one of the newspapers his brother used to paper an upstairs room at the Labour in Vain. Rushing to check, he enters the room unannounced to see "a lace-maker's upturned buttocks and a red-faced apprentice's erection." "'I'll just be a minute,'" says Whilky. (p. 251)

(Some readers are surprised that Whilky is literate, but far more of the nineteenth-century poor could read than is popularly supposed. There is no other explanation for the huge sales of one-page sensationalized biographies of the condemned at the foot of the gallows at public executions. There were many religious groups who taught the poor how to read so that they might have access to the Bible, and an enterprising fellow like Whilky would not wish to be disadvantaged in his struggle against the establishment.)

Whilky is also not without a touch of redeeming self-knowledge. When he meets some of the travelling players, he makes a little confession: "'I'm a bit of a performer myself,' smiles Whilky broadly. 'I pretend to give a bloody shit about my lodgers and their gittish little problems.'" (p. 245) Unlike Dr. Henry Chiver, Whilky knows he is a hypocrite.

Before we judge Whilky too harshly, we must consider the age into which he was born. The rich grew fat breaking the bodies of little children, and the poor and the nearly poor had to be resourceful to survive. Often, they could not afford to be honest. In *The Dress Lodger*, market-stall holders sell their wares in the dim light of evening to exhausted workers too tired to examine carefully what they buy and the children of the poor "know a hundred ways to sell bad fish." (p. 3) Dr. Clanny and Lord Shaftesbury the reformer are the great exceptions, not the norm. A man born to the upper classes could be admitted to the Royal College of Surgeons with no qualification other than a kinship to a well-known medical figure. (pp. 24–25) That would give him a licence to operate. There were few obstacles to success in nineteenth-century England for a person born to wealth. The title of Doctor, an officer's commission in the army, membership in Parliament – it was all his by natural right.

Sometimes, the homage paid by Holman to Dickens is very evident. The melodrama of the scene where Whilky compels Henry Chiver to cut up

Audrey's body – "'Take up the knife, sawbones'" (p. 286) – is reminiscent of some of Dickens's great set pieces. I think of Madame Defarge thirsting for blood at the foot of the guillotine.

There is as much coincidence in *The Dress Lodger* as there is in any of Dickens's novels. The client who tries to cheat Gustine out of her fee turns out to be Audrey's father's bookkeeper. In *A Tale of Two Cities*, Sydney Carton is the spitting image of Charles Darnay. I have no problem with it. Life is full of melodrama and coincidence. I find that so-called "realistic" novels have too little of either to be convincing. Life, as I live it and see it, continues to startle me every day.

Also like Dickens, Holman has a gift for the single, striking image. On that one outing into the clean countryside for the Sunday picnic, Gustine tries her first artichoke. "'It tastes like spring,'" she says in a line that could not be simpler or more moving. (p. 176)

In an interview with fellow New York novelist David Liss, printed on the last pages of my paperback edition of *The Dress Lodger*, Sheri Holman speaks about her use of a narrator: "Because my novel is set so long ago, I wanted to give the flavor of the period without writing a pastiche – thus the 'Dear Reader' (after Dickens) and the use of the plural mystery narrator." It is only towards the end of the novel that we find out who has been telling the story: "Have you now guessed in whose hands you rest? Why, even here in our own backyard, we must make obvious introductions. We are the citizens of the Trinity pit, dear reader: the murderers and drunkards, the prostitutes and unbaptized babies of Sunderland." (p. 256) The use of the multiple dead as narrators is from a source earlier than Dickens. I once asked Thornton Wilder if, since the dead speak in *Our Town*, he believed in a personal afterlife. He told me that he didn't and that "the last act of *Our Town* is a fancied construction, largely drawn from Dante's *Purgatorio*, whose whole purpose is to call the audience's attention to what we fail to grasp while living." I find that Wilder's explanation of his purpose applies just as well to the narrative voices of *The Dress Lodger*.

By the time I had read and reread Holman's novel, I had come to admire her work very much for reasons that I hope are now obvious. I had also come to like her, mainly for her introduction of a character seemingly extraneous to the narrative. I refer to "the Student of Life," a journalist trying to write an honest portrait of the British working class who pops in and out of the story, leaping to wrong conclusions and without for a moment understanding anything of what he observes. I thought it was a lovely little comment by Sheri Holman on writers in general, including herself, who try to bear witness to a specific time and place and so often get it wrong. I like people who are prepared to poke a little fun at themselves.

This is a remarkable novel, full of fascinating period detail and wonderful characterizations. It is a nineteenth-century novel that could never have been written in the nineteenth century. The Victorian and pre-Victorian audiences were oddly prudish in an age of brutality, and they required that the stories written to entertain them contain a morality that accorded with their own view that divine reward and punishment came in this life. They would never have accepted a story about a child prostitute, especially one in which the prostitute comes to enjoy a long and happy life.

The Dress Lodger is postmodern in that it uses nineteenth-century history and nineteenth-century techniques to tell a story that is surprisingly contemporary. What could be more contemporary than Whilky's theory of a Grand Plot by the rich against the poor? We live now in an age addicted to conspiracy theories. Much of the Arab world believes that September 11 was part of an elaborate plan by Israel to discredit Islam, and there are many in the inner cities of America who are convinced that AIDS has been deliberately spread among the poor by the white establishment.

Just as Holman let the dead speak so does she give the dying Eye the gift of prophecy. That prophecy will be the vehicle for a truly Dickensian happy ending. Gustine strains unsuccessfully to make out the Eye's last words, but we fortunate readers have the text:

> I can see ahead to 1848, when fifteen years later, the cholera, unappeased, comes once more for Britain. You are a matron now, happily married for the past ten years to that sailor who stepped off the pitcher and over the Quarantine. He treats you kindly and you go with him to visit his mother and your son at the Trinity Graveyard, you with no children in tow (your body was too ravaged for that) but happy nonetheless with your job as a nurse and your husband's love. All the babies you could want live down the street at Pink's house, where she is the mother of four, nearly a child a year since she married at seventeen a shortsighted, ferrety-looking young clerk who adores her. (p. 289)

The Eye foresees more cholera epidemics and the survival of both Pink and Gustine as nurses. Gustine will finally pass away "at home, surrounded by friends, of ripe old age," (p. 290) in the very year that Dr. Koch discovers a cure for cholera.

It is the happiest of endings, in absolute contrast to the misery of the novel. It is clearly a grafted-on ending but I don't care. I never believed any of Dickens's endings either, but I needed them as much as I needed this one. I know that Gustine's story could not have ended the way it does in the novel, but I could not bear any more unhappiness, and I thank Sheri Holman for ending this fine novel the way she did.

THE REMAINS OF THE DAY

Kazuo Ishiguro

(New York: Penguin, 1990)

Before Kazuo Ishiguro won the Booker Prize in 1989 for *The Remains of the Day* he was largely unknown to North American audiences. Those American readers who had come across his two preceding novels had seen his work as that of a Japanese writer. His name and the setting for the work seemed to make the conclusion obvious. Ishiguro is, however, an Englishman. He was born in Nagasaki in 1954 but came with his parents to Britain in 1960, where he has remained. In all his interviews since he won the Booker, Ishiguro has pointed out that he feels English and writes from an English perspective.

In his first novels, *A Pale View of the Hills* (1982) and *An Artist of the Floating World* (1986), Ishiguro created a country that resembles Japan, that is called Japan, but that is created in his imagination and only coincidentally resembles the place of his birth. As a result, I never felt in his earlier work that I was visiting a real world that the author knows and understands intimately and has succeeded in recreating for the reader. The novel, I believe, must present the portrait of a complex and believable protagonist moving through a world that I accept as being as real as my own. There was something about the Japan of Ishiguro's first novels that never quite convinced me.

He did, however, create fascinating characters, and the narrative structure, the same in both the earlier works and *The Remains of the Day*, is wonderfully effective. In all three novels, the central character reflects on his or her past life. As they review the events that have brought them to their present situation, the reader perceives much more clearly than they how they have prevented themselves for so many years from seeing how false was the premise on which they built their lives.

Ishiguro's characters are still, late in their lives, able to persuade themselves that they acted from worthy motives, but the irony is – and irony is Ishiguro's main writing technique – that the more his protagonists rationalize and deceive themselves the more we see to what degree they have wasted their lives.

Ishiguro is writing about people who wear masks to deceive both the world and themselves. What happens during his novels is that the masks begin to slip a little. We see the truth very early on, but the protagonist, clinging to self-deception, will only occasionally be forced to confront the sad lie he or she has lived.

In *A Pale View of the Hills*, a Japanese widow lives alone in an English country house, reflecting on her two marriages, one to a Japanese and one to an Englishman. Each marriage produced a daughter. Her first child was absolutely miserable when she was brought over from Japan to England, never able to make the necessary cultural adjustment. Her mother did make the transition, but was unable or unwilling to help her child. Her second daughter is completely Westernized and has little to do with her Japanese-born mother, who is still tormented by the memory of her first, now dead, daughter. Most of the time she is able to convince herself that she made the right decisions. But not all the time.

The same theme is found in Ishiguro's second novel, *An Artist of the Floating World*, whose protagonist is closer to the end than the beginning and must continually protest self-justification. A retired painter and art teacher, he relives the years before the Second World War when he gave himself whole-heartedly to the cause of Emperor and Nation. During that period of Shinto extremism and Japanese militarism, not only did Mr. Ono reject all Western influences, particularly in art, but he denounced a pupil and colleague to the Japanese police as a deviator from national policy. In his old age, he must still claim that he believed he was serving Japan's best interests. To do otherwise would be to face a terrible truth about what he had done in those pre-war years.

In Ishiguro's third novel, *The Remains of the Day*, he deals again with an aging protagonist trying desperately not to face up to a wasted life, a life guided for too long by wrong choices. But this time Ishiguro is on surer ground. In the earlier work we learned a great deal about the structure of the Japanese family and the traditional relationship between a Japanese teacher and his students, but I never felt that the structures were being analyzed by a participant, an insider. Since its birth the novel has always contained a strong didactic element, but it is vital that the reader feels the writer has mastered his material. It is with *The Remains of the Day* that Ishiguro comes into his own. He has a compelling grasp of the subtleties of the English class system, a system whose structures are unbelievably difficult for an outsider to grasp. (I speak as one who passed the decanter the wrong way at one memorable regimental dinner and thus defined myself for the whole of my brief military career as having come from beyond the pale.) It seems to me that Ishiguro has a perfect understanding of what separates the "upstairs" from the "downstairs" world. I have no idea how he did it; he must have listened for years with a perfect ear and watched with a remarkably keen eye.

The narrative movement of *The Remains of the Day* is very easy to summarize. At the beginning of the novel we meet a butler, Mr. Stevens to his fellow servants and Stevens to his employer and all those who live or visit upstairs. He has been at the great English country house of Darlington Hall for more than thirty years. It is July 1956, and Lord Darlington has been dead for three years. The estate has been bought by Mr. Farraday, an American gentleman. Stevens, who comes with the property, is running the house with a skeleton staff of four, assisted by some daily cleaning help from the village.

The new owner is taking a holiday before settling in at Darlington Hall, and he encourages Stevens to take a week off at the same time. He even offers to lend the butler his magnificent vintage Ford so that Stevens might see something of the English countryside. Stevens, a devoted servant for more than three decades, has travelled not at all.

At first Stevens is reluctant to act on his new employer's suggestion, but it occurs to him that a trip to the west of England might solve a pressing problem. In recent months he has noticed a few difficulties with his "staff plan," the organizational chart he has elaborated for the administration of the house. The demands of running the household are far less exigent than in the glory days of the thirties, when he had a staff of twenty-eight, and he thinks he can solve the problem with the addition of just one key servant. It is clear to the reader that one part of the problem is that Stevens is getting older, but Stevens, on the same evidence, comes to a different conclusion. It is a lovely example of the dramatic irony at which Ishiguro excels.

Stevens decides to combine a motoring trip with a visit to Cornwall. He has just received a letter from a former housekeeper at Darlington Hall, Miss Kenton, in which she mentions that she is now separated from her husband. She had left her employment some twenty years earlier and Stevens wonders if she could be tempted back.

He makes a leisurely journey towards her home, stopping overnight at bed-and-breakfasts and little country inns. As he travels, he reflects on the events of his life, his adult years having been spent entirely at Darlington Hall in the service of the late Lord Darlington. His memories form the greater part of the novel as we go back with him to the twenties and thirties.

Lord Darlington was one of the many members of the English aristocracy who believed in the interwar years that Germany had been too heavily penalized by the Treaty of Versailles after the First World War. It is a view with which I cannot agree, although it is still the conventional wisdom on the subject. Its proponents forget, or choose to ignore, the fact that after the Franco-Prussian War, only thirty-four years before Kaiser Wilhelm II launched the First World War, Germany had imposed very similar conditions on defeated France, seizing two French provinces and demanding that France pay the whole cost of the war. France paid its debt to Germany, and for the life of me I cannot think why, in 1919, what had been sauce for the goose might not prove acceptable fare for the gander. In my opinion, the mistake made by the Allies in 1918 was to offer an armistice instead of fighting on until a crushed Germany begged to surrender. Such an action would have made it impossible for Hitler to claim later that in 1918 Germany could have fought on but was stabbed in the back by what he called "the November criminals," a group made up, he claimed, of Jews, homosexuals, and communists. (My own belief is that the Allied leaders in 1945 realized the mistake that had been made in 1918. They understood that Germany had to be seen to be annihilated if another demagogue were not to rise up later and claim that Nazi Germany had not really been defeated. It was Hitler, and not the vindictiveness of Allied leaders, that made the horror of Dresden necessary.)

In 1923, however, the mistake made by the lenient allies in 1918 was not seen as such, and German whining about the unfairness of the

Versailles Treaty found many sympathetic listeners in England and elsewhere. In *The Remains of the Day*, Lord Darlington is anxious to curb British hostility to Germany and arranges an unofficial but international symposium to discuss a pro-German strategy. Very much under the influence of a German friend, Karl-Heinz Bremann, Darlington invites a brace of British cabinet ministers, who arrive incognito, a pro-German Frenchman known only as M. Dupont, and an American. The visitor from the United States, Mr. Lewis, once he realizes the meeting is to encourage pro-German feeling in England, denounces the other participants, Lord Darlington in particular, as a bunch of amateurs: " 'Gentlemen like our good host still believe it's their business to meddle in matters they don't understand.' " (p. 102) It is hard to disagree with Mr. Lewis, the unheeded voice of reason at the meeting at Darlington Hall, particularly if we note Darlington's musings to his butler. Reflecting on a conversation he had in Berlin with Baron Overath, an "old friend of my father," on the alleged cruelties of Versailles, Darlington blames everything on England's ally in the First War: " 'I was jolly well tempted to tell him it's those wretched Frenchmen. It's not the English way of carrying on.' " (p. 76)

Stevens accepts his employer's views without question. His loyalty is absolute. Speaking of Lord Darlington, he says, "I for one will never doubt that a desire to see 'justice in this world' lay at the heart of all his actions." (p. 73)

Unfazed by any criticism that he lacks training or professional qualification, Darlington believes that, like the Conservative Party, he was born to lead. He works all through the twenties and thirties to promote Anglo-German friendship and comes under the influence of Mrs. Carolyn Barnet, a British fascist, and her leader, Sir Oswald Mosley, who visits Darlington Hall three times in person. During his Mosleyite phase, Lord Darlington commits three explicitly anti-Semitic acts. He refers to a certain newspaper as "that Jewish propaganda sheet" and instructs Stevens to cease giving donations to the local charity because its management committee is "more or less homogeneously Jewish." (p. 146) More seriously, Darlington instructs Stevens to dismiss two Jewish maids. The housekeeper, Miss Kenton, protests vehemently: " 'I will not stand for such things. I will not work in a house in which such things can occur.' " (p. 149) As Stevens remembers the incident, he recalls that his "every instinct opposed the idea of their dismissal," (p. 148) but the argument he offers Miss Kenton is, in Stevens's mind, unanswerable:

> "The fact is, the world of today is a very complicated and treacherous place. There are many things you and I are simply not in a position to understand concerning, say, the nature of Jewry. Whereas his Lordship, I might venture, is somewhat better placed to judge what is for the best." (p. 149)

The girls are dismissed, and Miss Kenton, for an undisclosed reason, decides to stay on at Darlington Hall. There is no doubt, however, that, had she had Stevens's authority, she would have refused to act upon Darlington's instruction. It seems to me that Ishiguro wants to make it clear that Stevens always had a choice available to him and that his subservience to his lordship was an act of free will.

One year later, repelled by the ugly behaviour of Mosley's Blackshirts, Darlington makes a half-hearted suggestion to Stevens to trace the two maids: "'It was wrong what happened and one would like to recompense them somehow.'" (p. 151) It is clear to us, who are privy to Stevens's memories, that his employer was not so much vicious as stupid and easily manipulated, but Stevens, even decades after the fact, cannot bring himself to criticize his master. He has dissolved self and identity in his role as servant.

Stevens is not alone. He is a member of the Hayes Society, the association of butlers, and subscribes to *A Quarterly for the Gentlemen's Gentleman*. In the columns of the magazine, at the meetings of the Hayes Society, and in conversations with servants visiting Darlington Hall from other great houses, Stevens has participated for decades in the ongoing debate as to what makes the perfect butler, what qualities figure in the creation of such icons as Mr. Marshall of Charleville House or Mr. Lane of Bridewood, the same Mr. Lane who first realized the display potential of highly polished silver, a discovery that made him a hero in the world of butlerdom.

Over the years, Stevens has established to his own satisfaction the three primary criteria to be met by the perfect butler. The first is that "great butlers are great by virtue of their ability to inhabit their professional roles." (p. 42) Personal considerations cannot enter into the performance of their duties. Stevens's father was a butler before him in a great house, and is much admired by his son. Stevens Senior was able to serve with total professionalism a visiting general whose stupidity had caused the death of the butler's son, Stevens's older brother, during the Boer War. (p. 40) Stevens is fond of relating his father's story of an English butler "who failed to panic on discovering a tiger under the dining table," (p. 42) and is convinced that the ability to suppress one's emotions, to sublimate them in the work, is the key to greatness. He argues that it is a peculiarly English gift: "Continentals are unable to be butlers because they are as a breed incapable of the emotional restraint which only the English race is capable of." (p. 43)

The second criterion is that the butler possess a dignity in keeping with his position. Again, Stevens cites his father, whose silent, intimidating presence was sufficient to reduce two drunken guests to mumbling apologies. (pp. 39–40) Stevens believes that many years later, he, too, achieved on at least one occasion the perfect dignity for which he strove. His father has come out of retirement to work as an underbutler at Darlington Hall, only to lapse into senility. He lies dying in an attic room while his son is doing the serving honours downstairs at Lord Darlington's 1923 pro-German conference. When Miss Kenton tells him that his father has died and suggests that he leave his duties to tend to the body, Stevens answers in typically inflated prose, "'Miss Kenton, please don't think me unduly improper in not ascending to see my father in his deceased condition just at this moment. You see, I know my father would have wished me to carry on just now.'" (p. 106) It is a moment that Stevens would always recall "with a large sense of triumph." (p. 110)

The third criterion for a perfect butler is contained in one of the conditions for admission into the Hayes Society, that "the applicant be attached to a distinguished household." (p. 113) Stevens understands "distinguished" to have "a meaning deeper than that understood by the Hayes Society." He has thought through his philosophical position – a great touch, I think, by Ishiguro – and dismisses the snobbery of earlier generations, even including his father. Stevens would now call "distinguished" only those gentlemen who were "furthering the progress of humanity." (p. 114) Thus, a great butler is one who "has applied his talents to serving a great gentleman – and through the latter, to serving humanity." (p. 117) He elaborates on his view: "[T]hose of us who wish to make our mark must realize that we best do so . . . by devoting our attention to providing the best possible service to those great gentlemen in whose hands the destiny of civilization truly lies." (p. 199)

When the prime minister visits Darlington Hall to confer in secret with the German ambassador von Ribbentrop, Stevens's cup is full: "Who would doubt at that moment that I had indeed come as close to the great hub of things as any butler could wish?" (p. 227)

In 1936, young Reginald Cardinal, the son of an old friend of Darlington's, challenges Stevens to consider the harm his employer has unwittingly committed: "'Are you content . . . to watch his lordship go over the precipice? . . . Over the last few years, his lordship has probably been the single most useful pawn Herr Hitler has had in this country for his propaganda tricks.'" (p. 224)

The spur to Cardinal's challenge to Stevens, the old retainer for whom Cardinal has a real affection, is the planned visit to Hitler's Germany by Edward VIII, England's new pro-Nazi king. But Stevens is adamant: "'I have every trust in his lordship's good judgement.'" To do otherwise would be to abandon the very foundation on which he has so carefully constructed his butler's life.

These are all the events that go through Stevens's mind during that July week in 1956 as he motors slowly towards Cornwall and the reunion after twenty years with the former housekeeper.

When Stevens and Miss Kenton do meet, the encounter is brief. She comes to his hotel to tell him that she is now reunited with her husband and has no inclination to re-enter domestic service. Stevens accepts her decision and prepares to leave. Before heading back to Darlington Hall, he decides to take a little fresh air on the pier, to smell the sea and see the illuminations. He gets into conversation with a complete stranger, by chance a retired servant, and astonishes them both by breaking into tears. He recovers by focusing his thoughts on his duties towards his new employer, the American Mr. Farraday.

I find the novel remarkable for its understatement and the delicacy of its irony. A first rapid reading of the text might suggest that Stevens is in complete control of himself, except for a moment of weakness as his father lies dying, until the surprising bout of tears at the end on the pier. But a careful rereading reveals the terrible turmoil, the agony, that Stevens lived through. As Stevens had risen higher and higher in the ranks of domestic service, "for some years my father and I had tended – for some reason I have never really fathomed – to converse less and less." (pp. 63–64) The reader can see what Stevens cannot, that by becoming an even more perfect butler than his father had ever been he is no longer a person, he is a role, and roles do not have personal relationships. Stevens also avoids the temptations of the flesh. As Miss Kenton remarks, he has "'a curious aversion to pretty girls being on the staff.'" (p. 156)

Stevens is incapable of articulating any feeling not appropriate to his position. When Miss Kenton laments her cowardice in not leaving with the Jewish maids, Stevens protests, "'The whole affair caused me great concern, great concern indeed.'" Miss Kenton demands to know why he had not shared that concern with her. "'Do you realize how much it would have helped me? Why, Mr. Stevens, why, why, why do you always have to *pretend*? . . . I suffered all the more because I believed I was alone.'" (pp. 153–54)

Embarrassed by the personal turn of the conversation, Stevens takes refuge in the third person, a typically fine use of language by Ishiguro to underscore his point: "'Naturally, one disapproved of the dismissals. One would have thought that quite self-evident.'"

Stevens is not nearly as politically naive as his expressionless facade would suggest. Of Darlington's reception of von Ribbentrop et al., and of Darlington's several visits to Nazi Germany, he says, "Anyone who implies that Lord Darlington was liaising covertly with a known enemy is just conveniently forgetting the true climate of those times." (p. 137) They would not attack Darlington so readily, Stevens argues, if *The Times* were to publish a guest list of all those who attended the many German banquets given to honour the Nuremberg Rally. It is evident that, in spite of his loyalty to his employer, the pro-German attitude of Darlington Hall troubled him deeply.

But Stevens has chosen to have no faith in his own judgment. On one occasion, some of Lord Darlington's fascist guests decide to use Stevens as an object lesson in the failure of democracy. They want to show how foolish it is to entrust a vote to the unthinking lower orders, and so they ask him a number of political questions to which he always answers, "'I am sorry, sir, but I am unable to be of assistance in this matter.'" (pp. 195–96) We understand that Stevens feels the expression of political opinion is not appropriate to his function, but the drunken guests see it as proof positive of ignorance. Stevens is untroubled by the ordeal. His social betters know what is best, and unlike some of the new generation of servants, he believes it impossible to adopt "a critical attitude towards an employer and at the same time provide good service." (p. 200)

Nevertheless, the verdict of post-Second World War history is against Lord Darlington and his ilk of the twenties and thirties, and Stevens is finally forced to confront the terrible truth, that he sacrificed the whole of his working life to an idol with feet of clay. We have waited all through the novel for his insights to catch up with ours, for the moment when must confront what he has done: "I carried out my duties to the best of my abilities, indeed to a standard which many may consider 'first rate.' It is hardly my fault if his lordship's life and work have turned out today to look, at best, a sad waste." (p. 201)

In his conversation with the retired servant on the pier, Stevens makes it clear that his own rationalizations give him little comfort: "'All those years I served him, I trusted I was doing something worthwhile. I can't even say I made my own mistakes. Really – one has to ask oneself – what dignity is there in that?'" (p. 243)

We might have foreseen Stevens's sad admission. Much earlier in the novel, when speaking to a friend of his new employer, he had given the reply of Peter and denied that he had ever worked for Lord Darlington. (p. 123) He explained it later to a puzzled Mr. Farraday as a quaint English custom, designed to avoid revealing past employer-servant confidences.

One of the most carefully worked aspects of this portrait of the butler is Ishiguro's handling of Stevens's relationship with Miss Kenton. Even before their interview in the little Cornish hotel in 1956, it was clear that she had always loved him. Through all her years at Darlington Hall, from 1922 to 1936, she tried to break through his armour. She criticized his work, she criticized his father's work, she made fun of him, she imitated his motivational talks to the staff, she made cocoa for him, she stopped speaking to him, she let him hear her crying behind a door, and she even tweaked away the novel he was reading to improve his English. There was never a response. Stevens never abdicated his role. She confesses to him twenty years after the fact that her leaving service to marry Mr. Benn had been "'simply another ruse, Mr. Stevens, to annoy you. It was a shock to come out here and find myself married.'" (p. 239) Of her frequent running away from Mr. Benn, she says, "'I get to thinking about a life I might have had with you, Mr. Stevens. And I suppose that's when I get angry over some trivial little thing and leave.' " (p. 239)

In spite of her protestations that she has come to love her husband, it is clear that her ardour has never cooled. If Stevens could seize the moment, she would leave with him. But his response is typical of his denial of self and life:

> I do not think I responded immediately, for it took me a moment or two to fully digest these words of Miss Kenton. Moreover, as you might appreciate, their implications were such as to provoke a certain degree of sorrow within me. Indeed – why should I not admit it? – at that moment, my heart was breaking. Before long, however, I turned to her and said with a smile:
>
> "You're very correct, Mrs Benn. As you say, it is too late to turn back the clock. Indeed, I would not be able to rest if I thought such ideas were the cause of unhappiness for you and your husband."
> (p. 239)

Despite his flood of tears in front of a perfect stranger on the pier, Stevens will change nothing in his life. He will change nothing because he has learned nothing, not from his disillusionment with the late Lord Darlington and not from his heartbreak over Miss Kenton. His final resolve is to become the perfect butler to Mr. Farraday. The American likes to joke, and Stevens has already devoted much time to developing his "bantering skills." He vows to practise his bantering with renewed effort so that "by the time of my employer's return, I shall be in a position to pleasantly surprise him." That is the final line of the novel, and it is with that promise to respond to his employer's every need that we leave the poor, foolish Stevens.

The Remains of the Day is a *tour de force* as a commentary upon the English class system. Ishiguro knows exactly why the villagers Stevens meets on his journey would see him, in his employer's expensive car, as some great visiting gentleman while a doctor can identify him immediately as a servant. By a slip of the tongue or the cut of a jacket, an upper-class Englishman can recognize at a hundred paces those who do not belong, and Stevens's convoluted prose, while it may deceive the plebeians, can leave no doubt as to his status in the mind of his social superior. How fitting it is that, in the first paragraph of the novel, Stevens makes a grammatical error typical of those who try too hard when he says, "I was up on the step-ladder . . . when my employer had entered," misusing the past perfect tense, and it is the mark of genius to have Stevens end the novel with the magnificently split infinitive, "to pleasantly surprise him."

Ishiguro's novel is as fascinating a study of the management of a great household as Samuel Richardson's *Pamela* (1740), the first real novel in the English language. It also honours the didactic tradition of the novel in that it introduces a curious reader to a world he or she is unlikely otherwise to enter. And like *Pamela*, *The Remains of the Day* succeeds wonderfully in creating a complex protagonist who is as believable a person as ourselves.

There is also comedy in Ishiguro's work, strangely enough, such as when young Reginald Cardinal is on the eve of marriage. His father realizes that he has never discussed the facts of life with him, and he asks his old friend Lord Darlington to do the necessary. Lord Darlington, just as afraid of sex as is Sir David, delegates the task to Stevens of all people, and we have two pages of comic delight (pp. 89–90) in which neither Stevens nor young Cardinal have the slightest idea what the other is talking about.

But nothing can distract us from the novel's great achievement, the delineation of a man who has denied everything of value in his life in the service of a false ideal. Stevens is unique, but, as in all great novels, his human failings find resonances in our own lives. I cannot be the only reader compelled to examine my own past and to lament those long periods in my life when I too worshipped at the wrong shrine. It is very, very hard to face the fact that a belief one thought gave meaning to one's life turns out to be at best an illusion and at worst a lie.

Poor Stevens touched me profoundly. I wish him well at perfecting his bantering skills. He has little else to look forward to.

A GESTURE LIFE

Chang-rae Lee
(New York: Riverhead, 1999)

The protagonist of *A Gesture Life* is a man we assume at first to be Japanese. His name is Jiro Kurohata. When we meet him in the sleepy little American town of Bedley Run, less than an hour's drive north of New York City, he is better known as Franklin Hata or, even more succinctly, "Doc" Hata. It is sometime in the early 1990s, and Doc Hata, now over seventy years old, is the comfortably retired owner of a medical supply business. As he once explained to his friend Mary Burns,

> "People call me Doc, but I'm not a physician. I own the medical supply store in the village. Many years ago some customers and other merchants got to calling me that, and somehow it stuck. I wish some-times it wasn't so, but nobody seems to want to call me Franklin. I don't mind, but I would never wish to mislead anyone." (p. 45)

Doc Hata's days are quiet and ordered. After his morning laps in the swimming pool of his home – a house and garden he has made exquisite by the work of his own hands – the hours pass in pleasant exchanges with acquaintances and neighbours until his evening meal and his evening reading. Yet it is an empty existence. He has no hobbies and, when we meet him, he seems unwilling to enter upon intimate relationships with any other human being.

Doc Hata has an insatiable need for the good opinion of others. The first line of the novel is "People know me here," followed a little later by, "I somehow enjoy an almost Oriental veneration as an elder." Again and again throughout the novel, Doc Hata will reiterate the point. In an argument with his adopted daughter, Sunny, he tells her, "'I am respected and valued in this town. I'm asked to comment at all the critical council meetings. You have little idea what my position is. People heed my words.'" (p. 95) He has played golf twelve times in his life, always as a business activity and always with wholesalers who liked him because he would look after them when they got drunk after the game. He has enjoyed the business-centred conversation at conventions and the like, but only because the exchanges were never about subjects that were profound or consequential.

Now, in his retirement, Doc Hata is feeling a deep sense of unease in spite of his material prosperity in a town that seems to have accepted him. For whatever reason, Doc Hata, living a quiet, middle-class life most people would envy, yearns for the rest that death would bring. At his most depressed, he reflects that "older folks like me might be better off just falling asleep forever." (p. 19)

While burning some old documents, Doc inadvertently causes a fire in his family room and spends some time in the local hospital. As he lies in the hospital bed, without the little rituals that have structured his life, memories of the past he has long been able to subdue come flooding into his mind, often as a result of the questions put by the friendly staff. It is only now that we begin to understand the terrible burden that Jiro Kurohata carries within his hidden, innermost self.

The explanation of that burden is to be found not only in the recollections of Doc Hata, but also in the nature of the Japanese society that found and nurtured him.

Japan has been a unified, homogeneous, single-race society since the first Japanese emperor, Jimmu Tenno, came to power in 660 BC. Over the last twenty-seven centuries, the Japanese evolved a belief we call Shintoism. Shintoism taught that the Japanese were a people of divine origin, ruled by an emperor who was a living god. The Japanese worshipped him as they worshipped their ancestors and the spirits of the gods who lived in the nature around them, in the rivers and waterfalls of Japan, in the trees, and, above all, in the mountains.

Japan, in the eyes of its people, had only one problem: a complete absence of natural resources. To remedy the deficiency, the nation turned to its neighbours. In 1592, the Japanese regent Hideoyoshi mounted a hideously cruel invasion of the nearby peninsula of Korea. The Koreans ultimately pushed the invaders out, but Japanese interest in Korea persisted, and in 1910, less than a century ago, flushed by recent victories in wars first with China and then Russia, Japan invaded Korea again and annexed the country as a subject colony.

As Japan joined the worldwide movement to industrialize in the twentieth century, however, it needed more raw materials than Korea could provide. And so in 1931 Japan seized Manchuria, the northernmost province of China, and installed a puppet emperor. It renamed the province Manchukuo, and in 1937 moved south out of Manchukuo to attack the main body of China itself. Within the year, Japanese troops captured the great Chinese city of Nanking. In a six-week orgy the Japanese caused the death of three hundred thousand civilians by shooting, bayonetting, burying alive, or mass rape. (There were far more Chinese victims in that one city than there would be Japanese victims of the atomic bombs in 1945 in Hiroshima and Nagasaki combined.)

In 1941, Japanese expansion continued with the December attack on Pearl Harbor, only the first of many Japanese military successes in the Pacific.

Shintoism was now at its height. The function of every individual Japanese was to serve the Nation and the Emperor. Shintoism had never been a religion as we in the West understand it; rather it was a patriotic way of life expressed in religious terms. Many Japanese had no difficulty in following Buddhism at the same time to satisfy their deeper spiritual needs. But Shinto nationalism governed the whole of their daily lives. Because of their view of themselves and their emperor, they regarded all other races as innately inferior. Thus, as the Japanese conquered more and more of the nations of the Pacific Rim, more and more conquered peoples became victims of Japanese military brutality. These included Malaysians, Manchurians, Filipinos, and Chinese, but the worst treated were the Koreans, a people despised by the Japanese since the conquest of 1910. The women among the vanquished suffered most. To feed their military brothels during the Second World War, the Japanese forced young girls into prostitution, two hundred thousand at least from Korea alone. In the novel, five terrified Korean girls arrive sometime in 1943 or 1944 at a remote wartime outpost in Burma. They are under the supervision of a middle-aged Japanese woman to service the sexual needs of two hundred Japanese soldiers. Two lose their lives violently and three are forced to have sex until they die, their private parts mashed to a pulp.

This is the burden our protagonist, Doc Hata, has carried with him for fifty years. He was there when the five girls lost their lives.

We are told (p. 224) that Doc Hata's full family name, Kurohata, means "black flag" in Japanese. It is a fitting name because, in traditional Japan, a black flag would be flown outside a village where there was disease. Doc Hata has suppressed his wartime memory for fifty years, but it is there, a disease deep within him. Just as a Japanese village with a contagion put out its black flag to warn away strangers, so Doc Hata has created a facade that the outside world may not penetrate.

And the worst part of Doc Hata's burden is that, during the Second World War, he had fallen in love with one of those pitiful girls.

Western history books refer to these sex slaves as "comfort women." They are rarely referred to in Japanese history books, and *never* in Japanese school texts. There is sometimes a vague mention of a women's auxiliary volunteer corps from the subject nations, but never an explanation of what these hundreds of thousands of women "volunteered" for.

The post-war Japanese government never had to face the accusations of those few wartime victims who survived the abuse. When General Douglas MacArthur occupied Japan in 1945, in order to make the country function he needed the co-operation of the emperor, the government, and the Japanese people. MacArthur decided to absolve the Japanese of war guilt, with the exception of twenty-eight leaders whom he put on trial. Seven were hanged, including the wartime prime minister Tojo.

And that was it. That and a ban on the teaching of state Shintoism, plus an admission by the emperor that he was not God.

No other admissions and no reparations were demanded of the Japanese. The surviving "comfort women," so often Korean, wrongly felt that the shame was theirs, and it was not until the 1990s that a brave few of them came forward to demand an apology from the Japanese government. In 1995, Prime Minister Tomiichi Murayama offered a limited admission of,

I quote, "a mistaken national policy," and his successor, Keizo Obuchi, offered "deep remorse and heartfelt apology" in 1998 to South Korea for the Japanese colonial rule from 1910 to 1945. Neither apology made any reference to comfort women.

In 1998, three Korean women won a decision against the Japanese government in a Japanese district court. The government was told to pay the three women, collectively, seven thousand dollars (US) to compensate them for years of wartime sexual abuse. On March 30, 2001, the Hiroshima High Court overturned that ruling. The Japanese government need not pay the women the money, because, as the court put it, "no serious constitutional violations occurred."

My wife, Pearl, and I were in Tokyo in 1998. We were able to meet Haruki Murakami, the author of *The Wind-Up Bird Chronicle*, which I was preparing to review. As part of our conversation, I showed Mr. Murakami an article from that day's Tokyo English-language paper. The article voiced a threat against China and Korea that, if they persisted in making up lies about the existence of so-called "comfort women," they would succeed in provoking "even greater" anti-Chinese and anti-Korean feeling among the Japanese.

Murakami was very frank with me.

We are lost, the Japanese, . . . we have been working so hard . . . but where are we going? . . . They are saying, now, that there was no massacre at Nanking and that there were no comfort women. . . . Japan has not faced up to its past. Everyone had to face responsibility for the terrible Japanese actions. . . . Until Japan faces its past, we are not living the truth.

Most Japanese do not agree with Murakami. They suppress the memory, or choose not to know. But, in Murakami's opinion and in mine, they know they committed evil and that knowledge is a canker in the collective Japanese soul.

How does our benevolent, small-town American Doc Hata, over seventy years old by the 1990s, handle the burden as he lies in his hospital bed?

Let us first go back to his beginnings as his memories reveal them to us.

We learn that he was born Korean, not Japanese. He was born in Japan, but in a ghetto of mostly Korean hide-tanners and renderers, the most despised of occupations, handling as it did the unclean bodies of dead animals. When he is asked by one of the comfort women, Kkutaeh, if he had a Korean name, he denies it.

> "I don't have one," I told her immediately. But this was not exactly true. I'd had one at birth, naturally, but it was never used by anyone, including my real parents, who, it must be said, wished as much as I that I become wholly and thoroughly Japanese. (p. 235)

The child Jiro Kurohata escaped from his ghetto by scoring high on "achievement tests" at school. Such intelligence in a Korean made him, in the eyes of the Japanese authorities, almost Japanese. His natural parents were only too willing to give the prodigy up to the office of the children's authority, "which in turn placed me with the family Kurohata, and the day the administrator came for me was the last time I heard their tanners' raspy voices and their birth-name for me." (p. 236)

When the elderly Doc Hata reflects back on his adoptive parents, "I think of them most warmly, as I do my natural parents, but to neither would I ascribe the business of having reared me, for it seems clear that it was the purposeful society that did so, and really nothing and no one else. I was more than grateful." (pp. 72–73)

Chang-rae Lee makes it clear that the young Jiro Kurohata in pre-Second World War Japan was absolutely imbued with the values of Shintoism. Neither he nor his natural parents could conceive of a greater glory than becoming an honorary Japanese. After his adoption as a son of the factory-owner Kurohata, his first duty was not to self or even parents but to the tightly knit, "purposeful" Japanese society that would rear him in love of country.

When war came, "one naturally accepted the wartime culture of shared sacrifice and military codes of conduct," (p. 68) "fulfilling my duty for Nation and Emperor . . . I was grateful for being part of what we all considered the greater destiny and the mandate of our people." (p. 120) Jiro Kurohata was even more grateful than most for the chance that

> my truest mettle would show itself in the crucible of the battlefield, and so prove to anyone who might suspect otherwise the worthiness of raising me away from the lowly quarters of my kin. (p. 120)

Kurohata is trained in field and emergency medicine so that, while "not a true physician," he could "aid and sustain" his comrades. (p. 120)

The South African writer J.M. Coetzee wrote in one of his lectures that the great question of all animals, including the human animal, is "Where is home and how do I get there?" Right up until the last years of the war, Lieutenant Kurohata had an answer to the question that satisfied him completely. Home was Japanese society and, temporarily, the Japanese army in occupied Burma.

Nothing causes him to question his certainty. When his superior, Captain Ono, beats a private soldier almost to death for brushing against him, Kurohata records the action without comment. It is part of Bushido, the Japanese code of knightly conduct for the warrior. When Captain Ono asks that he be given a Burmese prisoner, sentenced to beheading for stealing, "for purposes of instruction," Kurohata makes no moral judgment on what follows. Captain Ono etherizes the man, opens his chest, stops his heart beating by administering an electric shock, and then massages the heart back to life with his hands. The last two procedures are repeated several times until the man dies. It is demonstrated as an emergency battlefield procedure. To Kurohata, "It was nearly magical. . . . Though to me it seemed more academic than anything else." (p. 76)

It is frighteningly clear that Kurohata and his comrades are living in a self-contained moral universe. Chang-rae Lee made two brilliant decisions to heighten the horror felt by the reader who is not part of that universe. First, the whole novel is delivered in the voice of Jiro Kurohata, later Doc Hata, in the quiet, formal English, full of dry, objective understatement, that is the equivalent of the formal Japanese of a well-educated person. Second, the narrative juxtaposes the horror of Kurohata's wartime past with the sleepiness of Bedley Run, an American town in Westchester County, in what has become known as John Cheever country, where the greatest human problem is that of a white male facing the angst of middle age. (There is even a reference to John Cheever's novel *The Swimmer* in the text.)

Kurohata's crisis, the first of his life, comes shortly after the arrival in the camp of five young Korean girls, the comfort women who will service two hundred Japanese soldiers.

The young lieutenant sees no ethical problem. He had encountered these comfort women before, at the Japanese officers' club in captured Singapore, when one had jumped to her death from a second-floor window, deliberately landing on her head. His reaction at the time was typically without emotion. "The girl was the first dead person I had ever seen. She was neither homely nor pretty. She was just a girl, otherwise unremarkable, perhaps fifteen or so." (p. 108) Another of the victims begs him for help in Korean, but he replies, " 'There's no place to go. . . . You must stay in the house,' " (p. 111) and there is no hint that she has disturbed the ordered Japanese world in which he has found his place.

The only feeling Lieutenant Kurohata records on the arrival of the comfort women is sexual desire: "[I]t was the notion of what lay beneath the crumpled cotton of their poor clothes that shook me as if I had heard an air-raid siren." (p. 165)

But it *was* possible for a Japanese soldier to have a different reaction to the comfort women. We meet a Corporal Endo, who is, significantly, from Kurohata's own hometown in Japan. Chang-rae here is surely making the point that both Corporal Endo and Lieutenant Kurohata must have been subject to the same cultural influences as they grew up. Yet Endo is capable of making an independent choice. Initially eager to have his share of the comfort women's services, Endo is lucky enough to draw the coveted lot as customer number one. Corporal Endo has an extensive collection of pornography and an unenviable case of extreme acne. One would expect him to be eager to be the first in line at the comfort house, a dreadful little hut with five compartments. In each compartment, there was no furniture other than "a wide plank of wood . . . its shape . . . like the lid of a coffin. This is how they would receive the men." (p. 179) "Like the lid of a coffin" – what a perfectly chosen simile to suggest the hellish existence those poor little girls would endure for the rest of their brief lives.

Yet Corporal Endo doesn't want to be first in line at the hut. As he confesses to his lieutenant,

"[Y]esterday after I saw them arrive in the camp I suddenly didn't think about it anymore. I don't know why. I know I must be sick, Lieutenant. I do in fact feel sick, but I didn't come to ask for any treatment or advice. I don't want my lot anymore but I realized I didn't want any of the others to have it, either. So I thought I could ask simply that you hold it for me, so none of the fellows can get to it." (pp. 168–69)

Then Corporal Endo goes further: he drags one of the girls into the bush and cuts her throat. It is a superb narrative move by Chang-rae Lee. Endo has looked out on his little world of the Burmese outpost, and refused to accept its terms. He does what good he can by freeing a girl from unspeakable horror, knowing that he will pay with his life. He is beheaded the next day, not for murder, but for depriving the camp of a valuable asset. His action is a perfect example of tragic defiance.

How can I say that his action was good? I quote the words of the dead girl's own sister, Kkutaeh, " 'I am only thankful for what he did. I am happy for my sister now.' " (p. 238)

After the death – the heroic death – of Corporal Endo, the reader can offer no excuse for Kurohata's lack of action. Endo has shown us that, in a world of satiric compromise, the heroic gesture is still possible. The individual is everywhere responsible for his actions. But Kurohata sees no problem and, anyway, could never find it within himself to be disloyal to the code in which he has grown up. As the aging Doc Hata remembers, "I feared, simply enough, to be marked by a failure like Corporal Endo's, which was not one of ego or self but of an obligation public and total." (p. 229)

Kurohata has been assigned the medical care of the comfort women and he continues to exercise his duties.

> The older woman, Mrs. Matsui, had brought over one of them after their first full evening with the enlisted men; the girl could hardly walk and was bleeding freely from her genital area, which was bruised and swollen nearly beyond recognition. She was weakened from the blood loss, and I had the orderly wrap her in blankets and instructed Mrs. Matsui to give her an extra ration of [food]. (pp. 226–27)

But Captain Ono orders that the girl be sent back to the comfort house immediately. His instructions are that Kurohata may remove the girls only in case of disease or if a malady is imminently life-threatening. Kurohata accepts the order without question. "All this was inviolable, like any set of natural laws." (p. 227) Lieutenant Kurohata still experiences no moral unease.

He discovers that his superior, Captain Ono, has kept one of the girls apart: Kkutaeh, the sister of the girl Corporal Endo liberated from her hell. Ono has not permitted her to service the men, nor has he used her himself as yet. He has sadistic plans for the little Korean girl, who fascinates him with what he thinks of as the high-quality, almost Japanese, bloodlines he sees in her face. As he tells Kurohata, whom he asks to keep a medical eye on Kkutaeh, already pregnant by some unknown lover or rapist, "'I'm letting the pregnancy go, in fact, to see how long she'll stay that way, once she begins servicing the whole of the camp. She was pregnant before even I was able to take my pleasure.'" (p. 270)

The problem is that Kurohata has fallen in love with the girl. He goes to see Captain Ono to tell him that "'I cannot let you visit her tonight, or on any future day. . . . I wish her to be my wife. I will marry her when the war ends. I have already decided this.'" (pp. 269–70)

It has been a delicate little affair. While Kkutaeh is sleeping, or pretending to sleep, in Kurohata's tent, he makes love to her. "[I]t was all quite swift and natural, as chaste as it could ever be. . . . I said then, *I love you*, and she didn't answer. *I love you*, I said again, in Korean, not whispering it this time but speaking it as clearly as I could." (p. 260) They confide in each other. Kkutaeh tells Kurohata how her father gave her and her sister up to the Japanese in order to save his son. Kurohata tells her how he plans to go to medical school to become a real doctor. He dreams of the future life they might lead together – a tender, naive little dream, like an oasis of words in this terrible, terrible place.

"I stayed awake until almost morning, thinking of other places you might like to see."

"What were they?"

"I thought of the rocky seasides on Shikoku, the steep cliffs above the water, the humble fishing villages there. Because you said you liked the water, and swimming. And then of course there is Tokyo, which I have not yet been to, but which must be wondrous in all its activity. They say it is a hundred Kobes, put all together." (p. 256)

When he confronts Captain Ono, his dream is shattered. Captain Ono laughs at him. "'You are an immense fool,' he said. 'I almost feel sorry for you. . . . The girl is telling stories, and you are believing them. Did she tell you how much she thought of you, too, how much she loved you? . . . Perhaps she suggested how she would like to meet you again, after the war?'" (p. 269)

His sneers drive Kurohata to violence. He has a hidden scalpel, but Ono pistol-whips him into unconsciousness before he can use it. Kkutaeh tells Kurohata later that he was not executed only because she agreed to have sex with the captain: "'He said he wouldn't kill you, but only if I agreed to his bidding. . . . All he really wanted was a last small concession from me. What was left of my will. So he has that. But the doctor has always had my life and my death.'" (pp. 292–93)

When next Captain Ono comes to Kkutaeh, this time with a gift of sweets, Kurohata is behind him, once more with a scalpel. But again he cannot bring himself to use it, although he feels Kkutaeh willing him to strike. It is finally Kkutaeh herself who takes the scalpel and drives it into Ono's neck. It is this moment, the moment of his failure to act, that Kurohata will have in his mind for the rest of his life, however hard he tries to repress the memory.

Fifty years later, in a quiet American town, old Doc Hata will yearn to have that moment back. What should he have done? He should have killed the girl to liberate her from what awaited her. Captain Ono was irrelevant. As a comfort woman, Kkutaeh's fate was sealed, so he should have killed her and then faced his own death as Corporal Endo faced his. Kkutaeh defined Kurohata's failure within moments of her killing Captain Ono. She tells him,

> "[R]eally you are not any different from the rest. I'm sorry I gave myself to you, not for me but for you. Perhaps it was a second's hope. For that I'll be sorry to my death. But if you loved me, Lieutenant, if you truly loved me, you could not bear to be with me. You could not see me like this, you could not stand for one moment longer the thought of my even living." (p. 300)

His attraction to Kkutaeh is calf love, almost a romantic pose, and Captain Ono recognizes that in one of his taunts: "'What do you think you are doing, protecting her honour? I suppose you imagine she's your maiden, and you her swordsman.'" (p. 269)

A measure of love is what one is prepared to sacrifice for it, and in the end Kurohata sacrifices nothing. He could not sacrifice his feeling of belonging, of finding home in the Japanese army, and he could not sacrifice his love of Nation and Emperor. He lacks the courage to free Kkutaeh by killing her and dying himself.

Later in the chronological story, Chang-rae Lee will make the point again about love involving a willingness to sacrifice. When his friend Renny Bannerjee tells Doc Hata that he is in love with the real estate agent Olivia Crawford, Bannerjee says, "'I have a terrible weakness for that woman. It's quite specific. Something in me wants to hand over all my money to her.'" (p. 38) The point is made in the idiom of comedy, and we smile, but the meaning is deadly serious.

After Kurohata fails his moment of reckoning, it is Kkutaeh who is dragged off to a clearing by thirty Japanese soldiers, the same clearing where her sister died, to be raped and chopped into pieces. Chang-rae Lee wisely chooses to describe, not the scene with its butchery beyond words, but the aftermath. The aging Doc Hata remembers the returning Japanese soldiers:

> Some were half-dressed, shirtless, trouserless, half-hopping to pull on boots. They were generally quiet. The quiet after great celebration. They were flecked with blood, and muddy dirt, some more than others. One with his hands and forearms as if dipped in crimson. Another's face smudged with it, the color strange in his hair. One of them was completely clean, only his boots soiled; he was vomiting as he walked. Shiboru carried his saber, wiping it lazily in the tall grass. His face was bleeding but he was unconcerned. He did not see me; none of them did. They could have been returning from a volleyball match, thoroughly enervated, sobered by near glory. (pp. 304–05)

All that remains for Kurohata to do is, literally, to pick up the pieces: "I could not feel my hands as they gathered, nor could I feel the weight of such remains. And I could not sense that other, tiny, elfin form I eventually discovered, miraculously whole." (p. 305)

In the memories that flood Doc Hata's mind as he lies in his hospital bed, there is a curious and lengthy hiatus. We know nothing of Kurohata's life between the time of Kkutaeh's death and 1963, when he chooses to set up a business in a little American town. There is so much we are not told. Why did he not commit ritual suicide when the emperor surrendered, like his commander, Colonel Ishii? Why did he not go to medical school as he had told Kkutaeh he would? Why did he leave the Japan he had served so loyally, a Japan that had honoured Kurohata by elevating him from Korean to Japanese status?

We know why he chose Bedley Run over other small towns. It was because of a newspaper article about the older section of the community, a village that made Jiro Kurohata, now Franklin Hata, think of the small city on the southwestern coast of Japan where he had lived in his youth. But why had he not returned after the war to that very city?

Doc Hata provides very few answers. He reveals much about certain past events but, although there are passages of introspection, we rarely see the inner truth of the man. It is not that Doc Hata is lying to us; rather, he is suppressing the things he does not want to face.

When we meet Doc Hata we know that an accidental fire has put him in the hospital. He'd had a shortness of breath in his swimming pool, which had in turn caused a train of thought leading him to reflect on the emptiness of his retirement. It was at that moment that he caused the accident of the fire. As I read on through the novel, I realized that burning old papers was a typical Doc Hata solution to a problem by purposely putting it behind him. When he spies on his adopted daughter, Sunny, and sees her in a degrading situation with two men, one man masturbating himself while the other performs oral sex on her, Doc's reaction is foreseeable. As he climbs down from his hiding place, "[I]t was then that I wished she were just another girl or woman to me, no longer my kin or my daughter or even my charge, and I made no sound as I grimly descended, my blood already trying to forget." (p. 116)

When Sunny leaves home, Doc Hata methodically repaints her bedroom and erases all signs of her from the house. It is as if she were never there. Is that what he did after the war in Japan, try to forget? Blocking everything out, acting as if it never happened?

What we do know is that, when Kurohata leaves Japan to become Franklin Hata of America, he gives up something very precious to him – a sense of belonging, a sense of being home. It is something he will spend the rest of his life trying to recreate. The defeat of Japan meant the end of the comradeship of the army: that, too, had been a home for him.

When Doc adopts a daughter, he thinks she needs a mother. "I had aimed to learn of a suitable woman through old friends back in Japan, depending on a small network of comrades from the war for a reputable contact, but so few Japanese of good background and means wished to leave their country, especially in those boom days." (p. 51) I found that a fascinating reference; I think it's the only one in the novel that refers to Doc Hata's post-war days in Japan. It appears he had kept in touch with wartime comrades, but so many questions remain unanswered. Did Doc ever discuss Japan's wartime aggression, the specific phenomenon of comfort women, the death of Kkutaeh? Did he ever discuss with his one-time comrades whatever was causing him to leave Japan for the United States? Again, the mystery.

There is, however, little mystery in Doc Hata's decision in Bedley Run to adopt a child. After founding a successful retail medical supply business, after buying and beautifying a comfortable, suburban American home, he bribes an adoption agency to provide him with a girl-child. Initially, the agency woman assumed he wanted a boy; he was, after all, going to be a single male parent, but "I interrupted her immediately and explained how I'd always hoped for a daughter. . . . I found myself speaking of a completeness, the unitary bond of a daughter and father. Of harmony and balance." (p. 74) The reason for his choice of a girl is not really clear to him – "I was (as I think of it now) strangely unmovable on the issue" (p. 74) – but it becomes clear to us when he confesses, "I thought only of the moment of her arrival, which I had hoped would serve to mark the recommencement of my days." (p. 74) That one word "recommencement" tells the reader what Doc is increasingly aware of, that his life since 1944 and the death of Kkutaeh has been one long period of non-living. He will give to his daughter what he could not give to Kkutaeh.

The seven-year-old girl is from the Korean city of Pusan, "likely . . . the product . . . of a night's wanton encounter between a GI and a local bar girl . . . it was obvious how some other color (or colors) ran deep within her." (p. 204) One could imagine they stood a chance of being happy together, the unwanted child of mixed race and the middle-aged Japanese, desperately anxious to be accepted, to be part of a harmony, a society, a home. But from the moment Sunny sets foot in Doc's perfectly groomed house, she weeps and shivers. It is not a house for a child. As Doc reflects later, "[E]ven after several years, Sunny felt no more at home in this town, or in this house of mine, or perhaps even with me, than when she very first arrived at Kennedy Airport." (p. 55)

Doc doesn't understand why, but Sunny, as she grows up, discerns a part of the truth. Much later, as a thirty-two-year-old, she will tell him, " 'I never needed you. I don't know why, but you needed me. But it was never the other way.' " (p. 96) The widowed neighbour, Mary Burns, with whom Doc has a brief affair, also gets very close to the truth when she tells him,

> "I think you treat her wrongly . . . like a grown woman . . . as if she's a woman to whom you're beholden. . . . But you act almost guilty, as if she's someone you hurt once, or betrayed, and now you're obliged to do whatever she wishes, which is never good for anyone, much less a child." (p. 60)

Doc will never admit it to himself, but there is no doubt that Sunny has become a surrogate for Kkutaeh, whom he failed to liberate from the nightmare she was about to enter. He smothers not only Sunny with his generosity but everyone with whom he has contact. He has tried not to, he has tried to create a balance, a harmony not unlike that of a Japanese garden. When he first bought the house in Bedley Run and "received welcome cards and sweets baskets from my immediate neighbors, I judged the exact scale of what an appropriate response should be, that to reply with anything but the quiet simplicity of a gracious note would be to ruin the delicate and fragile balance." (p. 44) But he lavishes help in all directions, to the local policewoman, Como, and to the young couple who buy his store when he retires, a young couple who are obviously unsuited to business and who eventually fail but who resent his constant interference and offers of assistance.

As she becomes a teenager, Sunny, too, resents the obligation his generosity has put her under. There is nothing that will kill or even prevent love as quickly as being the recipient of charity. In a fit of anger, she tells him,

> "But all I've ever seen is how careful you are with everything. With our fancy big house and this store and all the customers. How you sweep the sidewalk and nice-talk to the other shopkeepers. You make a whole life out of gestures and politeness. You're always having to be the ideal partner and colleague." (p. 95)

Her father responds with: "'And why not? Firstly, I am a Japanese! And then what is so awful about being amenable and liked?'" (p. 95) But Sunny counters with the stunning "'You burden with your generosity.'" She does not understand that Doc believes there is a contagion within him, that somehow, ever since Kkutaeh, he has been the harbinger of many tragedies: a child's fatal illness, the death of the child's mother in a car crash, the death by cancer of a friend. Doc often refers to his family name, Kurohata, the black flag that should warn people to stay clear.

He tries to tell himself that he had no choice, that his childhood made him the way he is. The dictatorship of his need to belong has been with him ever since he was twelve.

> I have feared this throughout my life, from the day I was adopted by the family Kurohata to my induction into the Imperial Army to even the grand opening of Sunny Medical Supply, through the initial hours of which I was nearly paralyzed with the dread of dishonoring my fellow merchants. (p. 229)

It is hard to imagine a North American shopkeeper paralyzed by the fear of letting down, of dishonouring, the other shopkeepers on the street.

When Doc speaks of "the alarming fragility of a person's early years, how critically the times and circumstances can affect one's character and outlook and even actions," (p. 67) he is offering the age-old excuse of all those who know they have failed at some critical point in their lives.

As Sunny grows more and more rebellious, Doc knows that he should be firmer, more insistent, but, as always, he chooses the easier path, trying to find harmony, to build consensus.

When Sunny gives up the relatively mild defiance of deliberately playing the piano badly, she enters the real rebellion of promiscuity. Como tries to shock Sunny out of her new direction by relating what Sunny's friend Jimmy Gizzi, a drug dealer, gang leader, and mother abuser, says about her: "'How generous you are to all the guys. What a good sport you are. He said you never get tired.'" (p. 90)

At one level, Sunny is doing what adolescents often do, acting out in their own extreme, naive way that which they see and hate in their family life. In her generosity with her body to Gizzi and his low-life associates,

Sunny is imitating the gestures that make up the whole of her father's otherwise meaningless life. At the same time, Chang-rae Lee is creating a parody of what happened in the Burmese jungle in 1944. In both situations, women had endless sex. The difference is that Sunny is choosing to do it out of defiance, while Kkutaeh's young friends had been given no choice.

Kkutaeh! She died so early in the novel, but her presence is on every page.

At nineteen Sunny has an abortion. It is late in her pregnancy, and Doc has difficulty finding a doctor willing to perform the procedure. In the end, he has to assist personally during the operation, and we remember that this is not the first time he has handled a dead fetus. We are drawn back again to Kkutaeh and that terrible clearing in the jungle.

During his affair with Mary Burns, Doc makes reference to once having had a wife. He can only mean Kkutaeh, and he lets Mary know that " 'it wasn't a subject that was very pleasing to me.' " (p. 49) But the memory of Kkutaeh forces itself through Doc's effort to suppress it, an effort of will that he has had to sustain through every waking moment of the last five decades.

Eventually, Sunny leaves home, and Doc will know nothing of her life and whereabouts for another thirteen years. As he tried to put the death of Kkutaeh behind him, so he will put the loss of Sunny in the past. Years later he will refer to her as just a Japanese girl who came over to study for a while and then returned home.

Doc Hata will take the advice he has so often given to other people, to persevere, to survive. The past will become no more than the past. But it is not, especially in his case, good advice. The past is always with us, crying out to be faced.

Doc is no more successful as the lover of his neighbour Mary Burns than he is as the father of the girl he adopted. Mary is well-bred, tastefully dressed, no longer young, and shares with Doc a love of gardening. He helps her to plant shrubs at the tomb her late husband prepared for both himself and his wife. There is a walk in the woods, and then, in a secret clearing – not the first clearing we have been in, so ingeniously does Chang-rae Lee bind together the disparate parts of his novel – their mutual attraction overcomes them and they undress. She will tell him much later that she was surprised, "at first, to find herself deeply attracted to an Oriental man," (p. 52) but she is willing. It is Hata who draws back at the final moment of passion.

I felt awfully young, touching her, and the wanting I had wished never again to know was rushing back to me, a disturbing shiver in my fingers and in my mouth and in my eyes.

I stopped everything then, perhaps too abruptly, for Mary Burns had the impression that she had done something terribly offending or wrong, and I knew I could not convince her otherwise, at least for the moment. We quickly dressed. (p. 315)

What had come between them was the shadow of Kkutaeh. Doc Hata's sexual desire for Mary Burns was, as he said, a wanting he had never again wished to know. Since Kkutaeh, he had never before allowed himself to lose control of his feelings. When he and Mary finally do sleep together, it is no more than "a pleasing conviviality," something to assuage Hata's dreadful loneliness. He has discovered that "in my town and every town, especially when you reach my age, you sadly find that the most available freedom is to live alone." (p. 68) For one moment, his self-control slips, and he wonders aloud to Mary if she should not move in with him. To the great relief of them both, "the whole thing did expire and without further discussion." (p. 140) Mary sees in him what Sunny saw. "'*You always try, Franklin, but too hard, like it's your sworn duty to love me.*'" (p. 95)

The final straw for Mary Burns comes after her daughter, a prodigal spendthrift, asks her how much money she can expect as her inheritance. To Doc there's nothing wrong with the query; as he sees it, the daughter wants to plan a well-ordered future. The relationship between Doc and Mary ends with Mary's comment to her lover, "'You're a marvel, I think.'" (p. 351) Doc records the comment without a trace of irony and without the slightest understanding of how he offended her. The truth is that, just like Sunny, Mary Burns could not envisage a life with a man who can never show passion or righteous anger, whose every action is a calculated gesture to maintain harmony.

Once the relationship is over, Doc Hata relegates it to the past, persevering with his life, surviving. As Mary lies dying of cancer in the hospital years later, he does not visit her. "[T]he last thing I wished to do," he tells himself, "was to upset her or cause her distress in any way." (p. 43)

There seems to be no chance of Doc's finding happiness or a life other than one filled with empty gestures. But then, by chance, in the neighbouring community of Beddington he finds Sunny, now thirty-two years old, the

manager of a failing store and the mother of a six-year-old boy. After a
thirteen-year separation, Sunny greets him warily. She pretends to her son
that Doc is just an old friend. She cannot recreate a family where a real one
never existed. As a "friend," she permits Doc a relationship with the boy,
whom he tutors and tries to pamper, even rescues from drowning. But,
except for once when out of the boy's hearing, Doc never refers to him as
his grandson. Doc Hata has come to understand what he did to Sunny, giving
her a home but not love, making her the means of his penance for the
betrayal of Kkutaeh instead of making her his daughter.

Over the weeks after their reunion the emotional distance between them
diminishes, and they are able to be open with each other in a way that had
never before been possible.

> "I wish I could have done better by you when you were young, but I
> was just opening the store then and circumstances were spare –"
> "Please –"
> "I'm not trying to excuse myself," I tell her firmly, enough that it's
> a surprise to me. "I'm not so naive as to be ignorant of how you must
> feel about things. You have not been anything but generous. But I
> know I'm on tenuous ground, and I accept it."
> "Do you?" she says, though not unkindly. And I note, too, that
> there is a certain give in her voice, a new gentility, and whether it's
> from the passage of time or a heart of pity . . . I don't care. (p. 281)

Doc sometimes dreams of the business they could have built together if
Sunny had never run away, but now he classes that dream of togetherness
with his youthful desire to be Japanese, with his enlisting in the Japanese
army, with his desire to be accepted in Bedley Run, with his lifetime of
obsession with belonging, with what he now sees as "my long folly, my
continuous failure." (p. 205)

He is more convinced than ever that any association with him will result
in disaster for the other person: "I'm at the vortex of bad happenings, and
I am almost sure I ought to festoon the facade of my house and the bumpers
of my car and then garland my shoulders with immense black flags of
warning, to let every soul know they must steer clear of this man." (p. 333)

But now there is some slight chance of happiness. Not for himself, but
for Sunny and little Thomas. To further that end, he will now accede to the

persistent urgings of his friend Olivia Crawford – surely the most persistent of all realtors – and sell his house. Together with his savings, that should
give him enough to achieve two objectives. The first will be to save from
bankruptcy the young man who bought his business. The man has lost both
wife and child, and Doc has not freed himself totally from the need to make
gestures of generosity.

Far more important, Doc will set Sunny up in his old business prem-
ises, with a flat above, to run whatever business she pleases.

> And with what remains, if Liv is right and all goes well, I'll have
> just enough to go away from here and live out modestly the rest of
> my unappointed days. Perhaps I'll travel to where Sunny wouldn't
> go, to the south and west and maybe farther still, across the oceans,
> to land on former shores. But I think it won't be any kind of pilgrim-
> age. I won't be seeking out my destiny or fate. I won't attempt to find
> comfort in the visage of a creator or the forgiving dead.
>
> Let me simply bear my flesh, and blood, and bones. I will fly a
> flag. Tomorrow, when this house is alive and full, I will be outside
> looking in. I will be already on a walk someplace, in this town or the
> next or one five thousand miles away. I will circle round and arrive
> again. Come almost home. (pp. 355–56)

The novel has come full circle. Jiro Kurohata has gone from being
almost Japanese, to being almost a tragic hero, to being almost an
American, to being almost a father, to being almost a grandfather, to being
almost home.

When the author Chang-rae Lee speaks of the immigrant experience,
he writes of what he knows. The son of a Korean doctor, he came to
America with his family in 1968, at the age of three. They finally settled
in Westchester County, the locale of the American section of today's
novel. Chang-rae Lee wrote of the immigrant experience in his first novel,
Native Speaker (1995), of what one gains and what one loses in the clash
between the old world and the new. *A Gesture Life*, his second novel, he
intended to call *Comfort Woman*. As part of his research he went to Korea
to interview as many of the survivors as he could. A Japanese soldier who
falls in love with one of the comfort women was meant to be only a minor
character, but the soldier grew and grew in the imagination of his creator

until he finally became Jiro Kurohata, who denied the girl he loved the liberating death she craved because he loved his Nation and his Emperor more. Because of his failure to act and to sacrifice himself and his code for love, Jiro Kurohata will become old Doc Hata, doomed, in his own words, never "to find comfort in the visage of a creator or the forgiving dead." Doomed to an empty life, a gesture life, doomed to come no more than "almost" home.

NO GREAT MISCHIEF

Alistair MacLeod

(Toronto: McClelland & Stewart, 1999)

I first read *No Great Mischief* when the publisher sent it to me in galley form, and I knew even then that the novel would achieve great success. It is the most perfect meditation on the impact of the twentieth century on tribalism and tradition, and it is, in large part, a lament, an elegy, for a culture and a way of life that, if it has not already disappeared, is already in its death throes. When I go to a funeral, I do not expect to hear the unadorned truth about the dear departed. *De mortuis nihil nisi bonum*, we say, and I get what I expect, an idealized version of the deceased. The same, I think, is true of the novel. Perhaps the bonds within the clan, *kwown* in Gaelic, were not really as strong as the novel suggests; perhaps a MacDonald would not recognize another MacDonald quite as easily as he does in the novel, nor be quite as kind; but these are mere cavils. Within the confines of the book the logic works very well, and to criticize *No Great Mischief* on the grounds that it idealizes a dead or dying culture is as inappropriate as shouting during a funeral eulogy, "Who on earth are you speaking about?"

With that caveat in mind, let us approach the novel itself.

The first line is, "As I begin to tell this, it is the golden month of September in southwestern Ontario." The man speaking is our protagonist, Alexander MacDonald. He is a married man with children, a successful orthodontist who lives in a world of teeth made perfect, "where the well-to-do sit with folded hands in attitudes of patient trust. Hoping that I might make them more beautiful than they were before." (p. 62)

The time is the recent past, about 1990. Our orthodontist narrator has left Windsor to drive to Toronto. He avoids Highway 401, preferring the quieter routes through villages where dogs still run down to the road to chase after cars. There is something about country life that is pleasing to him, and, as he drives, he reflects on the itinerant fruit pickers on the farms near the highway, from the Caribbean or Mexico or Quebec and New Brunswick, picking for wages they will take with them when they leave. "This land is not their own," he tells himself, and as he narrates the novel, a story told always in his own voice, he will return repeatedly to this theme of displacement. There will be many references to the itinerant fruit pickers of Southern Ontario, those foreign workers who are compelled by economic necessity to leave, at least temporarily, the place of their heart.

As I read, I began to wonder why this middle-aged orthodontist would feel such compassion, such empathy, for the dispossessed. I had no idea that orthodontists were such sensitive people. I was all the more surprised since Alexander MacDonald seemed to have urgent and pressing concerns of his own. He makes his semi-regular visits to Toronto, to a filthy rooming house on Queen Street West, so that he might bring comfort and companionship and alcohol to his oldest brother Calum, living the life of a drunken ex-convict on Skid Row.

Alexander also has a twin sister, Catherine, the wife of a wealthy mining engineer in Calgary, who lives in an upper-middle-class comfort much like Alexander's own. The paragraph that describes Alexander's remembered visit to his sister is a masterpiece of well-chosen detail:

> In the luxury of her understated living room we held the heavy crystal glasses filled with the amber liquid or placed them carefully on the leather-embossed coasters. In the bathrooms, discreetly located in angled alcoves, the toilets made no sound when they were flushed. The rushing waters all were stilled. (pp. 93–94)

That final sentence, with its echoes of Biblical majesty to describe what must be the most unnecessary piece of modern, middle-class, self-indulgent extravagance, is gorgeous. Later in the novel, when we meet country outhouses and buckets in the bedrooms, we will remember the expensive and pointless silence of Catherine's water closet. What is the purpose of a silent toilet if the human body itself is not silent?

However, there are more important questions. How is it, for example, that of five living siblings in the MacDonald family two have achieved such affluence while a third is sick, penniless, and alone? The answer is a part of the story that Alexander MacDonald promised to tell us in the first sentence of the novel. The story is made up of his memories and the memories that were told to him. However far back the story goes, it will always be told in the present tense, because it is the story of a people, a family, a clan for whom the past is so closely intertwined with the present that it is indistinguishable. The battles of centuries past could have been fought yesterday, and those who have died achieve immortality in the vivid stories of those who live. The oral tradition among the MacDonalds is very strong, and the past is always told in Gaelic. Phrases from battles fought long ago have become part of the everyday MacDonald conversation, and they have taken on mythic significance. Two in particular come to mind: "My hope is constant in thee, Clan Donald" and "If only the ships had come from France." There will be others.

To understand the story, the saga, that Alexander MacDonald will tell us, with all its references to a long-ago past fresh in the mind of every MacDonald in the novel, to understand the exile of the MacDonalds from their native Scotland, and to understand their deep love of Cape Breton, the place of their exile, we must go back a number of centuries. Scottish history is not only the background to the novel, it is a condition of it.

Let us begin just before the year 1300. Scotland, England's neighbour to the north, had always been a fiercely independent country. Twelve hundred years earlier, even the Romans had been unable to conquer it and had to content themselves with building a wall across the north of England to keep the Scottish warriors out.

But by the end of the thirteenth century, the situation had changed. The Romans were long gone, and England was strong and greedy for its neighbours' lands. Wales and much of Ireland had already been swallowed up, and Edward I of England turned covetous eyes upon Scotland. By 1290, Edward felt able to claim Scotland as a subject nation and put a puppet king on the Scottish throne. But Edward had never been able to subjugate the clans of the Scottish Highlands, and soon even his puppet turned against him.

After only a few years as a nominally subject state of England, Scotland declared itself free again, and in 1306, a new king, Robert the Bruce, was acclaimed by all the major Scottish clans.

In 1314 the English once more invaded Scotland, but were soundly thrashed by the Scots at the Battle of Bannockburn. It was at Bannockburn, where Scotland won back its independence, that Robert the Bruce turned to the leader of the largest Scottish clan, on whose support he relied absolutely, and said, "My hope is constant in thee, Clan Donald." It is an expression we hear over and over again in the novel as one MacDonald speaks to another, an expression of absolute trust of one MacDonald in another.

After the Battle of Bannockburn, Scotland is free, and we now move forward nearly three hundred years.

In 1603, Queen Elizabeth I dies without an heir. To avoid civil war, Parliament invites Elizabeth's cousin, James VI of Scotland, to become at the same time James I of England. One king will rule over two independent kingdoms. For nearly a century England would be ruled by Scottish kings: James I, Charles I, Charles II, and James II. But by 1688 the Protestant English suspected, with good reason, that James II was a secret Catholic and planned to restore England to the embrace of Rome. Accordingly, the English Parliament, with the support of the country, forced King James into exile. He tried to resist and raised an army in Ireland, but was smashed by the forces of the Protestant Dutch William and Mary of Orange, who had been invited to replace James on the English throne. Mary was a cousin of the Stuarts, but, like William, her husband, was staunchly anti-Catholic and thus eminently acceptable to the English.

Naturally, the end of the reign of James II sat even worse with the Scots than it did with the Irish. They rose up continually against the English to restore James and his family to the throne. They won some battles, like Killiecrankie in 1689, but more often they lost.

In 1715 and again in 1745 there were major Scottish uprisings, the two Jacobite rebellions. Both failed. The second rebellion was led by Bonnie Prince Charlie, the grandson of the exiled James II, but he and the clans were defeated at the Battle of Culloden in 1746. He might have won if the French had sent him the support they had promised, and thus we have the lament, heard constantly throughout the novel, "If only the ships had come from France."

From the Battle of Killiecrankie in 1689 to the Second Jacobite Rebellion of 1745-46, it became obvious to the English crown that the only way to destroy Scottish nationalism once and for all was to destroy the clans of the Scottish Highlands.

The English had taken the first step in 1707 by uniting England and Scotland in one political entity, the United Kingdom.

The second step came after Bonnie Prince Charlie's failed rebellion when the English government imposed a forty-year ban on the bagpipes, the kilt, and, above all, the wearing of tartan as an outward symbol of clan membership.

Third, and most important, the English Parliament accelerated a process that had already begun for economic reasons. It was a process that the English history books call the Enclosures and the Scots call the Clearances.

Landowners in the United Kingdom had become increasingly aware that they could make a much greater profit by producing wool than they ever could from the pitifully small rents their tenant farmers could afford to pay. Act after act was rushed through the English Parliament permitting both English and Scottish landowners to enclose vast areas of land for the grazing of sheep, dispossessing thousands of small tenant farmers, most in Scotland still loyal to the House of Stuart. In Scotland, the Enclosures or Clearances would serve a dual purpose, enhancing the profits of the rich and ridding Scotland of a threat to the English throne. Thousands of dispossessed Scottish Highlanders would be forced overseas, and there would be few corners of the world that would not benefit by receiving at least a few of these tough, hard-working exiles.

There was one way out, however, other than the drastic measure of seeking a new life overseas. Many Highlanders chose to join the army – the English army, the only one available to them. At least they would be fed and clothed, with a little money left over for their families. Thus it was that the English army came to have large contingents of its erstwhile Scottish enemies. When the English general James Wolfe faced Montcalm's forces at the Battle of the Plains of Abraham outside Quebec City in 1759 as part of England's Seven Years' War with France, it had been only fourteen years since, as a young officer, he had faced the Scots under Bonnie Prince Charlie at Culloden. Perhaps understandably, he did not trust his Highland soldiers, and so he placed them at the forefront of his attack, writing to a friend that it would be "no great mischief if they fall." (p. 109) And thus MacLeod has the title of his novel.

For those Scottish clansmen who chose to leave the British Isles, the new world of North America was a natural destination, and Newfoundland and Cape Breton Island, at the eastern tip of Nova Scotia, were the nearest points across the Atlantic to their beloved Scotland. And when the Scottish settlers arrived on Cape Breton Island, they looked around at the harsh, rain- and wind-swept island with its rocky soil, only 10 percent of which is arable, and they cried aloud, "It's just like home!"

Be that as it may, their profound love of Scotland grew to embrace Cape Breton, their place of exile. In the novel, the patriarch of the first MacDonalds to arrive will be buried alone beneath a great boulder at the edge of the cliffs of Cape Breton, looking across the Atlantic to the Scottish Highlands from whence he came.

More than two hundred years after the first MacDonald arrived, our protagonist's sister, Catherine, will visit Scotland and go to the ancestral village of Moidart. By the sea she encounters an old woman:

> "You are from here," said the woman.
> "No," said my sister, "I'm from Canada."
> "That may be," said the woman. "But you are really from here.
> You have just been away for a while." (p. 160)

A little later the woman says "You are home now," (p. 167) and they speak, in Gaelic, of times long gone by and of Bonnie Prince Charlie and his defeat by the English at Culloden and they weep together over a defeat that seems to have happened only yesterday.

I am reminded of something Alistair MacLeod said while commenting on how well his novel was doing in Scotland. I quote him exactly: "I am very pleased by how much Scotland seems to like me, although I have been away for 210 years. The MacLeod people came from the Isle of Aigue in 1791." Consider carefully the words he used. Like the characters of his novel, MacLeod is a Cape Bretoner who adores the place, but there is clearly an even older loyalty. Who but a Cape Breton Scot could say of Scotland, "I have been away for 210 years"? It is an absolute identification of himself with his dispossessed ancestors. There is no distinction between the self and the clan; the family and time itself is telescoped so that 210 years can lie within one person's lifetime.

One of the MacDonalds who left Scotland because of the Clearances was the patriarch who will begin our saga, Calum Ruadh, "Calum the Red." In 1779 he embarked with his second wife, Catherine, and his twelve children and his one son-in-law on a voyage to Nova Scotia in the New World.

He had left his dog with the neighbours, but, according to the story passed down from one generation to another and given to our narrator by his grandfather, the frantic animal

> swam after them, her head cutting a V through the water and her anxious eyes upon the departing family she considered as her own. And as they were rowed towards the anchored ship, she continued to swim, in spite of shouted Gaelic threats and exhortations telling her to go back; swimming farther and farther from the land, until *Calum Ruadh*, unable to stand it any longer, changed his shouts from threats to calls of encouragement and, reaching over the side, lifted her soaked and chilled and trembling body into the boat. As she wriggled wetly against his chest and licked his face excitedly, he said to her in Gaelic, "Little dog, you have been with us all these years and we will not forsake you now. You will come with us." (p. 23)

It's a lovely story, and I understand when our Alexander remembers his grandfather saying, "That always got to me, somehow, that part about the dog." (p. 23)

Like Calum Ruadh MacDonald, that first dog will be fruitful and multiply, and the descendants of both immigrants, human and animal, will share both life and loyalty in the one great family, Clan Calum Ruadh.

The voyage across the Atlantic was a terrible one. Catherine died of the fever, like her sister, Calum's first wife before her, but a granddaughter was born. After they arrived on the northern shore of Nova Scotia at Pictou's Landing, Calum wept for two whole days. When our narrator, Alexander, hears the story from his grandfather, the grandfather is visibly moved. It was as if the landing were yesterday:

> "He was," he said, composing himself and after a thoughtful moment, "crying for his history. He had left his country and lost his wife and spoke a foreign language. He had left as a husband and arrived as a widower and a grandfather, and he was responsible for all those people clustered around him. He was," he said, looking up to the sky, "like the goose who points the V, and he temporarily wavered and lost his courage." (p. 25)

How typical that Grandfather should choose a simile from nature. Throughout the novel, the MacDonalds, in particular the descendants of Calum Ruadh, are at one with the animal and natural world around them.

After two weeks to recover from exhaustion, Calum and his party take a small boat for Cape Breton Island. Although technically a part of Nova Scotia, "official" settlement was not yet permitted on Cape Breton, the starkly beautiful "land of trees," but, in practice, you could take as much land as you could squat on.

Calum Ruadh was an epic figure. He left Moidart at fifty-five and would spend another fifty-five years in his place of exile before he died at the patriarchal age of 110. Our author, Alistair MacLeod, calculated the numbers deliberately to show a love evenly divided between the place of leaving and the place of coming. Wherever they lived, loyalty, for the MacDonalds, was absolute, reciprocal, and universal within the clan. But it was not only the fierce loyalty to each other and to their own that would distinguish them over the years. Almost every descendant of Calum Ruadh would have red or raven-black hair, fair skin, and, above all, dark, dark eyes. This is why Catherine was recognized so quickly by the old woman of Moidart. This is why strangers in airports at the end of the twentieth century greet each other in Gaelic. This is why Alexander's nephew, the son of his sister, Catherine, is stopped on a bicycle trail in Calgary by a car full of men on their way to B.C.

> "What's your name?" said one of the men, rolling down his window. "Pankovich," he answered. . . . "What was your mother's last name?" "MacDonald," he answered. "See," said the man to the car in general, "I told you." And then another of the men reached into his pocket and passed him a fifty-dollar bill. "What's this for?" asked my nephew named Pankovich. "It is," said the man, "for the way you look. Tell your mother it is from *clann Chalum Ruaidh*." (p. 30)

By the time of Alexander MacDonald's grandparents, in the early twentieth century, logging and fishing in Cape Breton, although still the occupation of many, had become harsher and less likely to provide an adequate living. Cape Breton, "the land of trees," had suffered from clear-logging, and the fishing was less certain. Many turned to other work, in mining sometimes, and Alexander's father's father, Grandpa, was glad to get regular employment as the maintenance man in the local hospital. He won the job through the efforts of his friend and cousin, Alexander's other male grandparent, known to Alexander as Grandfather. Grandfather had worked as a carpenter on the construction of the hospital and was able to coach Grandpa on every detail of the hospital's inner workings so that he might triumph when interviewed for the position. Alexander's Grandpa and Grandma were always grateful to their friend and cousin, Alexander's other grandfather. As Grandma put it, "'He has always stood by us. . . . He has always been loyal to his blood.'" (p. 35)

This is only one of the innumerable examples in the novel of the positive side of tribal loyalty, the absolute reliance that one member of the clan or tribe may place on another.

Alexander's two male grandparents "were each a balance to the other." (p. 264) Grandfather, cautious and reflective, is a reader, always anxious to study to fill in the gaps in the oral tradition he passes on to his grandchildren. The other, Grandpa, also passes on the oral tradition, but he is full of fun and an appetite for life.

Grandfather is a man shaped by the circumstances of his birth. Born out of wedlock to a girl whose lover left to work as a logger in Maine, where he was crushed in an accident and from where he never returned, Grandfather has sought to make his life as neat and as ordered as his conception and birth were not. Describing him, Alexander tells us,

> After the death of his wife in childbirth, he lived for a long time by himself, rising at exactly six a.m. and shaving and trimming his neat reddish moustache. His house was spotless, and within it he knew where everything was all of the time. And in the little building behind his house where he kept his shining tools it was the same. . . .
>
> Before going to bed he would set out his breakfast dishes for the next morning; again with great precision, his plate face down and his cup inverted upon its saucer with its handle always at the same angle, and with his knife and fork and spoon each in its proper place, as if he were in a grand hotel.
>
> His shoes were always polished and in a shining row with their toes pointing outward beneath his neatly made bed, and his teapot was always placed on exactly the same spot upon his gleaming stove. (p. 33)

In those few paragraphs Alistair MacLeod gives us a skilful delineation of a trait that gains meaning with what we learn elsewhere about Grandfather's life. MacLeod does it throughout the novel, adding detail to detail until he achieves a perfect whole. I can think of no more fitting comparison than the way a perfectly shaped pebble is added to another perfectly shaped pebble until one has a cairn, a symmetrical pile of stones whose perfection makes the whole even more pleasing than its individual parts. It can come as no surprise to anyone that it took MacLeod more than ten years to write this novel, shaping each sentence, building each paragraph.

What I find incredible is that MacLeod used the same technique in the first short story he ever wrote. With "The Boat," published in 1968, he emerged as a fully formed writer. It is small wonder that, when he received the 2001 IMPAC prize in Dublin, the richest prize in English literature, he was hailed as one of the world's truly great writers. And that tribute is to a man whose entire output is contained in two volumes.

Our narrator's grandfather had been married for only a year when his wife died in childbirth, leaving him one child, a girl, Alexander's mother. He will spend the rest of his methodical life a lonely widower with a passion for holding the MacDonalds' oral tradition in his mind and supplementing it by reflection and reading. Grandpa, on the other hand, is the lusty progenitor of nine children who boasts that, as a young man, every time he returned from logging in the Nova Scotia woods and again stepped onto the soil of Cape Breton he would get an erection. Once he had regular work at the hospital, he could afford a house and two acres on the edge of town, where he and Grandma find tremendous happiness in each other. They sleep in each other's arms and they love physical contact in their daily life. When Grandpa is up a ladder on some household task, Grandma can never resist touching him behind the knees to make his legs buckle. She is as tolerant of all his weaknesses as she is aware of all his strengths. Alexander later remembers,

> Sometimes when he stayed too long at the taverns, as he sometimes did in his later years, he would exhaust his money and send a "runner" to Grandma, asking for more so that he might extend his socializing. She always gave it to him, saying, "He does not do this often. And it is little enough when you consider all he has given to us." (pp. 40–41)

One of the many exquisitely constructed little stories in the novel is about how Grandpa has too much to drink one Christmas Eve. He crumples and falls off his chair in a dead sleep.

"Whatever will we do?" she [Grandma] mused, and then brightening she said, "I know." And going to the box of leftover Christmas tree decorations she began to extract various ornaments and strands of foil rope and even a rather tarnished star. She placed the star at Grandpa's head and deftly strung the rope about his limbs, and placed little balls and stars at strategic places on his outstretched limbs. She strung some Christmas icicles across his chest, where they looked vaguely like outworn war medals, and then sprinkled him with some artificial snow. . . . And when she was finished her decorating, she took his picture. (p. 42)

Grandpa would carry a copy of that photograph on him until the day he died, and when it wore out from constant showing and re-showing, he would go to Grandma for the precious negative and have another copy made.

The love that these two people find in each other is only one of the many joys this novel has to offer. That love has its counterpart in the friendship between Grandfather and Grandpa and Grandma. As methodical Grandfather prepares the tax returns for disorganized Grandpa, Grandpa always sighs, dreaming of a refund, "My hope is constant in thee, Clan Donald." Grandma sums it all up in a line that is not only the final sentence of the novel but a litany repeated throughout the story, "All of us are better when we're loved."

Alexander learns an appetite for life from Grandpa and a more meditative habit from Grandfather. In his own person, Alexander creates a middle way between the two, the influence of his grandparents all the greater because of a terrible loss that Alexander endures at the age of three.

His parents had found work as lighthouse keepers on a little island just off the coast. When the ice was thick in winter, they could walk from the island back to their house and extended family on the mainland to visit and to shop in the town. One March evening they misjudged the ice as they returned to the island. Alexander, his sister, and three of his brothers had stayed on the mainland with the family. MacLeod's quiet account of what happens to Alexander's parents and one of his brothers is all the more terrifying because he describes, not the parents and the boy falling through the ice, but how little of the accident could be seen from the shore.

> Everyone could see their three dark forms and the smaller one of the dog outlined upon the whiteness over which they travelled. By the time they were halfway across, it was dusk and out there on the ice they lit their lanterns, and that too was seen from the shore. And then they continued on their way. Then the lanterns seemed to waver and almost to dance wildly, and one described an arc in what was now the darkness and then was still. (p. 48)

It is up to the observer, and to the reader, to imagine what that stillness meant.

The twins Alexander and Catherine, only three years old, will be taken in by Grandma and Grandpa. The dog, who survived the drowning, will return to the lighthouse on the island to protect what she saw as the family home. Certain that her vanished people will rise up out of the sea, she defends the island against all comers until the new lighthouse keeper, whom she attacks, puts four bullets into her loyal heart.

Alexander's three surviving brothers, led by the sixteen-year-old Calum, are deemed old enough to be independent. They will take over their parents' mainland clapboard cottage and abandon the schooling they had indulged in only sporadically. They will make a subsistence living from hunting and logging and fishing, and they will be a law unto themselves. As Alexander later remembers, he and Catherine were always entranced when Grandma and Grandpa allowed them to visit their older brothers in the old family house where no one brushed their teeth, where the bathroom was a bucket, where animals wandered in and out of the rooms, and where horses "would press their noses to the window, as if to see what was going on inside." (p. 73)

The brothers shoot animals from their windows, but only for food, and pee through the windows when the bucket seems too far away. As they grow older, to relax from the physical burden of their manual labour, they drive beaten-up, reconstructed cars to dances, fighting when challenged and always with the clan rallied behind them. They are hard and they are tough. When Calum, the oldest, standing in his boat in the fog, suffers agony from a rotting tooth and fails in his attempt to twist it out of his mouth with a pair of pliers, he ties a line from his tooth to his faithful horse Christy on shore and she yanks the tooth out of him. They are made of stern stuff, these MacDonalds, and the story of the tooth becomes another anecdote in the oral history of the clan.

It was the horror of that extraction that first inclined Alexander towards the study of dentistry, but his choice of career made his leaving Cape Breton inevitable. A professor at the University of Halifax warned him he would never make a living in a culture that valued teeth so little, and so Alexander will follow the road that leads him to wealth and Windsor.

But there is poetry along with the physical hardship in the lives of his older brothers.

> Sometimes, said my brothers, the blackfish [pilot whales] would follow their boat, and they loved applause and appreciated singing. If they vanished beneath the surface, my brothers would clap their hands in rhythmic unison like fans at a sporting event, and soon they would break the surface, sometimes so close to the boat as to be almost dangerous, drawn by the sound and the perceived good fellowship. They would leap and arch and then vanish again, although my brothers knew they were never far away but seemed like children involved in games of hide and seek, hoping to startle and surprise by their unexpected nearness. Sometimes when they were invisible my brothers would sing songs to them in either English or Gaelic and place small bets as to which set of lyrics would bring them whooshing to the surface, cavorting in their giant grace around the rocking boat. (p. 99)

As adults, Calum and the two brothers go into mining, where their strength and bravery will be at a premium. But always, between shifts, be it in Peru or British Columbia or Elliott Lake north of Sudbury, they will speak of the landscape of their youth. As time passes and their distance from home seems all the greater, they speak more and more often in Gaelic. They speak of the lighthouse and the gulls and the sea and the underground spring and Grandpa bringing hay across the ice with corks fitted to Christy's hooves so that the horse could find purchase on the ice.

This is a landscape Alistair MacLeod knows well. He is the son of an itinerant Cape Breton coal miner and was raised mainly on the family farm in Cape Breton. He worked as a logger and in hardrock mines in B.C. and Ontario to pay his way through university. He still keeps his miner's helmet and his headlamp at his summer home on Cape Breton. I have heard him say, "Cape Breton is like my mother: I will always be her child. . . . I know the songs and I know the landscape and I know how snow works and I know how boats work."

Alistair MacLeod understands well the longing that sometimes overcomes Calum and his brothers when they demand time off from their labour at the mine and drive back the hundreds of miles, defying all speed limits, to their beloved Cape Breton and their clapboard house and their pilgrimage to the island lighthouse.

Once, however, they will come back not out of longing but out of duty. They have been working as a team with other Cape Breton MacDonalds at a particularly lucrative contract at the uranium mine near Elliott Lake. There are other ethnic teams working at their side, the largest a contingent of French Canadians from Madawaska. Like the Cape Bretoners, the French of Madawaska owe loyalty not to any provincial or federal capital but to their home and to each other.

It was, I think, a marvellous narrative stroke by Alistair MacLeod to introduce another clan, another tribe, into the novel. It is clear to us that this group of French Canadians, without education or any loyalty other than to their own, are trapped in their culture. Some of them realize, but only dimly, that the same heritage that gives each of them identity and a home within their people is also a trap that prevents a full participation in the greater world outside. As we study this little group of isolated people, we realize that the same is true of Calum and the other Cape Bretoners. The two tribes illuminate each other. More than once, Alistair MacLeod has referred to Gaelic as "a beautiful prison." The same seems to be true of the French spoken by the group from Madawaska. Tribal loyalty certainly provides identity and mutual support, but there is the danger of the world passing your culture by and turning you into a quaint oddity of the past.

The novel contains a lovely fable about a king herring who guides schools of herrings to the hungry fishermen eager to feed their families. To the fishermen, the king herring is a benefactor; to the other herring he is a traitor. It all depends on one's point of view. Is one's culture a haven or a trap? The very sage Alistair MacLeod seems to me to suggest that it is both. That is why he and his creation Alexander MacDonald have both left the physical place of their heritage to live in the larger society. But there is still a terrible sense of loss, and Alexander MacDonald and Alistair MacLeod both carry their culture, that beautiful prison, in their heart.

At the uranium mine, the two tribes, one led by Calum MacDonald and the other by Fern Picard, live in an uneasy state of truce. Only rarely will the tribes come together in their shared love of drinking, dancing, and the folk music of their two heritages. It is significant that the fiddler who plays for them is a Métis, neither a Cape Bretoner nor a Madawaskan, and we are again reminded of the fate that can await an isolated, inward-looking culture.

Matters come to a head when a MacDonald, a cousin of our protagonist and another red-headed Alexander, is killed in a mining accident. It is rumoured that the accident was deliberately engineered by Fern Picard and his French crew so that they might bring in more of their own number, but before accounts can be settled the MacDonalds must take their dead cousin back to Cape Breton. It is at the funeral that Alistair MacLeod gives us one of the most exquisite passages of the novel. It is the description of the coffin.

> The casket was closed because he was no longer recognizable to those who once knew and loved him. Instead his picture was placed upon the casket's surface, the picture taken at his high-school graduation. His red hair was carefully combed and his dark eyes looked hopefully into the camera. There was a boutonnière in his lapel. Beside the picture there was a small stone chip from the original *Calum Ruadh* boulder. About the casket were the ferns and rushes from the *Calum Ruadh* land. It was still too early for the summer roses, the pink and blue lupins, the yellow buttercups or the purple irises with their splashed white centres. Still too early for the delicate pink morning glories growing from their tendrils among the rocks beside the sea. Growing low and close among the rocks and seeming to derive their sustenance from an invisible source, yet quick to die if plucked and removed. (p. 126)

The fragility of the Cape Breton wild morning glory, so easily wounded if transplanted, is a wonderful evocation of the fragility and impermanence of human life, a perfectly fitting comment on the death of this young man, driven by economic necessity to leave the native land and the culture that had nourished him.

After the celebration of the funeral, the MacDonalds are induced by the superintendent of the uranium mine to return to Elliott Lake. But the MacDonald team is now a man short.

Our narrator Alexander has just graduated from dental school. A life of relative ease awaits him. But the call of the clan is an imperative, and he goes, at least for the summer, to take his cousin's place. As it happens, he will not be the only Alexander MacDonald at the uranium mine. An American nephew of Grandpa's, by a brother who left years before for San Francisco, is seeking refuge from the Vietnam draft and will be taken in by the MacDonald team at the mine at Elliott Lake. But this new Alexander MacDonald is not like his cousins. He is unusually insensitive in an already difficult situation. He receives the friendly greeting of Marcel Gingras, "*Bonjour, comment ça va?*" with a curt "'Why don't you speak English? This is North America.'" (p. 224) Alistair MacLeod is too canny a writer to make every MacDonald into a saint, however idealized the novel may be. Worse, cousin Alexander is a thief. The theft of valuables from the French-Canadian team, together with the jealousies and suspicions, causes a fight during which Calum kills Fern Picard. The American cousin will flee, but Calum MacDonald receives life imprisonment.

As Alistair MacLeod has shown us before, loyalty to the family, the clan, the tribe can carry with it great benefits, but it can also demand a terrible price. Just as the Highland Scots lost their land because of their loyalty to Bonnie Prince Charlie, just as the dog of Alexander's parents lost his life because of his loyalty to his family swallowed up by the sea, so Calum MacDonald will lose his freedom because of his loyalty to an American with red hair and dark, dark eyes whose name is MacDonald. Calum himself, in his later years, will observe to his brother that the loyalties of the past have caused "too many bodies and too many wars." (p. 209)

Calum's imprisonment until his parole after ten years marks a slowing in the forward movement of the narrative. The MacDonalds will disperse. Catherine will marry rich and live in a "modernistic house" with silent toilets in Calgary, and Alexander will go on to orthodontistic prosperity in Windsor. And what of the other two, unnamed, brothers? They are unnamed by our author to stress the point that their first names are not important.

What matters is that they are MacDonalds. One will end up as a school-bus driver in B.C. Of him we know little. But the story of the last brother is a lovely one.

Waiting at a Glasgow railway station during a visit to Scotland he is hailed by a stranger as a MacDonald. He is offered a home and a job on a fish farm up in the Scottish Highlands. The incident is a kind of narrative counterweight to the earlier abuse of clan loyalty by the American cousin. I loved the conversation between the two MacDonalds at that filthy railway station. Says the stranger: "'We can always make room. We can always fit you in . . . we'll go to the bar. We'll talk about . . . Charlie's Year: 1745-6. If only the ships had come from France!'" (p. 263) And once again the past is a condition of the present. It's a delightful little story, and, if it's not true, it should be true!

The novel will end with two visits, both made by Alexander.

The first is to Grandma. Grandpa is long dead. He died in the fullness of his living, "from jumping up in the air and trying to click his heels together twice." (p. 264) It was Grandma who had encouraged him, after two failures, to make the third, fatal attempt. Now Grandma is in a nursing home at the age of 110. She is the last of her generation who lived fully in the Gaelic Cape Breton culture. She is the age of the founder of that culture, Calum Ruadh, and thus does Alistair MacLeod neatly complete the circle of his story.

Grandma's mind is wandering, but, like many in her situation, she has a profound memory of the far past. She and Alexander sing together in Gaelic, but she does not recognize him. When he does identify himself as *gille beag ruadh*, the little red-headed boy,

> She looks at me with bemusement, as if I am beyond the prepos-terous.
>
> "Oh, the *gille beag ruadh*," she says. "The *gille beag ruadh* is thousands of miles from here. Yet I would know him if I met him any-where in this whole wide world. He will always have a piece of my heart." (p. 272)

The memory is flawed but the love is perfect, and Alexander is bathed in the full force of his family's love for him and again invokes the litany "All of us are better when we're loved."

All that remains in the novel is Alexander's last visit to his drink-sodden brother Calum on Toronto's Skid Row. This is Calum of the clan Calum Ruadh, the Calum MacDonald hailed generously by Marcel Gingras, a member of another tribe, as "'the best miner we ever saw.'" This is the Calum MacDonald who was once flown two thousand miles to blast a rock face no one else knew how to bring down, and who could also spend a gentle afternoon with his retired old horse Christy and feed her and sing to her as they gave and received love one to and from the other. Now he shakes so much he can drink the alcohol his brother brings him only out of a plastic bowl. But he can look through the window of his pathetic room and see, not the filth and garbage of a Toronto back alley, but the cliffs and the beauty of Cape Breton and the grave of his ancestor.

Calum knows his death is imminent, and he has called his brother to him, as he did before at the cousin's funeral so many years before. "'It's time,' he says. 'Time to go.'" (p. 276) The call of the blood is absolute, and Alexander comes to the rooming house to take his brother home to Cape Breton.

As they drive, they talk as they talked during the visit six months earlier that began the novel, when they leaned "into one another like two tired boxers in the middle of the ring. Each giving and seeking the support of the other." (p. 191) It seemed to me that only in his conversations with Calum and with his sister, when the talk is of memory, does Alexander really come alive. After all, he is an orthodontist, and as Grandpa once pointed out, (p. 107) how much is there to say about thirty-two teeth?

When the two brothers get to the causeway across the Canso Strait that has joined Cape Breton to the mainland since 1955, MacLeod demonstrates his mastery of pure narrative excitement.

Calum takes the wheel. The police have warned them not to try to cross the storm-swept causeway, but Calum, so close to his beloved Cape Breton, finds once again his old strength.

> The car springs forward. The red engine light is on, the engine is roaring, and the water comes in at the bottom of the doors. The windshield wipers are thick with ice and stop dead. He rolls down the window and sticks his head out into the gale to see where he is going on the invisible road. We are hit by one wave and then another. The car rocks with the force of the blows. The causeway is littered with

pieces of pulpwood and dead fish. He weaves around the obstacles. The wheels touch the other side.

"Here," he says, "you can do the driving now. We're almost home." (p. 281)

At that moment, he dies. Alexander tells us:

> I turn to Calum once again. I reach for his cooling hand which lies on the seat beside him. This is the man who carried me on his shoulders when I was three. Carried me across the ice from the island, but could never carry me back again.
>
> Out on the island the neglected fresh-water well pours forth its gift of sweetness into the whitened darkness of the night.
>
> Ferry the dead. . . . Peace to his soul.
>
> 'All of us are better when we're loved.' (p. 283)

As I finished the novel, I realized that, apart from a brief reference to the Vietnam War, there had been only two pages of references to the great figures of the outside world or to the great events of that world. (pp. 245–46) This has been a very sharply focused study of culture and loyalty within the tribe and the negative and positive implications of that loyalty.

One might also see the novel as a contrast between the spiritual emptiness of the modern city, with its perfect teeth and silent toilets, and the densely felt, mythic past of an isolated culture, but it is a contrast, not a contest. The victory of the city was inevitable.

The Gaelic Cape Breton culture was doomed when logging and fishing and farming could no longer provide a sufficient living and the young people had to leave the place of their heart to make a living elsewhere. That is why our narrator, throughout the novel, is so interested in the immigrant, itinerant fruit pickers of Southern Ontario. Any culture that cannot provide work for its young is in great danger. Cape Breton Island culture was doomed the moment it was no longer capable of renewing itself economically.

In the sixteen short stories he has published over the last thirty-three years, now reissued by McClelland & Stewart as one collection, *Island*, MacLeod has always written of the tribalism and the loyalty and the harshness of life on his cherished Cape Breton. In the short stories, even more than in his novel, MacLeod makes specific references to the end of the Gaelic culture.

In the first great short story, "The Boat," the Cape Breton past is sold in shops. Tourists buy tapes of the old Gaelic songs that few people understand any more. In his final short story, ironically called "The Clearances" (1999), Germans are buying the shoreline of the island for vacation homes. The way of life begun in 1779 by Calum Ruadh MacDonald is over.

In *No Great Mischief* it is Alexander who is telling the story. To whom is he speaking? Who is the internal audience? His wife may not be able to feel the story as he does; she is from somewhere in Eastern Europe where the men of her family were killed or disappeared into one of Stalin's gulags. It is not a culture she is likely to miss. Exile for her means asylum, not alienation.

It is more likely that Alexander is telling the story to his children, new MacDonalds, that they might know from whence they came, that they might understand when a stranger offers them kindness because of the way they look. He is playing for them the role his grandfather and grandpa played for him.

The novel is above all a love song to Cape Breton Island and, at the same time, it is a lament. Within the novel, it is a lament by a middle-aged meditative orthodontist. Outside the novel, the work is a love song and lament by a sixty-five-year-old recently retired professor of English at the University of Windsor. Alistair MacLeod is lamenting the end of the Gaelic culture of seven generations of his family in exile from the Scottish Highlands.

But a part of the lament is also a celebration of the one great truth his Cape Breton culture had to teach: "All of us are better when we're loved."

FIMA

Amos Oz
(Orlando, Florida: Harcourt Brace, 1994)

Fima is set in Jerusalem in 1989. The novel was first published in Hebrew in 1991 and translated into English in 1993.

In the years that have followed the publication of *Fima*, the world has seen the Oslo Accords, the establishment of the Palestine Authority, the withdrawal of Israel from Gaza and large portions of the West Bank, the murder of Israeli prime minister Yitzhak Rabin, and the election of Benjamin Netanyahu.

But there are still massacres and a dreadful loss of life, both Israeli and Palestinian. In 1989, the time of the novel, Israel was led by Yitzhak Shamir of the right-wing Likud Party. Israel's present prime minister, Netanyahu, is also of the Likud.[*] Yasser Arafat is still the Palestinian leader and still, as Abba Eban pointed out, never misses an opportunity to miss an opportunity. While Arafat continues to enjoy the support of most Palestinians, in spite of well-documented and massive corruption in his administration, about half of Israeli voters see Netanyahu as dangerous, divisive, and anti-peace. The same percentage had the same view of Shamir in 1989.

---

[*] As I reread this book review, first given in 1996, I am depressed by how little has changed by 2003. If I replace Netanyahu by Sharon and if I add Arafat's unbelievable refusal of Barak's offer of land for peace in the summer of 2001, I might have given this talk last week.

Amos Oz is among those Israelis who fear the hawkishness of Netanyahu. Unlike most Israeli left-wing doves, however, he sees Netanyahu's election as regrettable but understandable. Oz's attitude is easily comprehended in the light of an interview he gave to *The Times* (October 24, 1990).

"You must understand that for years Israel has undergone a collective Salman Rushdie experience. In other words, we have been living under a death threat issued by Muslim religious leaders and Arab politicians, which has never been withdrawn. This would have been enough to drive even the sanest society insane, and we are not the sanest. We have been through persecution, oppression and isolation. What is surprising to me is not that so many Israelis have become hawkish, but that so many Israelis have managed to remain politically sober and realistic."

Amos Oz has for years played a prominent role in the Peace Now movement, arguing that both Jews and Palestinians have a legitimate right to a homeland and that some form of compromise is essential. He sees obstacles to such a compromise on both sides: he sees successive Israeli governments as stubborn and inflexible and Arafat as both cruel and stupid. Oz finds it remarkable, however, that Israel, faced with outrageous provocation and judged internationally – outside the United States – by a wickedly unfair double standard, has remained as democratic and devoted to a peaceful solution as it has. For all its blemishes, Israel has responded with relative restraint to unending murderous atrocities within its own borders. No other nation – and certainly no Arab nation – would have exercised such self-control. Nevertheless, Amos Oz, like Fima in the novel, knows that, if peace is to come, it will involve the giving up of land, land hard won by Israeli blood in wars forced upon it by its Arab neighbours.

Amos Oz is a *sabra*, a native-born Israeli. He was born in Jerusalem in 1939 to a fervently Zionist family. At the age of fifteen, he renounced right-wing intellectual Zionism and city life to live on a kibbutz, to live what he believed was the healthy life of a peasant soldier on a socialist commune. He was a kibbutznik from 1954 to 1990, at which time he left the kibbutz for the desert town of Arad so that his chronically asthmatic son could benefit from the clean, dry desert air.

It was on the kibbutz that the writer changed his family name from Klausner to Oz, "strength" in Hebrew. After taking his degree at the Hebrew University in Jerusalem, he began to write short stories. His writing was, in part, a glorification of Hebrew, a tribute to the Jewish state's ability to resurrect a language that had not been used as a means of communication between people for two thousand years. Unfortunately, his deliberate use of little-known, esoteric words became a barrier to the reader's comprehension, even that of an educated Israeli reader.

Amos Oz has modified his passion for Hebrew over the years, but, although he speaks perfect English, he has continued to write in Israel's national language, and I note that in *Fima* his protagonist is frequently irritated by clumsy and unacceptable constructions in Hebrew.

Amos Oz's protagonist is Efraim Nomberg Nisan, known to everyone as Fima. The reader is going to spend five days with him in 1989 Jerusalem, and much of the time will be spent in Fima's mind.

At the beginning of the novel, we receive a remarkably unflattering portrait of the book's central character, but we know at least, as Fima watches himself in the mirror, that this is a man who accepts his appearance, who is aware of his blemishes.

In the mirror he beheld a pale, rather overweight clerk with folds of flesh at the waist, whose underwear was none too fresh, who had sparse black hair on white legs that were too skinny in relation to the belly, and graying hair, weak shoulders, and flabby male breasts growing on a chest dotted with pimples, one of which was surrounded by redness. He squeezed the pimples between his forefinger and thumb, watching in the mirror. The bursting of the pimples and the squirting of the yellowish pus afforded a vague, irritable pleasure. (p. 8)

Fima views his body "not with disgust, despair, or self-pity, but with resignation."

He lives in Jerusalem, on a "shabby road at the southwest edge of Kiryat Yovel, a row of squat blocks of flats jerry-built in the late 'fifties." (p. 5) He is fifty-four years old, divorced, and living in a disorder and squalor that go far beyond what we would normally think of as acceptable bachelor conditions. "Fima's kitchen always looked as though it had been abandoned in haste. Empty bottles and eggshells under the sink, open jars on the countertop, blotches of congealed jam, half-eaten yogurts, curdled milk, crumbs, and sticky stains on the table." (p. 58) He is smelly, rarely changing his shirt or his underwear, and his clothes are so torn that he often has trouble putting his coat on. Nothing mechanical will obey him, and his daily routine is a catalogue of small disasters. He is a character out of traditional Jewish folk stories, either the shlemiel who always spills the tea or, even worse, the shlemazel on whom the tea is always spilled.

Yet Efraim Nomberg Nisan, or Fima, comes from a privileged background. We will learn, in bits and pieces, that he was born in the thirties in Jerusalem to Baruch and Lizaveta Nomberg. (Fima will add the name Nisan later.) Fima's father fled the Bolshevik Revolution for Prague and, later, for what was then Palestine, where he established a successful cosmetics factory and became a strong Zionist and a founding member of the Herut Party.

Our friend Fima – for it is difficult not to feel sympathetic towards him – had a comfortable, middle-class, Zionist upbringing. He received a B.A. in History from the University of Jerusalem in 1960 before beginning what his friends call his "billy-goat year," a frenzied 365 days of creative and sexual energy.

So frenetic is this one brief period that it is worth enumerating the exploits.

Fima meets a French girl, a Catholic guide for tourists in Jerusalem, and pursues her all over Europe. To give himself time for the chase, he tampers with the call-up date on his military identification card and is jailed by the Israeli authorities. His father intervenes with a senior Israeli official to get his son out. Fima meets the official's wife, eight years his senior, gets her pregnant and away from her husband, and then leaves her for a three-month stay in Malta. She loses the baby while he writes poetry and marries the woman who owns his Maltese hotel. After three months of marriage, Fima abandons his wife to go to Greece. In the Greek mountains, he meets three Israeli girls hitchhiking. In an idyllic episode, they sing, dance, and wear flowers. Fima falls in love with Ilia, sleeps with Liat, and marries Yael after taking all three girls home to Jerusalem to meet his father.

In August 1961, after Fima and Yael Levin marry, Fima's father buys them the apartment at the edge of Kiryat Yovel. At this point Fima's frenzy of action comes to an abrupt halt. Apparently incapable of further activity, he gets a menial job at a gynecological clinic, a position far beneath his qualifications, and produces the occasional political article for the newspapers, particularly *Ha'arets*. He appears to have retired into a life of the mind, his body exhausted by his billy-goat year.

His wife, Yael, is intelligent, hard-working, clear-sighted, and ambitious. After putting up with four years of Fima's indecisions and revisions, she goes off to the United States to work as a researcher for Boeing. Fima, by now completely mired in an interior world of confused thought, refuses to go with her and the inevitable happens. Yael meets a normally functioning human being, an American Jew, Ted Tobias. She and Fima lose touch after the divorce, but when she and her husband come to live in Jerusalem in 1982, they bring with them their three-year-old son, Dimitri, known as Dimi.

Both Fima and his father are enchanted by Yael's son, and Fima becomes the constant babysitter while Baruch Nomberg becomes a loving surrogate grandfather. Fima and Dimi become inseparable: Dimi is unusually intelligent and highly perceptive and can supply logical, sensitive, and often very funny endings to Fima's wildest and most imaginative stories.

Fima's love for Dimi, however, does nothing to change his way of life. He still lives in filth, and action is still sicklied o'er by the pale cast of thought. For the nearly twenty years since Yael left him, Fima has been debating, and the debate takes place largely in his own mind. He often envisages himself as Israel's prime minister, calling his cabinet to order to explore the possibilities of peace with the Arabs. He occasionally leaves the kingdom of his mind for endless, unresolved arguments with his father, and his father is a worthy opponent.

Baruch Nomberg, a long-time widower and a lover of beautiful, elegant older women, is a fascinating character. A brilliant raconteur, he can, without pausing, tell five different stories, all intertwined, each slipping easily into the next and each making a different moral point: "For fifty years now he has been conducting an extended seminar with Jerusalem taxi drivers on Hasidic tales and pious stories." (p. 67) He must indeed be a brilliant and compelling speaker; my own experience with Israeli taxi drivers is that it's impossible to get one of them to listen even for a moment.

Baruch is a generous man. He frequently leaves money in the pockets of his indolent son, and in his will he has a bequest to the ultra-orthodox for their Zeal for Torah Orthodox School and a similar bequest to the progressive, secular Society for the Promotion of Religious Pluralism. Baruch enjoys the vigour of argument, and he is willing to subsidize the ongoing and healthy conflict of views by giving money to both sides.

An activist in the establishment of the state of Israel in 1948, Baruch has lost none of his right-wing views. He has all the prejudices of those European Ashkenazi Jews who first came to settle Palestine. He trusts neither Arabs nor those Sephardic Jews who came to Israel out of the Arab countries after 1948 and again after 1956. Fima remembers how Baruch used to tease his wife about her attraction to Oriental food in the Sephardic market. Baruch called it her love for The Thousand and One Nights and Ali Baba and the Forty Thieves.

When his son points at the alleged injustices committed by Israel against the Arabs of the territory occupied by Israel after 1967, Baruch has his answer ready.

"Baruch, you are blind and deaf. We're the Cossacks now, and the Arabs are the victims of the pogroms, yes, every day, every hour."

"The Cossacks," his father remarked with amused indifference. "Nu? What of it? So what's wrong with us being the Cossacks for a change? Where does it say in Holy Scripture that Jew and gentile are forbidden to swap jobs for a little while? Just once in a millennium or so? If only you yourself, my dear, were more of a Cossack and less of a shlemazel. Your child takes after you: a sheep in sheep's clothing." (p. 74)

Baruch is impervious to his son's left-wing protestations. When Baruch attacks the Arabs for having forty states "from India to Abyssinia," including Iran, and for denying tiny Israel's right to exist, Fima stamps his foot in frustration, howling that Iran and India are not Arab states. Baruch remains unfazed:

"Nu, so what? What difference does it make to you?" the old man intoned in a ritualistic singsong, with a sly, good-natured chortle. "Have we managed at last to find a satisfactory solution to the tragic question of who is a Jew, that we need to start breaking our heads over the question of who is an Arab?" (p. 74)

Fima is profoundly sensitive to the suffering of Jews during the Nazi period – his thoughts and dreams are beset by images of *Ha Shoah*, naked, skinny children and uniformed men separating men from women – but he hates those "who went on and on about Hitler and the Holocaust and always rushed to stamp out any glimmer of peace, seeing it as a Nazi ploy aimed at their destruction." (p. 10) He cannot see history as a justification for aggression: "'Does every battered child have to grow up into a violent adult?'" (p. 94)

Fima fears the brutalization of Israeli society: "'These are hard times everywhere. We spend all our time trying to repress what we're doing in the Territories, and the consequence is that the air's full of anger and aggression, and everybody's at everybody else's throat.'" (p. 37) He sees that what he considers an insensitivity to Arab suffering is transforming itself into an insensitivity to all human relations. Bosses are curt to workers and medical staff to patients, and there is an "aggressive rudeness . . . in the bureaucracy, in the streets, in bus queues, and most probably also in the privacy of our bedrooms." (p. 159)

When his beloved Dimi participates with his friends in the cruel sacrifice of a stray dog, Fima "had a vivid picture of the last blood oozing from the gaping wounds, and the final spasms of the dying creature. In an instant illumination he realized that this horror too was the result of what was happening in the Occupied Territories." (p. 154) He writes a newspaper article on how insensitivity, violence, and cruelty flow backward and forward from the state to the Territories and from the Territories to the state, and he is horrified to find that he reacts more intensely to the death of Jewish settlers' children than he does to the death of an Arab boy. "Can a worthless man like me have sunk so low as to make a distinction between the intolerable killing of children and the not-so-intolerable killing of children?" (p. 203)

Fima doesn't accept the answer the Almighty gave to Job, that the limited intellect of humankind can never understand the cosmic plan that the Creator has for His creation. Fima seeks to understand everything and the moral implications of everything. There is nothing, whether it be trivial or important, that does not concern him, nothing that he does not worry to death for its underlying meaning. When he leaves a café and promises the proprietress that the weather will "brighten up soon," he frets about the moral justification for his promise. (p. 16)

Fima has three great friends, Tsvi Kropotkin and Uri and Nina Gefen. Either during visits or with twenty-minute phone calls, he harangues them incessantly on U.S. politics, magic realism in literature, Islamic fundamentalism, the Iran-Iraq war, Chekhov, and evolution.

When Nina Gefen, in an occasional fit of missionary fervour, comes to clean Fima's apartment, transforming it within half an hour from "Calcutta into Zurich," Fima "would lounge in the doorway . . . debating with Nina and himself the collapse of Communism or the school of thought that rejects Chomsky's linguistic theories." (p. 58) On such occasions, Nina and Fima sleep together, Nina because Uri is seeing other women, and Fima because Nina wants him to. Fima never acts, he reacts. A large part of his failure to act derives from his belief that all human endeavour is ultimately pointless. When he creates within the confines of his mind an Israeli of the future, an imagined Israeli whom he calls Yoezer and with whom he has debates, he always ends the discussions with the reflection that we'll all be dead in a hundred years.

Fima's conscious attempt to pay due attention to every single thing that happens in the world is a prelude to what he calls The Third State of Being. The first state is sleep, the second is being awake, and the third state, to which he aspires, is a state of supreme awareness, where the mundane details of life die away and ultimate truth is revealed in the oneness of all things. Fima knows that he can never attain that level and recognizes it as an abstract intellectual concept, but the doomed attempt to reach The Third State of Being (the title of *Fima* in its original Hebrew) provides his only motivation for continuing to live.

Before I read *Fima*, I would have guessed that a man who for nearly twenty years did nothing except argue the moral dimensions of everything with friends, strangers, his father, and God would be a terrible bore. But the truth is that I, like Fima's friends, find his apparently unrelated observations fascinating. I can think of few novels that I've been forced to put down every few pages to think through a point such as those made by Fima on his journey to The Third State of Being. During a phone call to his friend Tsvi, for example, Fima wonders why the German writers Günter Grass and Heinrich Böll always refer to the Nazis as "they," although both served in the Wehrmacht, wore the swastika, and gave the Hitler salute. "'Whereas,'" continues Fima, "'I, who have never set foot in Lebanon, who have never served in the Territories . . . regularly say and write "we." "Our wrongdoings." And even "the innocent blood we have shed." ' " (p. 176)

I spent some time thinking that one through, and the result seemed to me valuable. It is true, I think, that Israelis accept collective responsibility for their country's actions and mistakes in a way that the citizens of few other countries do. If an Israeli sees his country as committing an immoral action, the knowledge of that crime becomes a personal burden. For an Israeli the crime *is* the punishment. The knowledge that one's country has done wrong is the punishment for that wrong, and the Israeli does not slough it off by saying "they" instead of "we."

Amos Oz has always argued with the critics who see his novels as allegories, although reviewers have nearly unanimously considered at least two of his earlier novels, *My Michael* (1968) and *Black Box* (1988), to be allegories of the modern state of Israel. Oz prefers to see them as the record of individual experience. It seems to me possible to have it both ways. Certainly, Fima is a complete and wonderfully complex creation, but it is surely possible to read into the novel observations on the human condition in general and on Israel in particular. I am thinking specifically of the cockroach episode.

Fima is holding his shoe, about to dispatch a cockroach "strolling toward him, looking weary and indifferent."

The shoe froze in his hand. He observed with astonishment the creature's feelers, which were describing slow semicircles. He saw masses of tiny stiff bristles, like a mustache. He studied the spindly legs seemingly full of joints. The delicate formation of the elongated wings. He was filled with awe at the precise, minute artistry of this creature, which no longer seemed abhorrent but wonderfully perfect: a representative of a hated race, persecuted and confined to the drains, excelling in the art of stubborn survival, agile and cunning in the dark; a race that had fallen victim to primeval loathing born of fear, of simple cruelty, of inherited prejudices. Could it be that it was precisely the evasiveness of this race, its humility and plainness, its powerful vitality, that aroused horror in us? Horror at the murderous instinct that its very presence excited in us? Horror because of the mysterious longevity of a creature that could neither sting nor bite and always kept its distance? (pp. 78–79)

After peering into the mysteries of race hatred, Fima decides not to kill and closes the door of the cupboard gently, "so as not to alarm the creature."

If Oz does not want the reader to see his novels as allegories, then he should not write passages like this, a penetrating analysis not just of the roots of anti-Semitism but of the fear of "the other" that informs all prejudice.

At the level of individual experience, however, Fima's failure to kill the cockroach is one more example of how, Hamlet-like, he is so paralyzed by thought that action becomes impossible. He proclaims his own irritation at his inability to act: "What have you done with life's treasure? What good have you done?" (p. 111)

This great intellect, housed in an unexercised and unfit body, is capable of great tenderness. When he thinks back on his marriage to Yael, his memories are erotic and touching and beautiful. When he dreams of his mother, who died when he was ten, the images are poetic and beautiful: "Death had made her light and lovely. It had endowed her movements with grace but also with a certain childlike awkwardness. The sort of mixture of agility and clumsiness that is seen in newborn kittens." (p. 114)

Fima is so different from his father, Baruch Nomberg, but despite their political differences there is a great bond of love between them and more similarity than either would admit. It is even suggested physically: Fima "opened his eyes and saw his father's brown hand. . . . Then he realized that the hand was his own." (p. 11)

We should consider the implications of Fima's name. It is a diminutive of Efraim, and we remember from Genesis that Efraim (Ephraim) was the younger son of Joseph, who was the son of Jacob, who was called Israel after his struggle with the angel. We remember too that Jacob/Israel set his grandson Efraim above Efraim's brother, promising that "he and his seed shall become a multitude of nations." (Genesis 48:19)

Oz's protests notwithstanding, it is surely not too fanciful to see Fima not only as an individual but also as an allegorical figure. The family name that Fima took for himself, Nisan, is not only the first month of the Jewish calendar; it also means, in Hebrew, "banner," "emblem," or "symbol." If Baruch, a Jacob-like figure, represents the Israel of 1948, in the creation of which he played a role, then Fima can surely be a symbol of modern Israel.

We remember how fond Fima's friends are of his "unique combination of wit and absent-mindedness, of melancholy and enthusiasm, of sensitivity and helplessness, of profundity and buffoonery." (p. 27) We remember

Fima's obsession with the moral implications of every action. He is the embodiment of modern Israel, torn always between two extremes.

What other nation has daily demonstrations for and against every governmental decision? Close non-Jewish stores on the Sabbath? Demonstrations for and against! Fire back at Hezbollah in Lebanon? Demonstrations for and against! Withdraw soldiers from Hebron? Demonstrations for and against! Change the legal definition of who is a Jew? Demonstrations for and against! I can think of no other country so concerned with the morality of every single issue. The French government could blow up much of the South Pacific and Syria could murder twenty thousand dissidents with far less outcry in either France or Syria than an Israeli government would experience in Israel if it were to propose that El Al fly on the Sabbath.

Fima longs to regain his lost innocence, "an inner craving for the child, the youth, the grown man out of whose womb the chrysalis emerged," (p. 8) just as Israel must long for an earlier time when issues were clearer – in 1948, for example, when it was fighting for its very existence. The child Dimitri echoes that longing when he tells Fima of how he would like to sail away to a desert island, in the Galapagos perhaps, where life is simple.

What Yael says to Fima is true of both Fima and Israel: "'[T]hose eyes that were alert and dreamy started to fade and now they've gone dull.'" (p. 165) What has happened to the "'soulful, dreamy young man who inspired and entertained three girls in the mountains of northern Greece'"? (p. 164) She might as well have asked what happened to the glory and clarity of the dream of 1948.

There is no doubt in my mind that, at an allegorical level, Fima, with all his blemishes and loss of innocence, is Israel. When he walks past Shamir's residence, he imagines going in to debate the necessity of compromise with the Arabs. Doesn't every Israeli see himself as the equal of any Israeli leader? Every taxi driver we meet in the novel has an immediate answer to all of Israel's problems, if only the prime minister had the good sense to listen, and we are told how in the early days Fima's father, Baruch, used to argue with Ben-Gurion on the street.

Fima is both the individual and the symbol, but, in either role, he is treated compassionately by Amos Oz. We note the similarity to Oz's idol Anton Chekhov, whom Fima adulates and who is mentioned three times in the text. Chekhov also created characters who acted rarely and talked incessantly. The trick of genius is to make the reader care about people who think much and do little. Surely we do care about Fima. Certainly, he sleeps with too many women, but it is only when their husbands have ceased to pay them attention and it is rarely Fima who initiates the relationship. Typical is his meeting with Annette Tadmor in the office where he works as a receptionist.

> "Why aren't you looking at me?"
> "I don't like to cause embarrassment. There, the water's boiling. What's it to be, then? Coffee?"
> "Embarrassment to yourself or to me?"
> "Hard to say exactly. Maybe both. I'm not sure."
> "Do you happen to have a name?"
> "My name is Fima. Efraim."
> "I'm Annette. Are you married?"
> "I have been married, ma'am. Twice. Nearly three times."
> "And I'm just getting divorced. To be more accurate, I am being divorced. Are you too shy to look at me? Afraid of being disappointed?" (p. 39)

Fima doesn't stand a chance. This must be the wittiest seduction scene since Anne Bancroft had her way with Dustin Hoffman. Annette Tadmor is a wonderfully complex character. As she tells Fima, she worked hard at her marriage for twenty-six years, putting up with the dullness of a husband whose only answer was "*Azoy?*" ("So?") to anything she said. The final indignity came when it was he who had the pathetic mid-life crisis, walking out of a marriage in which he claimed he was suffocating.

When Annette and Fima first make love he ejaculates prematurely, but Annette consoles him the next day by complimenting him as the best listener she has ever met. She comforts Fima, concerned about his inadequacy, the way women have comforted men, poor insecure sexual creatures that they are, since the beginning of time.

Middle-aged men in this novel do not emerge as well-balanced human beings. Fima's friend Uri Gefen bolsters his fragile masculinity by myriad affairs, while the dreadful Dr. Eitan at the clinic takes out all his frustration in verbal cruelty visited upon his nurse. Yael, in her strength worthy of her namesake in Judges who slew the Canaanite oppressor, (4:21) makes the point succinctly to Fima. She has had her affairs during her marriage to Ted Tobias, but she doesn't whine about their significance. She is too busy being a tower of strength to her husband, her ex-husband, her ex-father-in-law, and her son.

> "I can't feel sorry for you. I don't want to be a mother to you all. That child, he's always scheming for something. . . . You'd think we're bringing up a prince here. And then you come around all the time, driving him crazy and making me feel guilty. . . . Don't come here anymore, Fima. You pretend you're living alone, but you're always clinging to other people. And I'm just the opposite; everybody clings to me. . . . Once, when I was little, my father the pioneer told me to remember that men are really the weaker sex. It was a joke of his. Well, shall I tell you something, now that I've missed my hairdresser's appointment because of you? If I knew then what I know now, I'd have joined a nunnery. Or married a jet engine. I'd have passed on the weaker sex, with great pleasure." (pp. 261–62)

Much of the novel contains this kind of tribute to the strength of Israeli women and lament on the frailties of men. Oz has commented often on the double burden women must bear, and not only in Israeli society.

For all of Fima's inadequacies, his acute awareness of everything around him provides great pleasure for the reader. There are marvellous descriptions of his walks through Jerusalem. One such excursion is in the Old Quarter, the Bukharian Quarter.

> In three or four hours from now the siren would be wailing here to herald the advent of the Sabbath. The bustle of the streets would subside. A beautiful, gentle stillness, the silence of pines and stones and iron shutters, would spill down from the slopes of the hills surrounding the city and settle on the whole of Jerusalem. Men and boys in seemly festive attire, carrying embroidered tallith bags, would walk calmly to evening prayers at the innumerable little synagogues dotted around these narrow streets. The housewives would light candles, and fathers would chant the blessings. . . . (p. 280)

Oz evokes the joy of Friday activity with a few brilliantly chosen details:

> The whole neighborhood was pullulating with feverish prepara-
> tions for the Sabbath. Housewives carried overflowing shopping
> baskets, traders hoarsely cried their wares, a battered pickup with
> one rear light shattered like a black eye maneuvered backward and
> forward four or five times until miraculously it managed to squeeze
> into a parking spot on the pavement between two equally battered
> trucks. (p. 278)

Fima remembers the Sabbath cooking of his childhood, and he reminds us
how vivid are the senses of children:

> The smell sometimes began to fill the world even on Thursday after-
> noon, with the washing and the scrubbing and the cooking. The maid
> used to cook stuffed chicken's necks sewn up with a needle and
> thread. His mother would make a plum compote that was as sweet
> and sticky as glue. And sweet stewed carrots, and gefilte fish, and
> pies, or a strudel, or pastries filled with raisins. And all kinds of jams
> and marmalades, one of which was called *varyennye* in Russian.
> Vividly there came back to Fima, as he walked, the smell and appear-
> ance of the wine-colored borscht, a semi-solid soup with blobs of fat
> floating on the surface like gold rings, which he used to fish for with
> a spoon when he was little. (p. 272)

The Jerusalem passages alone are worth the price of the book.

At the end of the novel, after five days of Fima's internal debate and
external argument, with action remembered but not undertaken, we arrive
at "the sad event" of the first sentence of the novel. Baruch Nomberg has
died suddenly while in the company of two lady friends. All of Fima's
friends, including Yael and her husband, are gathered in Baruch's apartment to commiserate with Fima and to witness the reading of Baruch's will.

Apart from bequests to various and competing charities, the bulk of
Baruch's estate goes to his son, "who is adept at distinguishing good from
evil, with the hope that henceforth he will not be content merely to distinguish but will devote his strength and excellent talents to doing what is

good and refraining so far as possible from evil." (p. 315) It is Baruch's plea to his son, and by extension to the Israel of which Fima is the emblem, to use the understanding of morality, of good and evil, not merely as intellectual exercise but as the basis of righteous action.

The last lines of the novel indicate a great pessimism on the part of Amos Oz about Israel's future, for Fima responds to his father's instruction with "Be good, but in what sense?"

But there was an annex to Baruch's will in which he left a modest apartment building "to my beloved grandchild, the delight of my soul, Israel Dimitri, son of Theodore and Yael Tobias." (pp. 315–16) Dimi's full name came as a shock; it was the first time it was used in the novel. It was then that it came to me: if Baruch represents the Israel of 1948, and Fima is the emblem of Israel in the 1980s, then Israel Dimitri is the Israel to come. I remembered then that, three times in the novel, Dimi is described as albino and as having crossed eyes. I also remembered what Dimi once said to Fima: " 'It's not fair: you can choose who you marry but you can't choose who your parents are. And you can't divorce them either.' " (p. 145) The full significance of that final assembly in Baruch's apartment became clear to me. All of them, Yael, Ted, Fima, the friends – even Baruch, present in spirit – are his parents, his forebears, in the sense that each has contributed or will contribute to Dimi's growth. His eyes are crossed and he looks in two directions. Which will he choose? Will Israel look to war or to peace? In his lack of pigmentation, Israel Dimitri is like the outline of a person in a child's colouring book. Every one of the parental figures will colour in one part until, at some time in the future, the portrait of a new Israel will be complete.

I remembered, too, what I should have remembered earlier: that with Rimona's son in *A Perfect Peace* (1983) and Boaz in *Black Box* (1988) Amos Oz had used a child with multiple parents before as a metaphor for Israel.

Finally, I remembered that Efraim, Fima's full first name, is not only a name, but also a Hebrew word meaning "fruitful," and I put together the names of the three generations, Baruch Efraim Israel. In English, it translates as "Blessed be a fruitful Israel." Amos Oz may protest all he wants against the labelling of his novels as allegories, but it is hard to see the benediction as no more than coincidence.

Fima is an allegory, yet Oz has succeeded at the same time in fulfilling the prime duty of the novelist by creating a fascinatingly complex character who never existed before and who moves through a world that is all too believable. Fima has joined the little world I carry in my mind, a world peopled with memorable individuals created by great novelists.

I am grateful to Oz for the character of Fima, and I am grateful for two other things, both very personal. Before I read *Fima*, I was never able to articulate precisely the great joy I find in my grandchildren. In Baruch's will, he describes Dimi as "the delight of my soul." I have used the expression ever since, although my gratitude is really to Oz's wonderful translator, Nicholas de Lange. In the original Hebrew, Oz wrote "light of my soul." The improvement – and I believe it is one – is by his translator. It is not blasphemous for a translator to fine-tune; "the wine-dark sea" is Chapman's phrase, not Homer's.

My other debt to Oz is for the brilliantly evocative walk Fima takes in the Old Quarter of Jerusalem. It brought back so clearly a similar walk I took in Jerusalem in 1981, and a moment in that walk when I said to my wife, Pearl, "I feel as if I am coming home." It took me ten years to work out the implications of that moment – I was already becoming like Fima – but at the end, unlike Fima, I acted. I undertook conversion and became a Jew.

There is much to be thankful for in this exquisitely written novel. I think of that lovely moment when Fima ends his walk through Jerusalem: "The early evening twilight had begun to gild the light clouds over the Bethlehem hills. And suddenly Fima realized sharply, with pain, that another day was gone forever." (p. 295)

How precious life is!

AMERICAN PASTORAL

Philip Roth
(New York: Vintage, 1997)

Just like "Swede" Levov, the protagonist of *American Pastoral*, Philip Roth was born in the Jewish neighbourhood of Weequahic in Newark, New Jersey, in 1933. There was some adolescent conflict between Roth and his hard-working insurance agent father, but by 1990, a fifty-seven-year-old Roth would be able to write a loving tribute to him in the memoir *Patrimony*, just as he had written affectionately of his mother in his 1988 autobiography, *The Facts*.

Roth attended Weequahic High, 95 percent Jewish and the Newark equivalent of Mordecai Richler's Baron Byng in Montreal. In his autobiography he remembers very few anti-Semitic incidents from his childhood; he and his schoolmates were as carefree as any young people in America and felt themselves to be as American as anybody else. From there, it was on to Law at university, a stint in the army, brief because of back problems, and Ph.D. work at the University of Chicago. Roth notes that there were fraternities he couldn't join, but other than that, he claims never to have felt seriously out of place just because he was Jewish. With his brother Sandy, a successful commercial artist with J. Walter Thompson, he seemed to have achieved all that the child of immigrants could wish.

At the age of twenty-three, in 1956, within weeks of completing his doctorate, Philip Roth threw everything away to court a manipulative, domineering, deceitful woman. One might well see a parallel between Roth's action and that of sixteen-year-old Meredith Levov in *American Pastoral*, who revolts so violently against what at first sight is the perfect family.

Roth had met Margaret Michaelson, a gentile and a divorced waitress with two children. She had a chaotic history of an abused childhood, a bad marriage, and serious mental imbalance. Roth gave up his studies and entered a tumultuous three years of romance and conflict. When Michaelson told Roth that she had just aborted her pregnancy by him so that he would not feel obligated to marry her, Roth, overcome by guilt, proposed and was accepted.

He went to tell his mother, who was horrified. Ten years later, he would remember and use her words when he wrote *Portnoy's Complaint*:

> "DON'T RUN FIRST THING TO A BLONDIE, PLEASE! BECAUSE
> SHE'LL TAKE YOU FOR ALL YOU'RE WORTH AND THEN LEAVE
> YOU BLEEDING IN THE GUTTER! A BRILLIANT INNOCENT BABY
> BOY LIKE YOU, SHE'LL EAT YOU UP ALIVE!"

Harsh words indeed, but his mother was right. Maggie Michaelson proved to be the *shikse* of Mrs. Roth's Jewish nightmares. In a fit of temper, two years after their marriage, Roth's wife told him that she had indeed tricked him into proposing. She had gone into Central Park and bought two ounces of urine from a pregnant woman. She had showed Roth the positive result of a pregnancy test and given him the news of the fictitious abortion. Their marriage ended the following year.

One might wonder why Roth gave everything up to marry such a harpy, but he answers the question in his autobiography: he saw Maggie as the moll in the getaway car. The reader might well pose the question: What could he possibly want to get away from? The Roth family, particularly the Roth brothers, seemed to be living the American Dream. Lou Levov, Meredith's grandfather in the novel, echoes what must have been the lament of Philip Roth's parents in real life:

> "What happened? What the hell happened to our smart Jewish
> kids? . . . Once Jews ran away from oppression; now they run away
> from no-oppression. Once they ran away from being poor; now they
> run away from being rich. It's crazy. They have parents they can't
> hate anymore because their parents are so good to them, so they hate
> America instead." (p. 255)

In 1959, having put aside all his parents' dreams for him and his own earlier academic ambition, Roth had to face the practical difficulties of earning a living for himself and Maggie and her two children. He began to write seriously and, within a year, produced a novella, *Goodbye Columbus*, and a number of short stories, including "Defender of the Faith." That is when Roth's troubles began with the American Jewish community. *Goodbye Columbus* was the story of a poor Jewish boy who falls in love with a girl from a nouveau riche Jewish family. Many American Jews objected vociferously to Roth's portrayal of the family's crass materialism. Worse, to them, was "Defender of the Faith," in which a Jewish soldier is depicted as both dishonest and cowardly. The community levelled the charge that Philip Roth was a self-hating Jew, a charge so often made against Canada's own Mordecai Richler.

Roth defended himself brilliantly in open debate. He argued that he was not writing uniquely about Jews but about the universal human condition. Since he was a Jew and since he did not want to write in abstractions, he used a Jewish reference, a Jewish framework, but his theme was always the general human lot.

It is true that in his writing he bears honest witness to a particular time, place, and culture, but his themes of intergenerational conflict and parental disappointment cross all cultural boundaries. The revolt of Merry Levov against her mother and father in *American Pastoral* is not a purely Jewish phenomenon.

Philip Roth does, however, see being Jewish as an immense advantage for a writer. As he puts it, being Jewish is the most intense and extreme way of expressing the old joke, Jews are just like other people, only more so.

I would agree with Roth's observation, and I think it derives from an important and basic difference in religious belief, in particular between Jews and Christians. For those who follow Christian teaching, this earthly life is a temporary and fleeting existence. It is a brief passage through a vale of tears, the valley of the shadow, before we enter a glorious life eternal. For the Jew this is not so. Judaism, as I understand it, teaches *totaliter aliter*, the total otherness, the total unknowability of God. All we Jews claim to know of God is the law he gave us through Moses our teacher, and that law governs the ways in which we live this life.

Although an individual Jew may make a personal act of faith with regard to a life after death, such a belief is not a required tenet of Judaism, which teaches that our concern is with how we live this life. Righteousness, or the lack of it, has no connection with any posthumous reward or punishment. Rather, one should live a righteous life only because God wishes us to do so. God will look after the life to come, if there is one, and we cannot know His intention.

It seems to me that this has very important implications. The believing Christian, approaching old age or death, might very well say, "Let this pass quickly that I might enter His glory." I know that my father, a deeply devout Christian, was sure that, when he died, Christ would be waiting to take him by the hand and lead him to reunion with my mother. Judaism offers no such consolation; all we know is that we hold this life as a gift from God, and we are responsible for living it to the full. That is why I agree with Roth that Jews, neither more nor less moral than other people, do live more intensely a life they perceive as being all there is.

In any event, Roth's defence that his Jewish characters were not only themselves but also vivid metaphors for the whole of humanity was not entirely accepted by his Jewish interlocutors.

But Roth went on writing. His first full-length novel, *Letting Go* (1962), was a rather disappointing look at the anxieties of a young Jewish male entering manhood. This was followed by the novel *When She Was Good* (1967), a thinly veiled attack on his ex-wife Maggie. According to Roth, she was still making his life a misery, pursuing him and demanding more and more money.

And then, in 1969, ten years after *Goodbye Columbus*, came *Portnoy's Complaint*. You might remember how the central figure, Alexander Portnoy, pours out his heart to his psychiatrist, describing his relationship to his parents, his obsession with gentile women, and his struggle to free himself from his cultural background. The passage that gave most ammunition to Roth's enemies was Portnoy's famous shriek of rage at the whole burden of history he is asked to carry: "'Jew Jew Jew Jew Jew Jew! It is coming out of my ears already, the saga of the suffering Jews! Do me a favor, my people, and stick your suffering heritage up your suffering ass – *I happen also to be a human being!*'" The author's counter to his critics was the one he had used ten years earlier. His protagonist was not only his own Jewish self but had a universal resonance; his cry was that of the young of every culture who reject their parents' values, reject a particular lifestyle that was not of their own choosing. However Jewish the particular, the theme is universal and would remain dominant in the rest of Roth's nearly twenty novels. (One notable exception is *I Married a Communist*, published in 1998, another attack on another ex-wife, this time the actress Claire Bloom who had written unflatteringly of her former husband.)

In most, though not all, of his novels after *Portnoy's Complaint*, including *American Pastoral*, Roth adopted a technique as old as English literature itself: the use of a narrator who is an alter ego of Roth, but not Roth. In, I think, nine of Roth's novels, it is Nathan Zuckerman who tells the story. Zuckerman is an American Jew, like Roth, born in the same year, 1933, but the use of this alter ego gives the writer an extra tool to work with. He can make Zuckerman more or less observant a Jew than Roth himself; he can make Zuckerman a little more naive or a little more skeptical than Roth himself; he can give Zuckerman problems in common with the novel's protagonist, to make him more or less sympathetic to the protagonist than Roth himself might be. The writer Roth can even argue with his narrator Zuckerman, as he does in the afterword to his autobiography.

Thus, when we read about the characters in the novel, we receive a further illumination through Zuckerman's reaction to them. In *American Pastoral*, the narrator, Zuckerman, and the protagonist, Swede Levov, both undergo prostate surgery. Swede's apparent recovery is made all the more wonderful because Zuckerman does not recover as fully.

The technique is, of course, borrowed from *The Canterbury Tales*. Chaucer the writer, the sophisticated man about the king's court, created Chaucer the pilgrim, a naive narrator who could marvel at the magnificence of some of his nouveau riche fellow pilgrims and thus point up their middle-class pretensions as even more absurd.

The use of an alter ego as narrator also gives the writer the advantage of distance from his story. Zuckerman may come to certain conclusions about the characters, but we cannot know if those conclusions are Roth's. And in *American Pastoral*, Roth, it seems to me, is especially anxious to pose questions about the immigrant experience without appearing to offer answers.

The novel begins with Nathan Zuckerman on his way to the forty-fifth class reunion of his Newark high school, Weequahic High. He is reminiscing about his old high school hero, some six years older than himself. Seymour Irving Levov was known as "Swede" to the school and to the community because he was blond, six-foot-three, and an athletic star. Twice the high school basketball team won the city championship with this young Viking as the leading scorer. To Zuckerman the child, Swede Levov was godlike. He was the quintessential American that the whole Jewish neighbourhood aspired to become. Zuckerman, a friend of Swede's younger brother Jerry, puts it succinctly. Levov was "the vanguard of the vanguard . . . our very own Swede . . . as close to a goy as we were going to get." (p. 10)

Zuckerman remembers how proud he was when, as a mature man, thirty-five years after graduation, he was recognized by Swede Levov in the crowd at a baseball game and hailed by his childhood nickname of Skip. One of the women in Zuckerman's party turned to him and said, " 'You should have seen your face – you might as well have told us he was Zeus. I saw just what you looked like as a boy.' " (p. 17)

Zuckerman also remembers his surprise when, ten years after their chance meeting, Swede writes to invite him to dinner in New York. As they dine, Zuckerman notes that Swede, in his late sixties, looks as marvellous as ever. He learns that Swede has a blond, gentile second wife, who is about forty years old, and three teenage sons, Christopher, Stephen, and Kent.

Swede's life and family seem picture perfect to our narrator: "*Swede Levov's life,* for all I knew, *had been most simple and most ordinary and therefore just great, right in the American grain.*" (p. 31) But it is all too perfect, and Zuckerman becomes certain "that more was there than what I was looking at," (p. 38) certain that there was a deeper reason for the meeting, something that Swede could not bring himself to broach. Apparently, all Swede wants is that Zuckerman, a writer, help him with a tribute he would like to prepare to his late father, Lou Levov, who had died a year earlier in his nineties.

Zuckerman is still mulling over the proposal when he arrives at the high school reunion. He meets Swede's younger brother Jerry and finds out that Swede has died only a few days before.

Jerry Levov is a brash, outgoing man, aggressive in his manner. A Florida doctor with an enormous practice, he has six children, four ex-wives, and a very loud voice. He is almost a stereotype and nothing like his discreet, goyishly handsome late brother.

Jerry fills in all the gaps that Swede had left out at the dinner. Swede had known he was dying of cancer. Jerry confides that his brother had spent the last twenty-seven years trying to recover from a family tragedy in 1968.

With what Swede had told him at dinner, with what Jerry told him at the reunion, and with what Zuckerman himself remembers of his Newark childhood and the Levov family, he begins to piece together what Swede Levov's life might have been like. For the next months he will write and dream about Swede Levov. In Zuckerman's own words, "I dreamed a realistic chronicle." (p. 89)

As Zuckerman dances off with his childhood sweetheart, we enter the life of Swede Levov, as recreated by Nathan Zuckerman, whom we will not meet again in the novel.

But first Zuckerman sets the stage. It is America in 1945. The war is over, the Depression is long past, and there is no more rationing. America has unique control over atomic energy, is governing Japan, and is helping to rebuild Europe. The GI Bill offers universal education. All things are possible. Children obey their parents. Parents know best.

How innocent it all was. At the reunion, Marilyn Koplik remembers that " 'the worst crime we could commit was chewing gum,' " and Joy Helpern explains to Zuckerman why she had never allowed him to unfasten her bra. Her brother Harold had to sleep in the kitchen of her crowded immigrant home, she tells Zuckerman, and if he had become her boyfriend, he would have come to her house and seen where her brother had to sleep. " 'It had nothing to do with you, sweetheart,' " (p. 84) she tells him. In a delicate, sweet, understated line, she has already said to him, " 'I *should* have let you undo my bra. Undo it now if you'd like to.' " (p. 78)

The post-war years were America's age of innocence, when every American was convinced that he or she lived in the best of all possible worlds – every white American, that is.

Nowhere was the spirit of patriotism stronger than in the Jewish section of Newark, New Jersey. Consider the American success of the Levov family.

The grandfather had come over from the Old Country in the 1890s. His son Lou had learned how to tan leather at the age of fourteen to help support the family of nine. Lou is one of a generation of hard-working survivors. After one failed attempt in business, he begins a pushcart enterprise, selling seconds in gloves, belts, and handbags. In 1942 he has a stroke of luck and wins a government contract for women's gloves for the armed forces. He opens a factory in Newark and begins to get department store contracts for leather goods. The dream comes true. Lou's older son

Seymour, already "Swede" the athletic hero, joins the Marines and catches the last months of the war as an instructor.

What could be more American than a self-made business success with a son who is a Marine?

In 1947 Swede goes to Upsala College on the GI Bill, refusing a contract with the Giants' farm club in favour of joining his father in the family business. At Upsala he dates the Homecoming Queen, a working-class Irish beauty, and they decide to marry. Lou is opposed to the match and has a fearsome interview, more of an inquisition, with Dawn Dwyer on how she and Swede would raise their children. She wouldn't be the first of Swede's gentile girlfriends that Lou had got rid of. But, finally, Lou can deny his perfect son nothing. As Jerry points out years later, "'Dad . . . he let you slide through. Everybody has always let you slide through.'" (p. 276)

Besides, Dawn Dwyer wasn't just the Homecoming Queen; she became Miss New Jersey and was the favourite to win at the Miss America pageant. As Swede's young admirer Zuckerman realized at the time, Swede had got it all. He had married a girl who almost became Miss America.

Swede was a tremendous success at the factory. The workers adored him as much as they feared his "impossible bastard" of a father. The big buyers from the department stores sent *him* gifts, and, during rare strikes, the picketers apologized to him personally for their actions.

What was best, for Lou, was that Swede loved the leather business just as much as he did. We share in their enthusiasm. At one point, when Swede is giving Rita Cohen a tour of the Newark Maid factory, we are treated to thirteen uninterrupted pages on glove production. I found it fascinating. I had no idea that, in the trade, the piece of a glove between the fingers is called a fourchette or that a young kid is called a cabretta. I am happy to learn, and the digressions never bothered me. They are in the great tradition of the novel. I am always mindful that, since the English novel was born nearly three centuries ago, it has been in part a teaching instrument, written for a newly risen middle class with an insatiable desire to learn. Although in some of his works Roth will use history in a very postmodern fashion, and although his themes strike us as very contemporary, he is in the main a traditional writer, notably in the elegance of his prose, the powerful thrust of his narrative, the didactic nature of much of his writing, and the omniscience of his narrator.

In 1952, Swede and Dawn have a little girl, Meredith, "Merry" for short, and the company continues to prosper, opening a second factory in Puerto Rico in 1958.

Swede, Dawn, and Merry move to the old-money village of Rimrock, very much against Lou's advice. He would prefer to see them in the fashionable and totally Jewish suburb of Newstead. But Swede and Dawn will have none of that. As Swede's brother puts it later, " 'She's post-Catholic, he's post-Jewish, together they're going out there to Old Rimrock to raise little post-toasties.' " (p. 73)

There are a few Jewish residents in the WASP heaven, but when one of them invites Swede to join the temple, he answers, " 'I didn't come out here for that stuff.' " (p. 314) Swede wants to be Johnny Appleseed. He walks five miles each way into the village to buy the Saturday newspaper and feels the equal of his architect neighbour, Bill Orcutt.

Swede loves being American. He loved his American childhood. He loved being a Marine. He has always loved the leather factory.

He has never been exposed to anti-Semitism. His wife, Dawn, has heard more offensive comments than he has. She remembers how her chaperone at the Miss America pageant had recalled 1945 as the year " 'the Jewish girl won. . . . I grant she was good-looking, but it was a great embarrassment to the pageant nonetheless.' " (p. 311)

That memory of Dawn's isn't enough to disturb Swede's tranquillity, nor are the missionary efforts of Dawn's mother. She keeps luring her granddaughter Merry to church services and persuades her to put a print of the Sacred Heart of Jesus on her bedroom wall, but, as Swede says, " 'It's harmless, it's a picture, to her a pretty picture of a nice man. What difference does it make?' " (p. 94)

And Swede seems proved right. Merry grows out of her Catholic phase – it was just one of her passionately felt fads.

Lou Levov is much more worried about Merry's future than Swede is. He has seen his own pastoral idyll destroyed, his own American dream of a factory burned to the ground during the race riots in Newark in 1967.

I cannot speak for every reader, but I adored Lou Levov. He seemed to me a close relative of Mordecai Richler's Izzy Panofsky in *Barney's Version*. Lou is larger than life, and Bill Orcutt pays tribute to him at the dinner party that ends the novel. " 'He's a very generous man. He doesn't hold anything back, does he? Nothing left undisclosed. You get the whole person. Unguarded. Unashamed. Works himself up. It's wonderful. An amazing person, really. A huge presence. Always himself.'" (p. 382) Then Bill Orcutt adds what I see as a Roth master stroke, "'Coming from where I do, you have to envy all that.'"

Bill Orcutt, later to become an adulterer, at least has the virtue of self-knowledge. A member of the establishment, quiet-spoken, always dignified, he envies the fullness, the Jewishness (in Roth's view) of Lou's massive personality. Orcutt's tribute must surely cause the reader to reflect on which model Swede chooses to emulate, his father with his full-blooded appetite for life or the Orcutts of this world, with their perfectly modulated voices and their restrained Episcopalian manners.

I loved it when Bill Orcutt appeared in a Hawaiian shirt and Lou made the puzzled comment to his son,

"I've noticed this about the rich goyim in the summertime. Comes the summer, and these reserved, correct people wear the most incredible costumes." The Swede had laughed. "It's a form of privilege," he said, repeating Dawn's line. "Is it?" asked Lou Levov, laughing along with him. "Maybe it is," Lou concluded. "Still, I got to hand it to this goy: you have to have guts to wear those pants and those shirts." (p. 334)

I even loved Lou at his most vitriolic.

"Get Nixon. Get the bastard in some way. Get Nixon and all will be well. If we can just tar and feather Nixon, America will be America again, without everything loathsome and lawless that's crept in, without all this violence and malice and madness and hate. Put him in a cage, cage the crook, and we'll have our great country back the way it was!" (pp. 299–300)

"Back the way it was"! The problem is that it never really was that way except for a lucky minority of white people. It wouldn't even have been "that way" for Lou Levov if he hadn't secured that first government contract back in 1942.

The whole point of the American pastoral dream is that it was a dream, fragile and short-lived. That magic, innocent period in the forties, fifties, and early sixties was like an extended Thanksgiving for some, and Thanksgiving is only supposed to last for twenty-four hours.

Lou can't understand how his world has changed. He can't understand how, at the dinner table in 1973, professionals and educated people will insist on the tolerance of pornography. Lou wonders where all the permissiveness has come from and what happened to the old, simple standards. He still can't understand what happened in Newark six years earlier when the black workers rioted. "'[E]verything I built up a day at a time, an *inch* at a time . . . they are going to leave it *all* in ruins!'" (p. 164)

Lou Levov is easy to love, but he has his limitations. He can imagine no experience other than his own, and he can never begin to comprehend black rage at a promise unfulfilled.

Sometimes, of course, Lou's limitations are funny, as when Dawn pays five thousand dollars for an abstract painting by their neighbour Orcutt, and Lou comments, "'Awful lot of money for a first coat.'" (p. 324) Lou laughs and we laugh with him.

But Lou's laughter hides a heart broken twice. Once by the burning of his beloved Newark in the 1967 race riots, and once by what his beloved granddaughter did the following year.

Dawn and Swede had been having trouble with Merry since she entered puberty. By 1968, she is an overweight, ungainly sixteen-year-old, and has a terrible stutter. They send her first to a psychiatrist, whose opinion is that the stutter is Merry's defence against a too-perfect mother. It is also to win the attention of her father away from Merry's rival, again her all-too-perfect mother. They try a speech therapist, Sally Saltzman. Nothing works. But there is something more serious. Merry has become violently opposed to the Vietnam War. Her parents and Lou also oppose the war – they are, after all, liberal Democrats – and all of them feel that Lyndon B. Johnson has betrayed America's ideals. But Merry's vehemence frightens them. She goes off every day to visit friends in New York City and sometimes stays over and then brings home Communist material.

Lou, who writes scurrilous daily letters to LBJ, gives his granddaughter copies and points out that no one in the family disagrees with her position. Her father reminds her of his impeccable liberal credentials. Even after the riots, he is keeping the factory open to provide work for the largely black neighbourhood, even after his competitors have moved production to the Far East, a move Lou has encouraged him to make.

When Lou and Swede both urge Merry to stay in Rimrock and organize anti-war protests, she refuses and, when criticized for the subversive literature she reads, she lashes out with "'You taught me to *learn* didn't you? Not just to study, but to *learn.*'" (p. 104)

And Swede has no answer. His liberal values prevent him from imposing his will upon his child. He can't compel his daughter, by force if necessary, to obey him, as his old-fashioned, Old Country brother Jerry would have done.

Then comes the explosion. Merry plants a bomb in the local post office, a symbol of hated federal authority, and a passerby, a doctor known for his kindness and good works, is killed.

Merry disappears and the family is distraught. Dawn is suicidal, and Swede enters an agony from which he will never fully recover.

After four months, there is an emissary from Merry in hiding. Posing initially as a student of the glove-making business – she gets the full tour – Rita Cohen has come for Merry's teenage scrapbook, the one she made on Audrey Hepburn. Later, again through Rita, there will be a request for five thousand dollars. Swede agrees to meet Rita at the New York Hilton not with five but rather ten thousand dollars.

The conversation between Swede Levov and Rita Cohen is wonderfully illuminating. Rita indulges in the whole invective of the rebellious young of the sixties. Of Merry, she says to Swede,

> "She hates you."
> "Does she?" he asked lightly.
> "She thinks you ought to be shot."
> "Yes, that too?"
> "What do you pay the workers in your factory in Ponce, Puerto Rico? What do you pay the workers who stitch gloves for you in Hong Kong and Taiwan? What do you pay the women going blind in the Philippines hand-stitching designs to satisfy the ladies shopping at Bonwit's? You're nothing but a shitty little capitalist who exploits the brown and yellow people of the world and lives in luxury behind the nigger-proof security gates of his mansion." (p. 133)

In contempt, Rita offers herself to Swede, spreading her legs, inviting him to degrade himself. She claims, untruthfully, that the offer – declined by Swede – is made at the suggestion of Merry, who, by the way, never sees a penny of the money Swede leaves at the hotel. Rita Cohen is like an evil spirit that Roth has dug up out of his childhood memories of Jewish folklore. "Egoistic pathology bristled out of her like the hair that nuttily proclaimed, 'I go wherever I want, as far as I want – all that matters is what I want!' " (p. 134) Swede recognizes, correctly, that she has no real interest in the welfare of the Vietnamese or of peasants anywhere. All he sees, he tells her, is " 'angry, infantile egoism, thinly disguised as identification with the oppressed.' " For once in his life, Swede speaks forcefully and out of deep conviction.

> "I haven't two minutes' interest in childish clichés. You don't know what a factory is, you don't know what manufacturing is, you don't know what capital is, you don't know what labor is, you haven't the faintest idea what it is to be employed or what it is to be unemployed. You have no idea what *work* is. You've never held a job in your life, and if you even cared to find one, you wouldn't last a single day, not as a worker, not as a manager, not as an owner." (p. 135)

If only he had spoken just once to his daughter like that, if only just once he had spoken with the justifiable authority of his years and experience. But the sixties weren't like that. All too often parents accommodated, compromised.

It seems clear that what Merry was rebelling against was the absence of strong opinion and deeply held values in her parents' lives, lives that epitomized the American Dream. Real conflict was impossible, and Freud and common sense both teach us that a child must win some kind of victory over his or her parents in order to enter adulthood.

There will be no contact between Merry and her family for four years, and for those four years Swede Levov will question himself endlessly and repetitively. The bombing must be, he thinks, his responsibility. His daughter's action must somehow derive from a mistake he made. I think his torment is not an uncommon one for parents of many cultures.

Could his father, Lou, have been right? By marrying outside his faith, could he have caused confusion in his child, neither Jewish nor Catholic?

Could he really have been an exploiter of his workers? Could it have been that one time when Merry was eleven and he had kissed her on the mouth the way she had asked him, the way he kissed her mother? But surely not, that was only the one foolish time!

Could it all be Dawn's fault? Could what Rita Cohen said be true? Could Dawn tolerate a Jewish husband but not a Jewish daughter? Could it be that kiss again, a rivalry between a beautiful Catholic mother and a fat Jewish daughter, a contest Merry had no chance of winning?

Could Merry be ashamed of her parents? Was Dawn right when she suspected that their neighbours laughed at them, at the "new Celtic neighbour. *And* her Hebrew husband"? (pp. 301–02)

Swede tries to blame the left-wing fanatics who corrupted his daughter. He addresses them in the quiet of his mind: "You hate us because we haven't failed. Because we've worked hard and honestly to become the best in the business and because of that we have prospered, so you envy us and you hate us and want to destroy us." (p. 214) He fantasizes conversations with the black militant Angela Davis and tries to find comfort in agreeing with her: "So he says to her *yes*, his daughter *is* a soldier of freedom . . . yes, the United States is responsible for oppression *everywhere*." (p. 166)

His introspection is punctured by attempts to hate his daughter, to reject her. That would bring a kind of closure. But there is no comfort and there is no answer. He is forced to consider the worst lesson that life can teach, that it makes no sense. He who had based his whole life on a belief in a great liberal democracy evolving as it should has to face the possibility of chaos. "There was no order. None. He envisioned his life as a stutterer's thought, wildly out of his control." (p. 93)

His whole carefully constructed world comes apart. He and Lou have to abandon their Newark factory. Swede and some of his employees are attacked; the streets are full of random violence. The little Jewish Eden of Swede's childhood, and of Philip Roth's, is now the car-theft capital of the world. Shops and homes are boarded up.

Lou's wife, Swede's mother, is now a twisted and bent old lady who cries when she thinks no one is watching her. Swede has an affair with Sally Saltzman, once Merry's speech therapist. Sally was close to Merry and so Swede wants to be close to her.

Dawn begins an affair with the neighbour, Bill Orcutt, but only after a stay in hospital for depression. She sells her cattle-raising business, a business she had begun only to show she was more than a pretty face, and we realize that Swede's Old Rimrock pastoral has not been a paradise for her. She had never even wanted to be a beauty queen; she had done it only for the money she needed to help her brother through college. She had wanted to become a teacher.

With Dawn's revelations, the reader is reminded that this was not only the time of the Vietnam protest, the explosion of distrust in government, the revolution of the young, and black anger; it was also when women in America began to question their assigned role in society.

All the old moral certainties are crumbling. The collapse of Lou's beloved Newark is the collapse of the whole American pastoral dream writ small. Only Lou himself goes on unchanged, sure of himself and his absolutes, allowing no room for doubt or moral ambiguity.

In 1973 comes a letter from Rita Cohen, the embodiment of evil. She invites Swede to come and see his daughter, allegedly working at the Animal Hospital in Newark under the name of Mary Stoltz. Rita claims to love Merry, to see holiness, even divinity, in her, but Rita has to go away and can no longer care for her. "You have to take over," she writes to Swede. (pp. 176–77) The truth is that she wants to destroy Swede and what he represents by showing him what has happened to his cherished daughter.

The reunion between father and daughter is heartbreaking. They see each other in the street, whereupon Merry throws "herself upon his chest, her arms encircling his neck. . . . 'Daddy! Daddy!'" (pp. 230–31) But she is filthy, gap-toothed, emaciated, living in a windowless, stinking room in a street entered only by an underpass "as dangerous as any underpass in the world." (p. 234)

Both Merry and her room are infested with vermin. She is a practising Jain, a member of that twenty-five-hundred-year-old Indian sect that teaches non-violence, destiny (Kharma), and the sanctity of all life. She will not clean herself or her abode in case she accidentally kills an insect. She wears a veil so that she will not inhale the tiniest living organism. She tells her father that, in her four years of wandering before she came to Jainism, she was involved in other bombings, killed three other people, and was raped twice. It is a scene to tear the heart out of any parent, and, overcome by the horror of the story, the filth and the stench, her father vomits on her face.

To Swede, Merry represents a total absence of order. He is driven beyond endurance by her serenity, a serenity as insane as was her rage four years earlier. It does not help that she no longer stutters. "Everything she could not achieve with a speech therapist and a psychiatrist . . . she had beautifully realized by going mad." (p. 246) She feels no remorse for her murders. In her Jainist view, the world is unfolding as it must. Her father cannot bear her condescension as she comforts him: " 'It's all right, Daddy. I can believe that you can't believe that you know what I'm saying or what I'm doing or why.' " (p. 244) There is no way that Swede Levov can accept what he perceives as his daughter's moral chaos. The only refuge he can seek is to believe that the daughter he once had is dead. Even as he clutches at that straw, he begs her to come home, but when she says " 'If you love me, Daddy, you'll let me be,' " (p. 266) he does just that and leaves.

He goes back to his Old Rimrock house and a dinner party from hell, but not before phoning his brother Jerry, who cannot comprehend why Swede did not drag his daughter out of the slum. We, too, may wonder, but we have to remember that, for the whole of Swede's carefully con- trolled life, his cardinal rule has been not to impose his will on other people, even his own daughter. It is Dr. Spock's foolishly permissive teaching taken to absurd lengths. (Even the good doctor, late in his life – too late – came to acknowledge what harm too literal a following of his earlier theories could cause.)

At the calamitous dinner party, the final event of the novel, Lou is raging against the permissiveness of the guests: the Umanoffs, the Saltzmans, and the Orcutts. Swede confides in his former mistress, Sally Saltzman, that he's seen Merry, and she in turn reveals that – through misguided liberalism and a belief in the confidentiality of the professional-patient relationship – she had harboured Merry during the three days that followed the bombing. At the same dinner party, Swede understands for the first time that Dawn, with her bright new facelift, is having an affair with Bill Orcutt. Once again, his world falls apart as he contemplates his betrayal by all those he had trusted. He begins to fantasize that one of the people he has told about Merry, his brother Jerry or Sally Saltzman, will phone the FBI and that her arrest will then be his responsibility. He even fantasizes that Merry might find her way to his house that very evening and that her dreadful appearance would cause Lou to have a heart attack.

To cap it all off, Jessie Orcutt, Bill's wife, gets falling-down drunk. Lou assumes a patriarchal role – " 'It's time to be a father again' " – and leads her into the kitchen, where he feeds her, spoonful by spoonful, with some of the solid food she so obviously needs, encouraging her with "'Yes, Jessie good girl, Jessie very good girl.'" (p. 422)

Suddenly, Jessie grabs the fork and goes for Lou's eye. She nearly blinds him, but all she offers as explanation is "'*I* feed Jessie.'" (p. 422)

Just as Swede had created for his daughter a world removed from real life because he believed that was best for her, so Lou feeds Jessie Orcutt the food he believes she ought to have. But just as Merry would revolt against a dream that was not her own, so Jessie turns against the well-meaning hand that feeds her in a wonderfully crafted little episode that is apparently unrelated to the general narrative but that in fact relates directly to the main theme of the novel.

I was lost in admiration of that emblematic passage, and I gasped again at Roth's final introduction of a Greek chorus in the person of Marcia Umanoff, the cynical professor of literature who bears witness to the final collapse of the American pastoral at the dinner party: "[S]he began to laugh at their obtuseness to the flimsiness of the whole contraption, to laugh and laugh and laugh at them all, pillars of a society that . . . was rapidly going under." (p. 423)

We know the end of the story from Zuckerman's dinner with Swede Levov at the beginning. We know that Swede and Dawn will divorce and that Swede will take another gentile, even younger, wife in a second chance at a life controlled by good sense and the classic restraints. But we also know that he is beset by grief and cancer under that unruffled exterior.

Was Jerry right when he said so brutally to his brother, "'You wanted Miss America? Well, you've got her . . . she's your daughter!'"? (p. 277) Was Jerry right that Merry in her violence is truer to the American spirit than Swede in his dream world?

In the sixteenth century, Queen Elizabeth I and her courtiers would play at a charade they called "the Pastoral." They would dress up as shepherds or shepherdesses and go into the garden and look after specially brought-in sheep. But it was only a pretty pretence, and after a few hours they always came back inside to the real world of plotting and politics. They knew the Pastoral was only a game and only meant to while away a little time. Swede did not understand that a child might not want to live the Pastoral for a lifetime.

But what is the alternative: to impose traditional values on one's children as Swede's brother advocates? Surely the novel suggests that that doesn't work either. Jessie didn't want to be spoon-fed, to be controlled by another human being, and it is hard to forget that Roth himself gave up a Ph.D. at twenty-six in order to escape with a moll in a getaway car.

We cannot know why it is only certain people who rebel, and why, of those, not everyone rebels violently. Is it just chance whether we have obedient or disobedient children? Surely it is significant that Merry Levov had temper tantrums even as an infant. Are some children born bad seeds, destined to bring sorrow to their parents? Is it all out of our control, as Swede Levov comes to believe? That answer would at least absolve parents of any responsibility.

As I finished this superb meditation on America's national trauma in the sixties, I remembered Zuckerman the narrator at the beginning of the novel telling the reader that he has retired to a remote Massachusetts village, convinced that he will never be able to understand any other individual human being. Is this true? Is each of us ultimately unknowable to anyone else? Certainly, the novel does not even try to answer this and other like questions. Why, for example, did Rita Cohen become a monster?

The last sentence of the novel is a question, "What on earth is less reprehensible than the life of the Levovs?" and in that question there is implicit another question of vital importance to each of us. How should we bring up our children?

After much consideration, I reached what I believe is Roth's own conclusion, that each of us should do our best. But what that best should consist of I have absolutely no idea.

WHITE TEETH

Zadie Smith
(Toronto: Penguin, 2000)

Since I was a very young boy, I have seen London as a magical place. It offers living history, theatres, bookstores, galleries, incredible parks, fabulous drinking places, and, above all, the constant movement of millions of human beings. When I came to London in 1954 from South Wales, I thought I had entered Paradise. I still love London: my wife, Pearl, and I visit it whenever we can, although I left it in 1964, after ten years, to make a better living in Montreal.

But when I read Zadie Smith's *White Teeth*, set mainly in London in the years leading up to 2000, I realized something that had never struck me before. When I arrived in the city in 1954, London was white. There were, of course, visible minorities, but they were few in number and they kept a low profile, hoping not to draw unwelcome attention from any natives resentful of their presence. It is significant that Zadie Smith chose *White Teeth* as her title. Brits all too often have white skin and brown teeth, regular dental care being a very recently acquired habit, and the white teeth of the darker immigrant was one of the markers that set them apart. We are reminded of their difference in some of the chapter titles, like "Teething Trouble" and "The Root Canals of Mangal Pande," one of Smith's many strategies to bind her sprawling novel together.

How things have changed since I first saw London. In the fifties and sixties, faced with an acute labour shortage, employers and transport authorities began to recruit directly in former colonies like the islands of the West Indies. There were also many on the newly independent Indian subcontinent who wanted to escape the political and social unrest that had come with independence. In one area alone, the old province of Bengal in the north of British India, there were such agonies of change as it became first East Pakistan and then independent Bangladesh that many fled to England and the hope of a better, more peaceful life. One such economic refugee is the Muslim Samad Iqbal, who came to London in 1973 and is one of the two chief characters in Zadie Smith's novel.

Those immigrants and their children have changed the face of London forever. New plays by Tanik Gupta are packing them in at the National Theatre. The commercial theatre is full of non-white actors like Cathy Tyson, Josette Simon, Adrian Lester, and David Harewood. London's newest public gallery, the Tate Modern, gives great prominence to the work of a black artist, Steve McQueen. The Iraqi immigrant Zaha Hadid is hailed by the conservative *Daily Telegraph* as "the prophet of the new architecture." The two biggest-selling authors, at the moment, are Salman Rushdie and Zadie Smith. The hottest dress designers are Ozwald Boateng and Hussein Chalayan. There are more than a dozen non-white members of the British House of Lords, and Cherie Blair, the wife of the British prime minister, frequently wears Asian clothes in public and declares them to be as British as she is.

In our novel, *White Teeth*, set in Willesden, a working-class/lower-middle-class district in northwest London, we have a melting pot of race and colour: "[Y]ou can walk into a playground and find Isaac Leung by the fish pond, Danny Rahman in the football cage, Quang O'Rourke bouncing a basketball, and Irie Jones humming a tune. Children with first and last names on a direct collision course." (p. 281)

We are, thank heaven, a long way from the old Conservative politicians like Margaret Thatcher, who declared publicly that she was afraid of being overwhelmed by alien cultures, or the far-right former Tory cabinet minister Enoch Powell, who prophesied rivers of blood. (p. 54)

That is not to say, however, that Britain has become a utopia of tolerance and mutual respect. Last year, there were two hundred thousand incidents involving racism. Zadie Smith herself has spoken about how one of her two younger brothers, a sixteen-year-old, has been stopped by the police and searched for drugs. His suspicious behaviour consisted of being black. In her novel, Zadie Smith does not ignore the very real racial tensions, even violence, in British society. There is widespread hostility to non-white immigrants, and British xenophobia sometimes spills over to include even white visitors from other cultures. Because of its low rents, a district like Willesden, already racially mixed, is a popular destination for young Australians on the London step of their two-year walkabout. In *White Teeth*, the Scottish landlord of a popular, crowded pub is moved to remark to the bar in general, " 'Is there some fuckin' sign in fuckin' Sydney that says come to fuckin' Willesden?' " (p. 412)

Usually, however, the target of the British fear of the stranger is the non-white immigrant. One such victim in our novel is the butcher Mohammed Hussein-Ishmael. He is regularly beaten up by every segment of society,

> decrepit drunks, teenage thugs, the parents of teenage thugs, general fascists, specific neo-Nazis, the local snooker team, the darts team, the football team and huge posses of mouthy, white-skirted secretaries in deadly heels . . . they all had one thing in common, these people. They were all white. (p. 405)

The authorities offer him no protection. We are told that, after he first set up his little store and "when he received a hammer blow to his ribs in January 1970, he naively reported it to the local constabulary and was rewarded by a late-night visit from five policemen who gave him a thorough kicking." (p. 404)

But much more frequent is the profound prejudice exposed in the casual remarks of "ordinary" people like Mr. Hero, the employer of Archie Jones, one of our protagonists. While ostensibly repudiating racism, he makes sure that Archie and his Jamaican wife do not attend any future company celebrations. " 'I'd spit on that Enoch Powell . . . but then again he does have a point, doesn't he?' " (p. 62)

Racist politicians in Great Britain would have us believe that the fear and the violence are a natural reaction by a people who have been a homogeneous society since the Norman invasion over nine hundred years ago. It is, they say, the understandable reaction of a people terrified of being taken over by foreign cultures. But this is nonsense. Out of a total population of nearly sixty million people, 93.7 percent are white and 6.3 percent non-white. It is ludicrous to suggest that fewer than four million people are going to overwhelm the remaining fifty-six million. It is the older immigrant who has a real reason to be afraid as he sees his children absorbed into the British mainstream, abandoning all the values and rituals that gave their parents their identity.

The problem, of course – if there is a problem – is that the immigrants of the last fifty years do not live evenly spread over the British Isles. They came where work was available, to London and to the industrial cities of the Midlands like Birmingham. Within those cities, like immigrants everywhere, they tended to live in clearly defined areas where earlier immigrants had established shops that catered to their tastes or where there were already appropriate places of worship. There are many such areas in London, including Whitechapel, Notting Hill, Brixton, and Willesden.

Zadie Smith chose to set her novel in Willesden. It's the area in which she was born in 1975 to a Jamaican mother and an English father. She has two younger brothers, born before her English father deserted the family, leaving his wife to bring up the three children. She appears to have made a very good job of it. Zadie Smith, who is now only twenty-seven, was a student at King's College, Cambridge, when she finished this novel at the age of twenty-three. After she completed her B.A. in English Literature, she drove a London bus until *White Teeth* was published. With an advance from Penguin Books of more than half a million Canadian dollars, she doesn't have to drive a bus any more and is now in the process of moving to Kilburn, a rather more prosperous area of London not too far from her native Willesden. She is close to her family and even to her much older half-brother and half-sister, the products of her father's earlier marriage. As a matter of fact, one of them is responsible for the genesis of *White Teeth*. Zadie Smith talked about the inspiration for her novel in a recent interview:

> "The seed of it came to me when my half-sister, Diane, visited me in Cambridge. . . . She mentioned that my parents had met at a party. And that just made me laugh so much because I couldn't imagine my dad at a party. I just couldn't. So I had to write about it . . . and it expanded from that simple thing." (Amazon.co.uk interview, "Eithne Farry talks to Zadie.")

The incident is easily recognizable in the novel – it is when the quiet Englishman Archie Jones meets the gorgeous, vivacious Jamaican Clara Bowden at a party – but Zadie Smith is quick to point out that the novel is not autobiography: "'My own family was much calmer – the Smiths would never keep up with the Joneses.'"

Her novel is not about the whole of British society; it is about those parts of London where native Brits and immigrants live together, where cultural cross-fertilization is inevitable, and where, in spite of the irrational fears of the Brits about being overwhelmed and the very justified fears of the immigrants that they will lose their traditional customs, a new hybrid identity is emerging. The process of creating a new kind of English man and woman is slow and painful, as it contains both a desire to assimilate and a fear of assimilation. Zadie Smith has little patience with those who want to preserve tradition and culture intact. As she says, "If religion is the opium of the people, tradition is an even more sinister analgesic, simply because it rarely appears sinister." (p. 167) The epigraph of her novel says it all: "What is past is prologue." What matters is not the history that led up to the present, but what we can make of the future. Zadie Smith's novel is about the struggle of the young to escape the confining culture of their parents, about race and class and the legacy of empire, and about the relations between the sexes, but it is also about a society struggling with all the baggage of the past towards a better time of tolerance, mutual accommodation, even fellowship.

She records all the disparate voices, the Arab voices, the Jamaican voices, the Bangladeshi voices, all the competing dialects, all the different accents that go to make up the song of modern London. She doesn't ignore the ugliness of some of the reality, but her novel is full of humour and hope as the little people of her rainbow society cope with that same reality. It is significant that the central narrative element is the friendship between two men, Archie Jones and Samad Iqbal, who have come out of vastly different worlds.

The novel proper begins on January 1, 1975, the year of Zadie Smith's birth, but later, in an extended flashback, we learn that Archie Jones and Samad Iqbal had first met thirty years earlier in the last days of the Second World War, both members of a bridge-laying tank crew so inept that they had earned the nickname "The Buggered Battalion." When their tank breaks down outside a Bulgarian village, two of the crew members are murdered by local partisans and the tank captain commits suicide as they are under attack. The descendant of a long line of British officers who had slaughtered and been slaughtered in the name of Empire all over the globe, the captain thus became "[t]he only Dickinson-Smith to die by English hands." (p. 80)

Samad and Archie are left alone. They have no idea that the war is over, and the villagers, enjoying the boost to the economy that comes from barter with the two strangers, see no reason to tell them. It's a hilarious piece of comedy.

The two men come to know each other well, and Samad realizes that the Englishman is absolutely without racial prejudice. The problem is that Archie is not only without prejudice but without beliefs or opinions of any kind. "'You don't stand for anything, Jones,' continued Samad. 'Not for a faith, not for a politics. Not even for your country. How your lot ever conquered my lot is a bloody mystery.'" (p. 104) This is Zadie Smith at her most thoughtful. There is no doubt that the ideal contained in the novel is a society where people of all cultures live in harmony. But at the same time Smith points out the concomitant dangers. Archie's vision of the future is a vague one – "'[W]hy couldn't people just get on with things, just live together, you know, in peace or harmony or something.'" (p. 169) The "or something" is the problem in Archie's philosophy. He has no idea how to get to the future. Zadie Smith is warning against the danger that, in throwing out ill-informed opinion like prejudice, we may throw out informed opinion at the same time and become empty cyphers like Archie Jones, without any thought-out standards or values. It seems to me that Zadie Smith sets out the problem very well. We must leave the past but we have not yet agreed upon the future. Like all first-class novelists, she offers the question but does not provide the easy answer. The only certainty is that the future cannot be based on the emptiness of Alfred Archibald Jones, who is incapable of making any decision whatsoever, allowing himself to be swept along by fate. When choice between two options is unavoidable, Archie tosses a coin and abides by the result. He accepts chance as co-existent with freedom.

His friend Samad Iqbal is Archie's opposite. Samad, sustained by his Muslim faith, has strong ideological views on dignity and honour. His inspiration is his great-grandfather Mangal Pande, a real historical figure. It was Mangal Pande who fired the first shot against the British oppressor in the great Indian Mutiny of 1857. Small matter to Samad that his illustrious ancestor missed his target and was executed by General Havelock a few days later. What was important was that Mangal Pande, a devout

Muslim, had refused to bite the end off a cartridge allegedly coated with pig fat, and had therefore maintained his honour, his culture, and his identity. Samad yearns to kill an enemy – as his great-grandfather, in spite of his heroism, had failed to do – but circumstances are against him. On only his third day in the army, a fellow Indian accidentally shoots him, rendering his right arm useless, and he is transferred as wireless operator to a tank crew of losers like Archie Jones. Marooned in the Bulgarian village, Samad is alone with Archie when they discover that a French collaborator with the Germans on their euthanasia program, a Dr. Marc-Pierre Perret, is sick and in hiding nearby. The war over, a group of Russians arrive to arrest the French doctor, but they did not anticipate meeting Samad Iqbal. He is both single-minded and a superb poker player. He and the Russians begin to play, initially for cigarettes:

> Cigarettes took them to medals, which took them to guns, which took them to radios, which took them to jeeps. By midnight, Samad had won three jeeps, seven guns, fourteen medals, the land attached to Gozan's sister's house, and an IOU for four horses, three chickens and a duck. (p. 101)

Samad trades in all his winnings with the Russians for the French doctor. He designates the weak and ineffectual Englishman Archie to carry out the actual execution in an ironic reversal of the Indian-English relationship that obtained at the time of his great-grandfather. Archie takes the doctor away and returns bleeding and limping badly. But Samad knows that the deed was done, and a bond of steel has been forged between the two men before they return to their respective countries.

Before these events of 1945 are revealed to us, we are witness to the narrative's beginning on New Year's Day, 1975. Archie Jones is sitting in his car on Cricklewood Broadway in northwest London. The post-war period had not been kind to Archie. He was unable to get any job more exciting than that of designing how circulars and brochures should be folded by the printing firm he works for. His one moment of glory was tying for thirteenth place in a cycling event in the 1948 Olympics, and even that moment is not recorded in the history books because of the carelessness of a recording clerk. In 1946 he had been swept by events into marriage with an Italian girl in Florence, but that was a failure almost from the beginning.

No one told Archie that lurking in the Diagilo family tree were two hysteric aunts, an uncle who talked to aubergines and a cousin who wore his clothes back to front. So they got married and returned to England, where she realized very quickly her mistake, he drove her very quickly mad, and the halo was packed off to the attic to collect dust with the rest of the bric-a-brac and broken kitchen appliances. (p. 7)

Archie Jones has long accepted that he is no more than a raindrop in the ocean of life, and he has always been content to go with the flow, but after twenty-nine years of marriage to a neurotic, alcoholic wife who has her whole family living with her, the situation has become too much even for the passive Archie Jones and he has moved out.

On New Year's Day, 1975, Archie is sitting in his parked car with a hose running inside from the exhaust. "He had flipped a coin and stood staunchly by its conclusions. This was a decided-upon suicide. In fact it was a New Year's resolution." (p. 3)

As it happens, he is parked outside the butcher shop of Mohammed Hussein-Ishmael, Mo for short, the same Mohammed Hussein-Ishmael who is regularly beaten up by his customers and the London police force. Mo has just finished his morning massacre of the local pigeons, which he hates as much as he hates white racists, and is understandably indignant at what is about to happen on his doorstep:

> "No one gasses himself on my property," Mo snapped as he marched downstairs. "We are not licensed. . . .
>
> "Do you hear that, mister? We're not licensed for suicides around here. This place halal. Kosher, understand? If you're going to die round here, my friend, I'm afraid you've got to be thoroughly bled first." (p. 6)

Archie is thrilled that fate, in the unlikely person of Mohammed Hussein-Ishmael, has intervened to give him a second chance at life, and uncharacteristically, in his euphoria, he gatecrashes a young people's New Year's party. There he meets Clara Bowden, the nineteen-year-old daughter of Jamaican immigrants, twenty-eight years younger than he is, magnificently tall, as black as ebony, and beautiful. He is on the rebound from his marriage, she is on the run from her Jehovah's Witness mother, her Jehovah's Witness boyfriend, and from the Jehovah's Witnesses faith itself.

We might wonder why this strong, intelligent, beautiful girl would be attracted to "a rather short, rather chubby middle-aged white man in a badly tailored suit," (pp. 38–39) or why she had been so devoted to the physically repulsive, compulsively nose-picking Ryan Topps, converted to the Jehovah's Witnesses by Clara's own mother, Hortense Bowden. Zadie Smith offers two insights that I find remarkable in their perceptiveness. The first is that young people are rarely in love with another person; rather they are in love with the idea of being in love. She puts it amazingly succinctly: "Clara was a teenage girl like any other; the object of her passion was only an accessory to the passion itself." (p. 32) The second insight is particular to the faith Clara Bowden has just renounced: "[A] residue, left over from the evaporation of Clara's faith, remained. She still wished for a saviour. She still wished for a man to whisk her away, to choose her above others so that she might *Walk in white with Him* . . . Revelation 3:4." (p. 38)

Six weeks later, Alfred Archibald Jones and Clara Bowden are married. There will be little contact with Clara's mother, who sees her daughter as godless and anyway believes that, although she likes what she knows of Archie, "Black and white never come to no good." (p. 330) Zadie Smith is careful to acknowledge that white racists do not have a monopoly on prejudice. Every character in the novel, except for Archie Jones, has his or her fair share.

Hortense Bowden, Clara's mother, has a personal reason for her cynical view of race relations. Her father was white. She was born during the great Jamaican earthquake of 1907, her birth the result of an encounter between a drunken English captain and the fourteen-year-old daughter of his Jamaican landlady. During the pregnancy, Hortense's mother, Ambrosia, had embraced the Jehovah's Witnesses version of Christianity.

It's worth a moment to consider this faith, so often referred to in the novel. It was founded by an American, Charles Powell, in the 1870s. It teaches a literal belief in the Christian Bible, with a great emphasis on the imminent end of the world. On that terrible day, 144,000 people, the Anointed, will join Jehovah God and Jesus Christ to rule in Heaven, another six million will be saved to enjoy an earthly Paradise, and the rest of humanity will be consigned to the grave. Hortense had been bitterly disappointed in 1925 when, on January 1, the universal destruction promised by the elders in Brooklyn had not materialized. She is ecstatic when a new date for the end of the world is set by the movement's elders, January 1, 2000. She now gives thanks for having been born during an earthquake: "'Lord Jesus, I live dis century! Well and truly I live dis terrible century wid all its troubles and vexations. And tanks to you, Lord, I'm gwan a feel a rumble at both ends.'" (p. 352)

Hortense is especially anxious that the Lord's fire and brimstone be visited upon the sharp-tongued woman who lives at No. 53. Speaking of her, and others like her, she says, with a snort, "'Some people . . . have done such a hol' heap of sinning, it *late* for dem to be making eyes at Jehovah.'" (p. 26)

Hortense Bowden is a delicious character who has added some of her own refinements to her faith. Her lodger Ryan Topps, Clara's one-time lover, ferries her around London in the sidecar of his Vespa scooter, and she keeps her motorcycle helmet in a heated oven so it will be "'warm and toasty on de col' marnins.'" (p. 337) She dreams of being one of the Anointed in Heaven with Christ, in spite of her church's teaching that all the heavenly positions are reserved for males, and she takes literally the injunction of Revelation 3:15, against having a lukewarm faith: "*So then because thou art lukewarm, and neither cold nor hot, I will spue thee out of my mouth.*" (p. 340) She sees "lukewarm" as an evil in and of itself. The result is that she serves all food and liquids either boiling hot or freezing cold, another reason for her daughter Clara's disenchantment with the faith. As Hortense's granddaughter will later put it, "'Revelation is where all crazy people end up. It's the last stop on the nutso express. And Bowdenism, which was the Witnesses plus Revelation *and then some*, was as left field as they come.'" (p. 340)

This Bowdenism is what Clara has run away from, but she doesn't find any salvation in the arms of Archie Jones:

> One month into their marriage and he already had that funny glazed look men have when they are looking through you. He had already reverted back into his bachelorhood: pints with Samad Iqbal, dinner with Samad Iqbal, Sunday breakfasts with Samad Iqbal, every spare moment with the man in that bloody place, *O'Connell's.* (p. 42)

Clara is speaking of the same Samad Iqbal who had shared a tank with Archie thirty years earlier and who had returned to his native Bengal in 1945 after telling Archie that he was looking forward to being married. The conversation between the two men in the tank is not only a superb piece of humour; it also anticipates the clash of cultures that will come to pass decades later.

> "Oh, but I have still some time to wait," he said, smiling wistfully. "Unfortunately, the Begum family do not yet have a female child of my generation."
>
> "You mean your wife's not bloody born yet?"
>
> "What of it?" asked Samad . . .
>
> "Where I come from," said Archie, "a bloke likes to get to know a girl before he marries her."
>
> "Where you come from it is customary to boil vegetables until they fall apart. This does not mean," said Samad tersely, "that it is a good idea." (pp. 84–85)

Twenty-eight years later, in 1973, after long waiting, forty-nine-year-old Samad Iqbal marries eighteen-year-old Alsana Begum. The couple decides to leave Bangladesh – formerly East Pakistan, formerly Bengal in British India – and all its political and economic chaos and make a new life in England. Samad seeks out Archie Jones, the only man he knows in the new country, and, after a year in the slums of Whitechapel in London's East End, where racist thugs in steel-toed boots kick in their windows, manages to buy a tiny house in Archie's home borough of Willesden. The upward move is made possible by Samad's working all hours at his bullying cousin's Indian restaurant, where, in spite of his wounded arm, he becomes a waiter of genius, and Alsana's sewing piecework for a Soho sex shop: "[M]any were the nights Alsana would hold up a piece of clothing she had just made, following the pattern she was given, and wonder what on earth it was." (p. 47)

Alsana is diminutive, except for her feet and her opinions, but contributes more than her share of the novel's humour. Like most immigrants, she masters basic English quickly but has trouble with idiomatic expressions. The result is frequent and engaging malapropisms, such as this particular gem: "'Getting anything out of my husband is like trying to squeeze water out when you're stoned.'" (p. 67) Alsana has a niece in London, Neena, a lesbian who works at a cobbler's and lives with her lover. Alsana, who has kept her Muslim Bangladeshi heritage intact, abhors the relationship. Her condemnation initially pours forth in long sentences but, after she no longer has "the time or energy to summon up the necessary shock each time," her reproach is abridged to the one phrase "Niece-of-Shame," as in the sentence, "'I came to collect my husband's shoes, not to chit-chat with Niece-of-Shame.'" (pp. 54–55)

Just as Clara discovers that Archie Jones has feet of clay, Alsana becomes disillusioned with Samad Iqbal. As she confides to Niece-of-Shame and Clara, "'We married old men,'" (p. 69) and "'men are the last mystery. God is easy compared with men.'" (pp. 67–68) Her view of her marriage as a failure comes slowly but it comes inexorably:

> "I liked him well enough. We met in the breakfast room on a steam-ing Delhi day and he fanned me with *The Times*. I thought he had a good face, a sweet voice, and his backside was high and well formed for a man of his age. Very good. Now, every time I learn something more about him *I like him less.*" (p. 67)

Alsana does not hesitate to generalize from her own situation. With ref-erence to Niece-of-Shame and the joy she and her lover find in each other, Alsana says, "'I'm as liberal as the next person. . . . But why do they always have to be laughing and making a song-and-dance about everything? I cannot believe homosexuality is that much fun. Heterosexuality certainly is not.'" (p. 246)

Lesbians and husbands are not the only groups of which the fiery little Alsana disapproves. She is as full of prejudice as the racist leader Enoch Powell, whom she dismisses with a curt "'Rivers of blood silly-billy non-sense.'" (p. 54) But Alsana is prepared to make exceptions. One such exception is Clara, the Jamaican wife of Archie Jones. Alsana and Clara have much in common. Both are young women disillusioned with the older men they married, and both become pregnant at about the same time.

> Black people are often friendly, thought Alsana, smiling at Clara, and adding this fact subconsciously to the short "pro" side of the pro and con list she had on the black girl. From every minority she

disliked, Alsana liked to single out one specimen for spiritual for-giveness. From Whitechapel, there had been many such redeemed characters. Mr Van, the Chinese chiropodist, Mr Segal, a Jewish car-penter, Rosie, a Dominican woman . . . all these lucky individuals were given Alsana's golden reprieve. (p. 56)

Thus does Zadie Smith again avoid the trap, so hard to avoid in a novel largely about racial tensions, of attributing bigotry to only one group, usually the WASP oppressor.

The years pass, and Clara Jones brings up her daughter, Irie, and Alsana Iqbal brings up her twin sons, Magid and Millat. They do so in the almost complete absence of their husbands.

Archie Jones and Samad Iqbal, bosom friends and bound forever by their shared experience in the 1945 execution of the French collabora-tionist doctor, spend every spare moment at O'Connell's Pool House.

The pool house is a gorgeous creation. Originally Irish, it was bought by an Arab immigrant, Ali, and his six sons in 1971, and transformed into a café serving only fried food. When Ali dies of "a fatal heart attack due to cholesterol build-up around the heart," (p. 213) his oldest son takes over the business. The only modification to the menu is that bacon and all other forms of pork are banned. Ali's death is attributed not to cholesterol but to his violation of Muslim dietary law.

Mine host at O'Connell's is now Abdul-Mickey, so called because the male children in Ali's immediate and extended family were all given the name Abdul. The aim was that one would not see himself as superior to another, "which was all very well and good but tended to cause confu-sion in the formative years." (pp. 161–62) This confusion Ali's children avoided by adding a second, English, name, and so the novel is enriched by Abdul-Mickey, Abdul-Colin, Abdul-Jimmy, and so on. Abdul-Mickey is foul-mouthed and acne-covered, but, as he reassures a new customer, "'don't you worry about my skin, it don't get anywhere near the food and it don't give me much trouble.'" (p. 384)

O'Connell's has been a home-from-home for Archie and Samad since they popped in for a quick fry-up on November 2, 1974, but they are not the only regular customers. In the corner sit two elderly, trilby-wearing Jamaicans, Denzel and Clarence. Clarence is obese and Denzel is emaci-ated, both are widowers, and the game of dominoes is their passion. They play interminably and are unspeakably rude to anyone who disturbs their concentration. They were not strangers to me as I read the novel. I had met them before, or some people very like them. In 1956-57, while I was a full-time student at the London School of Economics, I spent a year working the night shift at Wall's Meat Factory. As it happens, the factory was in Willesden, the locale of the novel, which was in the process of transforming its character from Irish to Caribbean and Indian. I was working at the factory and living in a basement room nearby, because, as was my habit, I had spent my scholarship money for the year on a few wild Soho days and nights.

Our meal break at the factory was at midnight, and I was invited to make up a fourth at dominoes by three elderly Jamaican fellow workers. I received a compliment I have never forgotten when a new Jamaican on the floor asked to take my place and was told, "We don' need you, rasclat, him good domino man!"

While Archie and Samad are enjoying Abdul-Mickey's bacon-free hospitality over the years, their children grow up together. Millat and Magid and Irie, who represent the post-post-colonial period, have no time for Samad's boasting of his great-grandfather's heroism in the 1857 Indian Mutiny or for Samad and Archie's reminiscences about the Second World War. They roll their eyes when their elders begin to talk, and Irie Jones speaks for all of them when she describes the past as "historical shit." (p. 440) The young of the novel are like most young people everywhere in that they attach no importance to any event that occurred before their birth. They see no reality other than modern multicultural London.

I am reminded of a friend, a history teacher, who told me that she was endeavouring to interest her class in the Napoleonic period only to be interrupted by a student who said, "Who cares what happened fifty years ago?"

Meanwhile, Samad Iqbal is fighting to keep his identity as a Muslim for himself and his sons. He is the terror of his twin boys' school governors' meetings. On one delicious occasion, he tables thirteen separate motions, the last one being that the school give up the celebration of Harvest Festival, essentially a pagan feast, in favour of a number of Muslim holy days. Samad makes a powerful case:

> "Where in the bible does it say, *For thou must steal foodstuffs from thy parents' cupboards and bring them into school assembly, and thou*

shalt force thy mother to bake a loaf of bread in the shape of a fish?
These are pagan ideals! Tell me where does it say, *Thou shalt take a*
box of frozen fish fingers to an aged crone who lives in Wembley?"
(p. 113)

The chair of the Board of Governors, Ms. Miniver, tries unsuccessfully to
head him off, but their exchange is typical of many such exchanges in the
novel where two cultures face each other without either having the slightest comprehension of the other.

"Only you've tabled twelve motions already this evening; I think
possibly somebody else –"
"Oh, it is much too important to be delayed, Mrs Miniver. Now, if
I can just –"
"*Ms* Miniver."
"Pardon me?"
"It's just . . . it's *Ms* Miniver. All evening you've been . . . and it's,
umm . . . actually not Mrs. It's Ms. Ms."
Samad looked quizzically at Katie Miniver, then at his papers as if
to find the answer there, then at the beleaguered chairwoman again.
"I'm sorry? You are not married?"
"Divorced, actually, yes, divorced. I'm keeping the name."
"I see. You have my condolences, Miss Miniver." (p. 111)

Not only is every one of Samad's motions to bring Islam into his
sons' school defeated; he succumbs to temptation in the form of Poppy
Burt-Jones, his sons' music teacher. Her flattery of this by now fifty-seven-
year-old man is irresistible: " 'I'm sure the Omar Sharif comparison's been
made before, Mr. Iqbal.' " (p. 118)

Samad confesses his attraction to Poppy to a fellow waiter, " 'I have
been corrupted by England,' " (p. 125) and is offered invaluable advice:
" '[Y]ou're as young as the girl you feel, if you get my meaning. . . . You've
got to learn this stuff, mate . . . Female organism, gee-spot, testicle cancer,
the menstropause – mid-life crisis is one of them. Information the modern
man needs at his finger-tips.' " (p. 126)

Samad's response is from the depths of his being: " 'But I don't wish
for such information. . . . I don't wish to be a modern man! . . . I should

never have come here – that's where every problem has come from. Never should have brought my sons here, so far from God.'" (p. 126) Samad is terrified of the total assimilation that awaits his sons: "'They have both lost their way. Strayed so far from the life I had intended for them. No doubt they will both marry white women called Sheila and put me in an early grave.'" (p. 349)

Samad confides his fear to Archie, who in turn consults Abdul-Mickey, who identifies the choices with great precision:

"[Y]ou tell Samad he has two options. He can either send them back to the old country, back to India –"

"Bangladesh," corrected Archie, nicking a chip from Samad's meal.

"Whereverthefuckitis. He can send 'em back there and have 'em brought up proper, by their granddads and grandmums, have 'em learn about their fucking culture, have 'em grow up with some fucking principles. Or . . .

"*Accept* it. He'll have to *accept* it, won't he. We're all English now, mate. Like it or lump it, as the rhubarb said to the custard." (pp. 166–67)

Archie brings to the problem the wisdom of Solomon. Unwilling as always to commit himself, he suggests adopting both options: send one child to Bangladesh and keep the other in London. After much agonizing, Samad decides to send Magid, the older twin by two minutes and the more intelligent of the two, back to a Muslim upbringing with his grandparents. Millat will stay in London. At nine years old, Magid is put on a plane in the middle of the night and Samad has to face the wrath of Alsana, who has not been consulted.

For the next eight years, Samad lives a life in which his wife barely speaks to him and in which he watches his son Millat go from bad to worse. Millat is a natural leader, incredibly good-looking, and one of London's great lovers. At the age of thirteen

he graduated from leader of zit-faced boys to leader of women. The Pied Piper of Willesden Green, smitten girls trailing behind him, tongues out, breasts pert, falling into pools of heartbreak . . . he was the best of the rest, on any scale of juvenile delinquency he was the shining light of the teenage community, the DON, the BUSINESS, the DOG'S GENITALIA, a street boy, a leader of tribes. In fact, the only trouble with Millat was that he *loved* trouble. And he was *good* at it. Wipe that. He was *great*. (pp. 188–89)

Yet Millat's only true friend is Irie Jones, the daughter of Archie and Clara. She and Millat – and Magid until he was sent away – have always been inseparable. But Irie has a problem with her image of herself. She is big and she is black and she can't accept that big and black can be beautiful. "Intent upon fighting her genes," (p. 236) she tries to have her hair straightened, but the process goes horribly wrong. On another occasion, her mother, Clara, is horrified to find her wearing excruciating corsets to reduce her bulk:

"What's up with you? What in the Lord's name are you wearing? How can you breathe? Irie, my love, you're fine – you're just built like an honest-to-God Bowden – don't you know you're fine?"

But Irie didn't know she was fine. There was England, a gigantic mirror, and there was Irie, without reflection. A stranger in a stranger land. (p. 230)

Irie Jones's only comfort is Millat Iqbal until fate introduces her to the progressive, intellectual middle-class in the form of the Chalfen family.

Marcus Chalfen, once Chalfenofsky, is a university lecturer in biology and a genetic engineer. His wife, Joyce, née O'Connor, is an academic, a horticulturalist, and a fervent believer in the virtues of cross-pollination for both people and plants. Her husband has devoted all his recent energies to developing a programmed mouse, a mouse pre-set to live a certain length of time, with specific illnesses and recovery at ordained intervals. In short, the mouse will live out a predetermined schedule. Marcus, the single-minded scientist, is blind to the implications of his genetic engineering for humanity, the abolition of free will and chance. He can see no further than his one rodent, FutureMouse.

Marcus Chalfen and his wife have long renounced their heritages. She is far from Catholicism, and in Marcus's family "therapy had long supplanted Judaism." (p. 270) They have rejected history in favour of a belief in themselves, a belief in the rightness of their progressive thinking. They represent the ultimate in political correctness and recognize no authority higher than their own version of liberal trendiness, a version they call Chalfenism. As part of their politically correct agenda, they send their son, Joshua, not to the private school they could well afford, but to the local comprehensive, where the nerdy but gifted boy falls in with Millat Iqbal and Irie Jones. The three are caught smoking marijuana, and the principal, a trendy liberal like the Chalfens, adopts the suggestion of the Chalfen family that, for two months, Irie and Millat will join Joshua at the Chalfen home twice a week, where they will benefit from a two-hour session of Chalfenism. I spent five years in the 1960s teaching in London with too many of the likes of the Chalfens and the principal, and I share Zadie Smith's obvious distaste for this particular shade of politically correct parlour pink. In the Chalfen family, Smith is sounding the second warning note of the novel. If we abandon all the prejudices and traditions of the past, we must not embrace instead the emptiness of Archie Jones or the arrogant intellectual narcissism of the Chalfens. I agree with Neena, the Niece-of-Shame, in her opinion of the Chalfens: "'[C]razy, nutso, raisins short of a fruitcake, rubber walls, screaming-mad basket-cases. Every bloody one of them.'" (p. 302)

The three teenagers each react differently to the Chalfen household.

Joshua, the son of the house, is embarrassed by his parents' trendiness, by his mother's fixation on the handsome Millat Iqbal, by his father's silly sexual references in front of Irie Jones, by his parents' desire to be pals, not parents, to the young. In rebellion he joins an extremist animal rights group, FATE (Fighting Animal Torture and Exploitation), violently opposed to the genetic engineering his father has undertaken with the FutureMouse project.

Irie Jones, however, is absolutely fascinated by the middle-class Chalfen home, where it seems to her both adults and children participate as equals in a democratic free-flow of intellectual conversation. How different the Chalfens appear from her own damaged parents, Archie with his war-wounded leg and Clara with her false teeth. She has already accepted that she will be judged by the native English standard of beauty, but she is intensely curious about her Jamaican past and has already idealized the relationship between the young, white captain and her Jamaican great-grandmother. Torn as she is between two worlds, Irie sees the Chalfen world as an intellectual haven, particularly when Marcus offers to pay for her future education. But Irie is a very sensible girl, and she comes to realize that the Chalfen world is not a perfect one. When Joyce reveals that her friend Marjorie, a psychiatrist, has told Joyce the conclusions of interviews she has had with Millat, Irie is horrified: "'What the fuck happened to doctor-patient privilege?'" and condemns the whole condescending structure as "middle-class mafia." (p. 371) Irie is content to keep on taking the fifteen pounds a week that Marcus pays her for filing, but the blinkers are off, and she sees the Chalfens for what they are, pretentious and empty people.

Millat Iqbal was never deceived by the Chalfens for a moment. When Joyce pays him thirty-five pounds a week for such household duties as babysitting Oscar, the youngest of her four boys, he knows that what she is really paying for is "the presence of Millat. That energy around her." (p. 294) But for all his apparent self-confidence, Millat has as great a need to belong as any other adolescent. This devotee of sex, Guinness, popular music, cigarettes, and gangster movies is increasingly drawn to a Muslim splinter group, frowned on by mainstream Islam and all the more attractive to Millat for that reason. The group's title is Keepers of the Eternal and Victorious Islamic Nation, with the acronym KEVIN – "'We are aware . . . that we have an acronym problem.'" (p. 255) But it is not easy to give up all the fleshpots of the West and, much of the time, Millat has "one foot in Bengal and one in Willesden." (p. 190) Sometimes he is able to effect a compromise. The Koran forbids an unmarried man to touch a woman, so Millat arranges to receive oral sex, while keeping his hands to himself, from "a very small redhead who understood the delicate nature of his dilemma." (p. 380) Finally, however, he dons the black uniform of KEVIN and leads a contingent up north to Bradford to burn copies of Salman Rushdie's *Satanic Verses*. (The year is 1989.) Millat is now as committed to KEVIN as he had been to sex and gangster movies, but he is still very much a teenager. When Alsana burns his adolescent possessions, as he had burned Rushdie's book, Millat weeps, and when Alsana confronts Joyce Chalfen, who Alsana feels is taking her son from her, Millat is enraptured: "As far as he was concerned, you could analyse it until the cows came home, but nothing beat being all dressed in black, smoking a fag, listening to two mammas battle it out over you in operatic style." (p. 379)

Millat's twin brother, Magid, far away in Bangladesh, has meanwhile undergone a conversion just as dramatic. He has become a pen pal of the scientist Marcus Chalfen; a devotee of Sir R.V. Saraswati, one of the rare pro-English Indian writers; a total admirer of all things British; and a serene atheist. He returns to London after an eight-year absence to attend law school, his studies to be financed by the ever-interfering Chalfen family.

Millat is appalled to see his brother at the other end of the religious spectrum, and Alsana barely recognizes her son: "'His underwear, he irons them. It is like sitting down to breakfast with David Niven.'" (p. 363) Magid, however, is pure English charm, and he wins over all at O'Connell's. The proprietor, Abdul-Mickey, speaks not only for himself but for the elderly, foul-mouthed Denzel and Clarence when he says, "'Speaks fuckin' nice, don't he? Sounds like a right fuckin' Olivier. Queen's fucking English and no mistake. What a nice fella. You're the kind of clientele I could do wiv in here, Magid, let me tell you. Civilized and that.'" (p. 384)

Samad's reaction to his anglophile, Chalfenist son is one of pure heartbreak: "'There are no words. The one I send home comes out a pukka Englishman, white suited, silly wig lawyer. The one I keep here is fully paid-up green bow-tie-wearing fundamentalist terrorist. I sometimes wonder why I bother.'" (p. 349) That last sentence, "'I sometimes wonder why I bother,'" is an exquisite touch by Zadie Smith. The feeling comes straight from the heart, but it is expressed in a turn of phrase so dear to the Cockney, and we realize from his own assimilated speech how futile is Samad's struggle to keep aloof from the culture of his adopted city. As the novel nears its close, Samad Iqbal will have to live with how his sons have been shaped by the colonial, post-colonial, and post-post-colonial history of his family. They have reacted in ways totally opposite to what he had planned for them, but the directions they have taken illustrate what Smith puts so bluntly: "[T]hey cannot escape their history any more than you yourself can lose your shadow." (p. 399)

At the end of the novel, Smith pulls all her narrative threads together, a little too neatly, perhaps, in what may be a flaw in this otherwise remarkable novel. As she gathers all her characters in Trafalgar Square on December 31, 1992, we see, for the first time I think, the puppeteer pulling the string, the wizard behind the curtain. But the flaw is not too serious, because the plot is the least important element of this novel. *White Teeth* is a celebration of character, a celebration of diversity, a chorus of competing voices.

On New Year's Eve Marcus Chalfen is going to unveil his genetically engineered FutureMouse at a great public meeting. His son Joshua will attend with his fellow members of FATE, the animal rights group, to protest his father's work. Millat Iqbal will be there with his KEVIN Islamic extremists to denounce godless science. Magid Iqbal will be there to support his mentor Marcus Chalfen. Abdul-Mickey will be there to discover if genetic engineering might help solve the problem of his family's hereditary acne. Irie Jones will be there because she works for Marcus Chalfen, and her parents will be there to support their daughter's employer. Samad and Alsana Iqbal will be there because Archie and Clara Jones will be there. Hortense Bowden and her Jehovah's Witnesses will be singing hymns at full throttle outside the hall to protest the intervention of genetic science in God's plan.

The meeting falls into anarchy. The guest of honour is revealed to be the same French doctor that Archie Jones was supposed to have executed in 1945. A flashback reveals that Archie bungled the execution as he has bungled everything else. Samad Iqbal "realizes that he has been lied to by his only friend in the world for fifty years," but, at the same time, after a burst of virulent Bengali invective directed at Archie, realizes also that their friendship will continue. They have no one else to turn to: "*'This incident alone will keep us two old boys going for the next forty years.'*" (p. 455) Millat Iqbal will fire a gun at Dr. Perret and Archie Jones will intercept the bullet, saving the scientist's life for the second time, "with no more reason or rhyme than the first time." (p. 461) Cheered on by Archie, not fatally wounded, FutureMouse will make a break for freedom, a freedom that will be illusory because his future has already been programmed into him.

The Iqbal boys are tried for the shooting, but the judge, unable to distinguish between the twins as to who discharged the firearm, will sentence each of them to four hundred hours of community service. The good-hearted Irie Jones will give birth to a child fathered either by Millat or Magid. She had slept with both within the same hour but gave Millat the first turn so that, just once, he might be ahead of his brighter and slightly older twin brother. Continuing to share her bounty, she takes Joshua Chalfen as her lover, and she, Joshua, her child, and her grandmother Hortense Bowden will later leave for Jamaica so that Irie may explore one half of her heritage and Hortense may experience the end of the world in her native country.

The novel has a Dickensian richness in all its characters, even the minor participants like the black voodoo woman Mad Mary, who speaks in rhyming couplets, or the dreadful war veteran J.P. Hamilton, who remembers slaughtering Africans, betrayed in the concealing jungle by the whiteness of their teeth.

There is a Dickensian theatricality in many of the scenes. One remembers Alsana protesting Samad's inadequacy as a wage earner by stripping off her clothes and putting them on the dinner table, demanding to know if they were edible.

There is Dickensian coincidence. Millat and Magid Iqbal, five thousand miles apart, each breaks his nose at almost the same time.

But, above all, there is Dickensian exuberance. Both Zadie Smith and Dickens exult in the glorious range of humanity.

The book is a wonderful chorus of voices rising up from a true cross-section of humanity. As we close the novel, nothing has really been resolved. Marcus Chalfen will no doubt engineer another FutureMouse, and Samad Iqbal will go on being frustrated by his sons. The novel is a perfect satire in that it ends much where it began, with imperfect people living in an imperfect world. No one has lived an epiphany, a moment of revelation – Irie Jones, for example, still does not know who she is – and the record is one of unrelieved human frailty. The only real change marked in the novel is that Abdul-Mickey will open the doors of O'Connell's to women for the first time on New Year's Eve, 1999. If the novel has a message, it is that our lives are governed far more by chance than we would like to think. One's heritage plays a part, but Magid and Millat Iqbal illustrate how difficult it is to know how one will react to that heritage. In the chaos that informs much of our lives as our plans go astray, it would seem that friendship and its cousin, love, are all that we have to cling to.

The ideal contained in the novel is embodied in a dream of Irie Jones, a dream of a world in which we recognize and celebrate difference but value more our shared humanity, a world in which the future is more important than the past: "In a vision, Irie has seen a time, a time not far from now, when roots won't matter any more because they can't because they mustn't because they're too long and they're too tortuous and they're just buried too damn deep. She looks forward to it." (p. 450)

As do I.

FELICIA'S JOURNEY

William Trevor
(Toronto: Vintage, 1995)

The year of *Felicia's Journey* is 1991, shortly before Ireland began its miraculous economic expansion. In a small town in the Republic, somewhere near Dublin, a seventeen-year-old Irish girl discovers that she is pregnant. Unemployment is rife in Ireland, and, like so many young Irish people, Felicia's lover, Johnny Lysaght, has gone to work across the Irish Sea in England. He impregnated Felicia during one of his visits home to see his widowed mother.

Felicia doesn't have Johnny's English address – he had always found a reason not to give it to her – and Johnny's mother, fiercely protective of her son and intuitively aware of Felicia's condition, won't give it to her. Felicia's only clues to Johnny's whereabouts are a postmark she sees on one of Johnny's letters in his mother's house and the one piece of information Johnny once let drop, that he works in a lawnmower factory.

Felicia steals her great-grandmother's pension savings and leaves the house she shares with her great-grandmother, her father, and her brothers and takes the night ferry to England. All she knows – or thinks she knows – is that the father of her unborn child works in a lawnmower factory somewhere north of Birmingham.

She will not find her lover, she will meet some very strange people, she will be robbed of the money she stole, she will have an abortion, and she will end up by prostituting herself and living on the streets.

It's a sad little story and not uncommon, and yet William Trevor's narrative won the British Whitbread Prize in 1994, a prize second in prestige only to the Booker. It was the third of William Trevor's novels to be so honoured. The Whitbread judges realized just how much was going on in Trevor's deceptively simple story.

Shortly after the novel begins, there is a discreetly given history lesson, made up of scraps of information passed on to the family by Felicia's father and great-grandmother. It is a lesson to pay attention to, as it helps the reader understand the little world Felicia has left behind her. For brevity's sake, I will give the details in chronological order.

Ireland lay under English rule for nearly eight centuries after the conquest of 1171. The Irish hatred of their English overlords was exacerbated during the Reformation, when Henry VIII's England became Protestant and Ireland remained staunchly Catholic, and when Oliver Cromwell later tried to dilute Ireland's Catholicism by making land grants to English and Scottish Protestants in Northern Ireland. Nothing was achieved except the creation of two solitudes who hated each other.

Again and again the Irish Catholics rebelled. They came closest to success in 1916 when a group of Irish patriots seized the Dublin post office and proclaimed a free Ireland. Although the Easter Rising failed and its leaders were shot by the British, the impetus it gave to the independence movement was unstoppable, and in 1921 the British government was forced to partition Ireland into the Protestant North, which would remain an integral part of the United Kingdom, and the Catholic entity of the Irish Free State in the South. Civil war erupted in the South between those who accepted Partition and those who wanted to fight on until the whole of Ireland was free, a conflict that would last two bloody years.

Felicia's family home in 1991 has become a shrine to the martyrs of the Easter Rising. The ninety-nine-year-old great-grandmother, incontinent and bedridden, with whom Felicia shares her sleeping quarters, had married one of the martyrs of the Rising only three days before the fatal battle began. Felicia herself is named after a Catholic Republican heroine who died on the 1916 barricades. A great family scrapbook has every detail of Ireland's struggle for freedom, and thus Felicia is the heir to the whole tradition of Irish sacrifice.

But there is about her no whiff of greatness. Mundane would be a generous description of her life. Her mother is dead, her father is the gardener at a convent, and her brothers are manual quarry workers. Felicia had the usual education from the nuns: the only lesson that she can remember is the story of Saint Ursula, who allegedly sailed the world without ever touching land so that her virginity would never be at risk. Felicia had once worked in a meat factory, but the factory closed and so she is now unemployed like most of the young women around her. Sometimes she thinks about the jobs she would like to do, and one of these reflections gives rise to what is to me one of the saddest sentences in the book: "You had to be trained to work a till in a supermarket." (p. 23) It is hard to imagine an ambition so limited as to make the operation of a cash register a task beyond one's capabilities.

Trevor draws an exquisite portrait of the dreariness of working-class existence at the time, an existence still lived under the shadow of the Church. Every breakfast is a fry-up, and any journey by a man from point A to point B will involve dropping into at least one pub on the way. The only chance of work for many is to leave the Republic for the North or for England. Many young Irishmen will take the easy way out of poverty and sneak across to England and join the British army, careful, however, to return to Ireland in civilian clothes when they come home on leave. The uniform of the army of the oppressor would not be welcome in the Republic, and a sensible young Irish soldier in the British armed forces would be well advised to concoct another explanation of how he makes his living across the Irish Sea.

How far is the Irish Republic that Felicia grew up in from the dreams of its founding fathers some seventy years earlier. The hallowed sentiments expressed in 1921 by Eamon de Valera, the father of an independent Ireland, have an honoured place in the scrapbook in Felicia's home.

The Ireland which we have dreamed of would be the home of a people who valued material wealth only as the basis of right living, of a people who were satisfied with frugal comfort and devoted their leisure to the things of the spirit; a land whose countryside would be bright with cosy homesteads, whose fields would be joyous with the sounds of industry, with the romping of sturdy children, the contests of athletic youths, the laughter of comely maidens: whose firesides would be forums for the wisdom of old age. It would, in a word, be the home of a people living the life that God desires men should live.
(pp. 26–27)

Unemployed Felicia is not living the life of which de Valera spoke. At her brother Aidan's wedding, the finery is tawdry and temporary, and the chatter is empty and meaningless. The industrial England she will find across the water will fall just as far short of what any of its pioneers might have dreamed.

All that Felicia had to look forward to were her dates with Johnny Lysaght. They meant dancing at the disco on a Friday night, slipping out for drinks at Sheehy's Pub, and ending in the field behind the gasworks where Felicia got her first kiss and more besides. The sophisticated reader will see the gropings as banal and rather sad, but for Felicia they were magic moments.

Now Felicia is pregnant and a thief, off to the English Midlands with stolen money to find her dream. It isn't a very well-defined dream: it seems to consist of finding Johnny, marrying Johnny, and living happily with Johnny ever after.

When Felicity leaves behind her family and Ireland, she has no passport, no birth certificate, and only the vaguest of destinations. As she passes through British customs, she encounters no real problem: it was common enough in rural Ireland to have no identity papers since, until recently, there was no real need of them. All she is carrying is the memory of poverty, a history that is too heavy to have meaning for her, and two carrier bags, in one of which is hidden her great-grandmother's savings.

This motherless child, with only the most tenuous identity, going off into a great unknown reminded me of the figure of the innocent in the medieval Morality Plays, the perfect target for the forces of Good and Evil who will struggle for her soul. The connection with the Morality Plays seemed to me to be reinforced by her name. It could not have been just a whim of the author to endow her with the feminine form of Felicity, one of the Cardinal Virtues that featured so prominently in medieval drama.

I thought back to the English Middle Ages, when the great mass of the English population was illiterate, and simple plays were a popular instrument of teaching the elements of the Christian faith. The Mystery Plays dramatized events in the life of Christ and occasionally earlier events like Noah and the Flood, and the Miracle Plays were based on the lives of the saints. These little exercises began sometime in the eleventh century and were usually staged by the guilds, associations of crafts- and tradesmen. Every year, on the day of their patron saint, the carpenters or the fishmongers or the blacksmiths would build a horse-drawn float and tour their community with their little play, a Mystery or a Miracle. Everyone knew the plots, and so the guilds emphasized the quality of pageant. They vied with each other as to who could produce the most gorgeous costumes. About 1450, the guilds added a third kind of play to their repertoire, the Morality. Allegorical, they always told the same story, the struggle between Good and Evil for the soul of the hero. Painters over the centuries embraced the theme, usually as The Struggle Between Good and Bad Angels for the Soul of a Child.

The crowds loved the Morality Plays, and they were particularly fond of the figure of Evil, always more exciting than Good. This figure of Evil came to be called Vice, the embodiment of all seven of the Deadly Sins: Anger, Envy, Sloth, Avarice, Pride, Gluttony, and Lust. As a glutton he was always fat, his lust often expressed by wearing a huge wooden penis, and he was dressed in red to remind the onlooking believers of the flames of Hell. Naturally, he never won and was either killed or driven off the stage by Good. But he was always the most spectacular character.

With the appearance of Mr. Hilditch in the early pages of the novel, I became convinced I was reading a modern Morality. Mr. Hilditch is the embodiment of Gluttony.

> Christened Joseph Ambrose fifty-four years ago, Mr Hilditch wears spectacles that have a pebbly look, keeps his pigeon-coloured hair short, dresses always in a suit with a waistcoat, ties his striped tie into a tight little knot, polishes his shoes twice a day, and is given to smiling pleasantly. Regularly, the fat that bulges about his features is rolled back and well-kept teeth appear, while a twinkle livens the blurred pupils behind his spectacles. His voice is faintly high-pitched. (p. 6)

It is important to remember that the medieval audience believed that one sin practised to excess would lead to the practice of all the others, and that Vice, while often a violent caricature of a person, would sometimes be portrayed in deceptively attractive garb. There would always, however, be one flaw, since the Devil, while cunning, is not capable of creating perfection. The unnaturally high voice that William Trevor attributes to Hilditch would have been a dead giveaway to a fifteenth-century audience.

Hilditch weighs 274 pounds and is the catering manager at a factory near Birmingham in the industrial centre of England. He is fifty-four years old and lives alone in the house his mother left him.

Having identified to my own satisfaction the innocent soul and the Bad Angel, I waited impatiently for the Good Angel to come around the corner. As I waited, I noticed that William Trevor was giving the same treatment to the English Midlands that he had given to Felicia's Ireland. As Felicia tramps on from one new town to another, from one industrial zone to another, in search of the elusive lawnmower factory, she is traversing a wasteland. Garbage and dead plants strew the public flower beds, the hanging baskets are rusty, and obscene graffiti deface the sculptures put up for the people's edification. "The scrubby grass she walks on is grey, in places black, decorated by the litter that is scattered around her – crushed cigarette packets, plastic bags, cans and bottles, crumpled sheets from newspapers, cartons." (p. 15)

The new towns built around Birmingham after 1945 were part of a dream of a brave new world, as potent a dream for a post-war England as de Valera's had been in 1921 for post-independence Ireland. Britain's post-war Socialist planners had also wanted to create an environment for happy, laughing, healthy children. But the reality in England in 1991 was all too often high-rise slums surrounded by pathetically abused public areas. The new England and the new Ireland were both dreams gone sour.

How ingenious of William Trevor, I thought, to stage a Morality Play with the backdrop of the wasteland that is so much of modern England. How dramatic to stage the struggle for the soul of a child against the background of a fallen world, a world after Eden, a world without the hope of the earthly Paradise our parents and grandparents dreamed of.

I watched the terrible Hilditch as he stalked Felicia. He speaks to her, offers to help find her boyfriend, recommends a local bed-and-breakfast, and tells her that his non-existent wife, Ada, would wish him to help a young girl who is lost and alone. He even takes her on sad wild goose chases to other towns and other industrial zones to hunt down Johnny Lysaght's factory. We know of course, and Hilditch guesses, that Johnny has in fact found work in the British army, but Felicia's search goes on.

The reader enters the mind of Hilditch as he remembers other girls he has helped. Their names are like a refrain: Beth, Elsie, Sharon, Gaye,

Jakki, and Bobbi. Some were fleeing abusive stepfathers or boyfriends, others were searching like Felicia.

Ominously, Hilditch interrupts his own thoughts – "Certain things you don't say aloud; and certain things you don't say even to yourself, best left, best forgotten." (p. 42) He calls such musings "going down Memory Lane." For Hilditch, no cliché is too hackneyed – he is a great lover of popular songs – and it is his very ordinariness that makes him so frightening, as well as the precision with which he plans every element of his life, especially the meals he prepares both at home and for the workers at his factory canteen.

We are privy to his thoughts, and William Trevor reveals the horror to us as delicately as Hilditch plans his meals: "[Hilditch] only regrets that the ordained brevity of this relationship is an element in those [exhilarating] circumstances also. Perhaps that, he reflects as he washes a pound of brussels sprouts, is how perfection in a friendship has to be, unenduring lest it lose its quality." (p. 52)

The reader is compelled to wonder why all the relationships were brief, because nowhere in the early pages of the novel does Hilditch admit directly that he killed Beth and Elsie and Sharon et al., nor does the author confirm it. It is possible that he just flirted with them. It is the ambiguity itself that works on the reader's imagination, and hint after hint only confirms our suspicions that Hilditch means Felicia the most terrible harm.

It is not until Chapter 10 that we meet Miss Calligary, a Jamaican immigrant proselytizing door to door for a fundamentalist Christian group whose centre is a residential building called the Gathering House. When Miss Calligary sees a distressed and pregnant Felicia in the street, she "strides forth to gather the girl in." (p. 81) The multiracial residents of the Gathering House are kind and gentle to Felicia, and they rejoice in her pregnancy. "'A child will be born in the Gathering House,'" one of the saved whispers to another, and, for the first time in England, Felicia feels safe: "[A]ll of it is more like a dream than reality: she has never in her life met people like this before, nor even known that such people exist." (p. 88)

Wonderful, I thought, the Good Angel has arrived in the person of Miss Calligary and the innocent child, and her child, will be saved from the force of Evil.

But my satisfaction with my perceptive analysis was short-lived. Warning bells began to sound. Miss Calligary is introduced to us in a red nightdress, and I thought it odd that William Trevor should choose to dress the Good Angel in the colour of Hell. Then the full import of Miss Calligary's name struck me, together with Felicia's feeling that her reception at the Gathering House was "more like a dream than reality." It was only at that point that I realized that William Trevor had been leading the reader – or at least this reader – in the wrong direction and playing a very clever game.

I must leave the novel for a moment to discuss a gem of early movie history that may seem at first irrelevant but is in fact at the very heart of an understanding of *Felicia's Journey*. In 1919, at the height of the Expressionist movement in Germany, the director Robert Weine created the movie *Das Kabinett des Doktor Caligari*. The plot is apparently simple. A hypnotist, Dr. Caligari, is touring country fairs with an assistant who is capable of great feats of strength while in a deep trance. The hero of the film suspects that Caligari and his assistant are responsible for a whole string of unsolved murders and chases the evil hypnotist to an asylum, where he is locked up as insane. In the last moments of the film, it is made clear that the story has all been a dream in the mind of one of the inmates, our erstwhile hero, and Caligari is not the villain but a kindly doctor who is also the director of the asylum. Nothing in the movie was as it first seemed to be.

It is impossible that William Trevor's choice of a name for his missionary was a coincidence, and Felicia's perception of the Gathering House as "more like a dream than a reality" confirmed that my facile view of the novel as a modern Morality had to be abandoned. After that very salutary evocation of the German Expressionist masterpiece, I decided to wait for the end of the novel before attempting any easy conclusions.

Unwilling to convert and reluctant to accept hospitality under false pretences, Felicia leaves the Gathering House only to have her diminishing funds surreptitiously taken by Mr. Hilditch. Frantic, she returns to her various bed-and-breakfasts and to the Gathering House, from which she is ejected in a most un-Christian way by believers horrified that she would think them capable of dishonesty. Any lingering hope the reader might have had in Miss Calligary and her movement as the force for Good is dashed. Whatever salvation might be available to Felicia, it will not be in the simplistic promises of the fundamentalists.

Friendless and alone, Felicia turns again to Hilditch, who, since he met her, has constructed a whole myth about a wife Ada. Now, he tells her, Ada has died in hospital. He has even strewn women's clothes all over his house to convince Felicia of a woman's presence.

Hilditch helps Felicia to get an abortion, and Felicia is tormented by imagined reproaches from the nuns, the Virgin Mary, and her own dead mother. But, in spite of her despair, Felicia finally recognizes the menace in Hilditch when he comes to her room and tells her of the other girls he's helped – " 'In their time of need they counted on me.' " (p. 155)

Felicia "knows the girls are dead . . . in the hoarse breathing, in the sweat . . . in the way he talks," (p. 155) and, panic-stricken, she waits for him to leave her room and then flees the house and, for a long time, the novel.

Her disappearance is a masterly contribution to the suspense. We cannot know whether Hilditch has caught up to her or not. Such shreds of evidence as we are given suggest she has become another victim. In his garden, Hilditch contemplates freshly turned patches of earth and, the day after the possible escape, he visits one of those stately houses of England that are open to the public for a small charge. "Already the Irish girl has joined the others in his Memory Lane. . . . He always plans an outing as soon after a parting as is possible, in an effort to combat the lowness of his spirits. The day after Gaye went he came to this selfsame stately home." (p. 158) On his return home, he burns all the women's clothes and accessories.

The novel has turned its whole attention on Hilditch. What had seemed to be a straightforward battle between Good and Evil has now become the dissection of an apparent monster. It seems to me remarkable that William Trevor, happily married for nearly forty years and a contented church sculptor before he turned to writing to support his family, should be able to exhibit the compassionate understanding we will shortly witness for a serial murderer, but the author has frequently reiterated his belief that blacks and whites are really no more than complicated greys.

Hilditch begins to be hounded by Miss Calligary and her associate. They had seen him with Felicia and view him as a Good Samaritan to a girl in distress. Intent on paying tribute and on saving this deserving soul, they confront him on his doorstep and shout compliments and scripture through his letterbox. Hilditch cowers in his house, convinced that they have stumbled on the truth. We learn from Hilditch himself that Felicia got away from him – "The Irish girl is roaming the streets" (p. 186) – and Hilditch can know no peace. Felicia, who knows about the other girls, is a constant danger.

Under the pressure of his fear, Hilditch makes a partial confession to Miss Calligary: "'I took her money to keep her by me, but even so she went away.'" Miss Calligary's reaction is foreseeable: "'[T]his man is not as he seems. . . . He has stolen a girl's money for some heinous purpose.'" (p. 199)

Indeed, the jovial Hilditch is not as he seems. We know that he never knew his father and was brought up by his mother. After her death, he emptied her house and made it his own, filling it with large, substantial furniture. We know that he is meticulous in his habits, and his memories reveal him to have been a compulsively neat child. He has been lucky at his work. He was an invoice clerk, but when a promotion became available, he took a catering course and was appointed canteen manager. We know that he adores the details of his job and his contact with the employees and the sales representatives. He actually practises for his encounters with other people:

By ten o'clock Mr Hilditch has read everything in the *Daily Telegraph*: the foreign news, the financial news, the sports news, the home news. He has no interest in sport, but usually finds himself acquiring information about sporting matters because he finds the knowledge useful in conversation. (p. 60)

This is clearly a man who wears a mask, a man who prepares a face to greet the faces that he meets.

Hilditch has endured his share of humiliations. Chief among them was his disqualification, thirty-six years earlier, from military service on medical grounds. He has bitter memories of the attitude of the recruiting sergeant, and he invents, for Felicia, a more pleasing personal history for himself: "'I've had a regimental career myself. . . . I came out when Ada was first ailing.'" (p. 63)

Now Hilditch is in his mid-fifties and fat and ever "closer to other, darker, aspects of the depths that lie within him." (p. 7) Desperately unhappy with who and what he is, he loves to drive around with Felicity, as he did with the other young girls of Memory Lane, and be mistaken for a husband or a lover. He tells a cashier at a café that he's Felicia's boyfriend – she is far enough away for him to take the risk – and he is delighted when they assume at the abortion clinic that he is the father of Felicia's baby.

As we become increasingly aware of Hilditch's mental state, William Trevor gives us every detail of Hilditch's daily routine, of clogged extractors and competition between suppliers. Trevor does in prose what Hitchcock used to do on film, stressing the banality and ordinariness of everyday events in order to increase our sense of underlying horror.

We know that Hilditch is incapable of a normal relationship with a woman. We do not yet know why, although the reason will become clear later. He tells us himself that he went once to a prostitute and, humiliatingly, was unable to perform. Our imagination – or mine at least – cannot begin to grasp what it is he did with the girls he trapped in his web. Only slowly does it become clear that he always killed them in the same circumstances. He would drive them out to a lay-by – a rest area on a country road – and do whatever it was he would do to make them die. The actual deaths are never clear – he doesn't dwell on them – they were only a means to an end, a means of ensuring that Beth, Gaye, Jakki, and the others would never truly leave him, that they would be joined to him forever in his mind in that collection of images he visits so often.

The murder always had to take place in his car – "It had to be the car; he couldn't do it in his house, no man could." (p. 196) The explanation of why the murders could not take place in his mother's house is also an explanation of the agony in the mind of Hilditch. Under the self-imposed order of the life he shows the world, Hilditch is a man in hell, and on occasion his inner torment breaks through the facade. "Tears flow from Mr Hilditch, becoming rivulets in the flesh of his cheeks and his chin, dripping on to his neck, damping his shirt and his waistcoat. His sobbing becomes a moaning in the room, a sound as from an animal suffering beyond endurance, distraught and piteous." (p. 151)

In a few ghastly passages towards the end of the novel, the reader discovers the source of the agony. Speaking of his late mother, Hilditch wonders,

> Had she always foreseen, when he was six and eight and ten, when he sat beside her watching *Dumbo*, and *Bambi*, when first he practised his signature, when he wrote down *Major Hilditch*: had she always known that she would turn to him when there was no one else? When the insurance-man winked and said no time for anything

today, did she foresee – already – what would happen in this house? The barman at the Spa said the wife had put her foot down, no more hanky-panky. After a few months the policeman didn't drop in any more. (p. 195)

His mother had turned to him "when there was no one else," when she had grown unattractive, and compelled him to incest. She would say to him, "'Be nice, dear,' in the special voice, the promise that the request will never be made again, broken every time." (p. 200)

Driven further into insanity by the fear that Felicia will expose him and, even worse, that the relentless Miss Calligary will find out not only about the girls of Memory Lane but about what he had been compelled to do in his childhood, Hilditch reaches the end of endurance. He is not without self-knowledge – he even reads about delusional insanity at his local library – but he is in the grip of an obsession about which he can do nothing: "The black woman knows; that's why she comes to his door." (p. 200)

Finally, this tormented man takes his own life, and our only possible reaction is one of compassion. To know all is to forgive all, and Felicia herself pronounces his epitaph on the penultimate page of the novel: "Lost within a man who murdered, there was a soul like any other soul, purity itself it surely once had been."

Felicia's Journey is one of thirteen novels by William Trevor, and it is typical in that, when we meet his major characters, the damage has already been done to them. We rarely if ever meet the perpetrators of the damage. When we meet Felicia she is already pregnant and Hilditch's sexual relations with his mother are more than forty years in the past. William Trevor's interest is in the victim. In Britain, he is often referred to as the poet of lost souls, the novelist of damaged lives. This gentle man, an Irish-born Protestant, now lives quietly in Devon, but in one of his rare interviews, Trevor confided to the magazine *Books in Ireland* in 1995 that he often visits Dublin and London and wanders the streets at night, talking to the homeless to discover who they are and where they are from and why they are there.

Before I read *Felicia's Journey*, my favourite work by William Trevor was *Miss Gomez and the Brethren* (1971). A Jamaican missionary, not unlike Miss Calligary, finds that the fundamentalist organization to which she has devoted her life is nothing more than a money-seeking confidence trick. Like Felicia, Miss Gomez has to begin again, financially poorer and with fewer certainties, but much freer of beliefs formulated by other people.

Felicia's Journey began as an apparent Morality Play and then became a brilliant psychological study of a deranged mind. In the last chapter of the novel, as William Trevor effortlessly returns to Felicia, the novel becomes a wonderfully evocative study of the plight of England's homeless. The author takes up again the theme of the beginning of the novel, when Felicia wandered through the wasteland of the New Towns, and again we are forced to consider how far we have fallen short of the dreams of those who believed so passionately that humankind was capable of building in our world a new Jerusalem.

Even before Felicia stayed briefly and dangerously at the home of Mr. Hilditch, she had begun to live on the streets among the lost and the fallen, and William Trevor puts a human face on those who share Felicia's lot.

[T]he homeless of this town have found their night-time resting places – in doorways, and underground passages left open in error, in abandoned vehicles, in the derelict gardens of demolished houses. . . . All ages lie out in the places that have been found, men and women, children. The family rejects have ceased to weep into their make-do pillows; those brought low by their foolishness or by untimely greed plead silently for sleep. A one-time clergyman no longer dwells on his disgrace, but dreams instead that it never happened. Rejected husbands, abandoned wives, victims of chance, have passed beyond bitterness, and devote their energies to keeping warm. . . . Men who have failed lie on their own and dream of a reality they dare not contemplate by day: great hotels and deferential waiters, the power they once possessed, the limbs of secretaries. Women who were beautiful in their day are beautiful again. There is no arrogance among the people of the streets, no insistent pride in their sleeping features, no lingering telltale of a past's corruption. They have passed the stage of desperation, and on their downward path some among the women have sold themselves: faces chapped, fingernails ingrained, they are beyond that now. . . . In their dreams there is occasionally the fantasy that they may be cured, that they may be loved. (pp. 101–03)

The passage is wonderfully moving, with a poetry deriving from catalogue, incremental repetition, and exquisitely chosen images, but Trevor continues with practical details of the lives of the vulnerable. For a while, Felicia takes refuge in a house where the landlord is trying to get rid of a sitting tenant by inviting in deadbeats. There is no way that a landlord in England can evict tenants, so many resort to making life so unbearable that the tenants leave of their own accord.

Felicia meets many of life's walking wounded, the same flotsam that so intrigues the author on his nightly perambulations. There are heroin addicts, of course, and there is the eighty-two-year-old Irish bag lady who has spent an incredible forty-one years on the streets. There is the middle-aged former prostitute who has found comfort in the companionship of a physically beautiful young man with a ruined mind. His only activity in life is to send birthday cards to bishops, all of whom he is convinced are lonely.

It's a strange world, but no stranger perhaps than the superstitious little world that Felicia left behind in her poverty-stricken Irish village or the soulless industrial landscape she once tramped looking for her Johnny.

As the novel ends, we leave Felicia in the debris of the streets, but it is a new Felicia, a Felicia sustained by self-knowledge and self-acceptance. She accepts the past as done. She can do nothing to undo it and it has led her to the present.

> The only guilt is that she permitted her baby to be taken from her: she shouldn't have done that, but there you are. She looks out now from where she is, and does not brood: what's done is done. She does not brood on her one-time lover's treachery. She walked away from a man who murdered girls. (p. 209)

Felicia is aware of the presence of goodness: she knows of a dentist who gives free dental care to the homeless, who "has dedicated her existence to the rotten teeth of derelicts, to derelicts' odour and filth." (p. 213) But Felicia cannot explain her goodness any more than she can explain Hilditch: "Her goodness is a greater mystery than the evil that distorted a man's every spoken word, his every movement made."

Felicia "seeks no meaning in the thoughts that occur to her, any more than she searches for one in her purposeless journey," (p. 212) and has not arrived at any great understanding of the cosmos, but she has arrived at a vital truth. She knows who she is. She has freed herself from her childhood and from dependence on men like Johnny Lysaght. She will trade her body now, in return for, say, a long-distance lift from a truck driver, but she trades in the full knowledge that it is a commercial transaction, a *quid pro quo*. It is a kind of freedom she didn't have when she was a handmaiden to her father and her brothers.

She has escaped not only the threat to her body by Mr. Hilditch but the threat to her soul by Miss Calligary. Not for Felicia is the easy absolution of simplistic fundamentalism.

Stripped of everything at the end of the novel, including superstition and imposed values, Felicia has no barriers between her and her essence, "the thing itself," and she is as serene as Lear in her self-awareness.

> The innocence that once was hers is now, with time, a foolishness, yet it is not disowned, and that same lost person is valued for leading her to where she is. Walking through another morning, fine after a wet night, she accepts without bewilderment the serenity that possesses her, and celebrates its fresh new presence. (p. 207)

The journey we have made with Felicia has been wonderful. William Trevor has created such psychological suspense and such complete portraits and has demonstrated such compassion for the human condition. His style is as perfect as his grasp of the human mind, and his text moves from present to past without strain. He interweaves reality and memory in a seamless whole. His craft is great, but the craft never shows, and we never hear the machinery moving.

His great achievement is to make of Felicia at the end of the novel a person who has succeeded. She is at economic zero, but in any sense that I understand the word, she is free. There is no human state more desirable. When she finds a person to love or a goodness to practise she will be free to choose her path in a way that few of us are. She has come through the Valley of the Shadow and her future is clear. It will be built on truth, hard truth, but her own truth.

THE STONE CARVERS

Jane Urquhart

(Toronto: McClelland & Stewart, 2002)

Although Jane Urquhart's novel *The Stone Carvers* moves from Bavaria in Germany to Ontario and later back to Europe, it has all the ingredients of a German fairy tale: a woodcarver, a mad king, a seamstress, a quest for perfection, a boy who follows the wild birds and lives under bridges like a troll, a beautiful young girl disguised as a crazy woman, a woman disguised as a man, a beautiful valley, and an ending in which everyone finds true love.

The Stone Carvers is not, however, a fairy tale. It is a novel about damage and loss and the redemptive power of love and art. In this, her fifth novel, Jane Urquhart draws more than ever before on the formative experiences of her early adult years.

She was born in 1949 in Northern Ontario into the family of a mining engineer, but came to live in Toronto at the age of five. After studying in Vancouver and at the University of Guelph, where she took her degree in English, she married the artist Paul Keele. The marriage ended when her husband was killed in a car accident. She found some solace in resuming her studies, taking a second degree, this time in Art History, in 1973. Then came a second and very happy marriage to the artist Tony Urquhart. She had written nothing during her university years or her first marriage, but that changed when Tony took her on a tour of the battlefields of Europe and Jane Urquhart came to the memorial at Vimy Ridge, the site of a major battle during the First World War.

The great powers of Europe, together with their empires, had gone to war in 1914 for a variety of reasons, none of them noble. Chief among them were British and German rivalry over African colonies and maritime supremacy, a French desire for revenge for France's defeat by Germany in 1870, and ethnic tensions in the ramshackle Austro-Hungarian Empire. Germany, as leader of the Central Powers, had a daring plan – the von Schlieffen plan – to attack France by moving the German armies through neutral Belgium and sweeping down the French coast to cut off assistance to the French by Britain. The German initiative was thwarted, however, when the French and British turned the German forces back in the north of France. Both sides began to dig in on two opposing fronts, separated by a no-man's-land of anything from two to three hundred yards, on a line from Flanders in Belgium to Picardy in France.

These "fronts" would move very little for the four years of the war for a very simple reason. By 1914 the two best means of defence in land warfare, barbed wire and the machine gun, had been both invented and perfected, while the only two weapons that could overcome those defences, the tank and the airplane, were in their infancy. The result was that the generals on both sides would hurl millions of men and their rifles against defences that were virtually impregnable. Long before the completion of the Vimy Memorial in 1936, there was a greater European memorial to humankind's folly, the flesh and bones of millions of men bound up in the mud and blood of Belgium and northern France.

Only rarely was there a significant gain of enemy ground, and it is ironic that Canada, fighting loyally at the side of Great Britain, should have found a new sense of its independence in one of these few clear victories.

On Easter Monday, April 9, 1917, the Canadian Corps, made up of four divisions, launched an assault on Vimy Ridge, a key position in the German line in the French province of Picardy. Earlier British and French attempts to capture the German stronghold had failed at a cost of 150,000 casualties, but the Canadian attack was successful, and within forty-eight hours Vimy was in Canadian hands. Nearly four thousand Canadians paid with their lives for the victory, and after the war a grateful France gave a hundred hectares of land to the young nation of Canada. The soldiers who had died in the attack would rest in Canadian soil for perpetuity. (It is a source of great pride to me that it was my first cousin, Captain Claude Williams MC, who led the Canadian machine-gunners out of the trenches and over the top at Vimy.) In 1923, the Canadian government decided to build a monument at Vimy. A Toronto sculptor, Walter Allward, won the competition to build the monument. It would take him thirteen years to complete the work, and his struggle forms a large part of the second half of Jane Urquhart's novel. The memorial, unveiled in 1936 and visible for sixty kilometres, would consist of two thirty-metre obelisks and twenty giant figures dominated by a hooded woman in mourning. Below would be a series of long walls on which Allward would carve the names of those 11,285 Canadian soldiers whose bodies were never recovered during the war, a significant portion of Canada's sixty thousand war dead.

Jane Urquhart was immensely affected by the sight of the Vimy Memorial. She found it "staggeringly beautiful . . . the landscape around it like a metaphor . . . scarred." (CBC Radio interview, April 4, 2001)

But she did not begin to write until 1977. Her first medium was poetry and her poems, in her own words, were

> loose bits of paper carried by the wind
> caught for a moment
> on the fence around this time.

In one collection of poems, *False Shuffles* (1982), a daughter makes a whole story of fragments passed down to her in the oral tradition from her mother and her grandmother. In another collection, *The Little Flowers of Mme. de Montespan* (1983), historical fragments are gathered like flowers in a bouquet to form a coherent narrative of a woman whose whole life was devoted to the "preservation of her flesh." In one of the poems of that collection, *"Le roi s'amuse,"* she introduces what will become her larger theme, the fragmentation of the self as a result of trauma:

> The man who touches you
> without love
> . . .
> he is the death
> of the child in you
> the beginning of dark
> . . .

Urquhart's short stories continued to demonstrate her fascination with fragments as metaphors. The title story of her 1987 collection, *Storm Glass*, examines a marriage through the ongoing argument between a husband and wife as to whether the shards of glass found on beaches should be called "storm glass" or "water glass," and all her novels that followed are replete with images of fragments. Her first novel, *The Whirlpool* (1986), centres on a woman who fishes victims and the fragments of their possessions out of the pool under Niagara Falls. In *Away* (1993), the last witness to the family saga, the granddaughter Esther, sticks notes to every object in the family home so that she might more easily weave the bits of history into a coherent narrative. In *The Underpainter* (1997), Austin Fraser the artist pieces together the remains of his friend's smashed china, representing the life Fraser unwittingly destroyed.

As Urquhart wrote over the years, she became more and more interested not only in fragments but in how the fragmented individual may be made whole again. She became increasingly interested in how, in the oral tradition, pieces of history are worked by the imagination into compelling stories, in how the self can recover from alienation caused by being transplanted as an immigrant or through psychic damage or catastrophic loss, and in how love and/or the act of creation can play their part in the healing process.

In her novels, with their strong narrative thrust, the reader can see the influence of the nineteenth-century writers like Dickens and the Brontës, whom Urquhart loves. Urquhart is also amazingly able to find the supernatural in the commonplace – her fellow novelist Margaret Atwood has defined both Urquhart and herself as "Ontario Gothic" – and Urquhart has confessed her preference for finding the extraordinary in seemingly ordinary people, "smaller histories from smaller archives."

All her themes have come together brilliantly in *The Stone Carvers*, and the journey to healing of Klara and Tilman Becker and the mending of fragmented lives seem just as important as Allward's obsession to complete the magnificence of the Vimy Memorial.

The novel opens with a brief description of the unfinished monument in 1934, but we do not yet know it is Allward's monument at Vimy. That story is yet to be told, and the novel proper begins with another story.

It is a story of the little German immigrant village of Shoneval, Ontario, and its beginnings. The story is made up of fragments put together by the nuns of the nearby convent and a pious spinster who divides her time between farming and service to the local church. The time is in the early 1930s, but the story, as the nuns and the spinster tell it, has its genesis in Bavaria in 1866.

We meet Father Archangel Gstir, a peaceful, contented soul who loves his church and his Bavarian mountains and all the glory of God's creation down to the little wildflowers he presses so carefully in his album. He receives a dual call, from God and his king, Ludwig II of Bavaria, to go to serve the German immigrants who had left for the wilds of Ontario and a fresh start in the New World. After six months of arduous travel, he comes through the torment of blackflies to his "first deep Canadian valley . . . [where he] fell in love at once." (p. 14) It is a desolate scene of mud and felled trees, but Father Gstir can see beyond the present reality.

> He saw all this, but he also saw how it would be later, with crops and orchards growing in the cleared areas, and with painted houses and barns, and with gardens sprouting flowers. He beheld all that was there in front of him, and all that he believed would be there in the future, and he knew he was home. (p. 14)

Father Gstir gasps with joy at his vision of a magnificent stone church that would be at the centre of the German-speaking community in this wonderful place, and he accosts two millers: "'You live here in this beautiful valley, this shoneval,' he told two men who were so whitened by flour that he almost believed them to be angels. 'God be praised!'" (p. 15)

Father Gstir plans to stir enthusiasm for the building of his great church by organizing a Corpus Christi procession with all its engaging pageantry. Joseph Becker, an immigrant carver, will contribute a crucifix and a Virgin and, later, an altar for the church, and thus does the grandfather of our narrator, Klara Becker, enter the story as she and the nuns remember it. It will take twelve years of effort by the priest and volunteer labour by his parishioners before the great stone church is finally consecrated in 1881 and another four years after that before the fine bell for which Father Gstir had always yearned arrives from Bavaria, but the good priest knows that well-wrought buildings have a permanence that is not accorded to human life, even in memory. With the woodcarver Joseph Becker he discusses how the ravages of time cannot affect the essence of a monument: "'Beautiful ruins are the skeletons of fine architecture . . . good bones from the beginning . . .

[my church] will become a wonderful ruin up there on that hill.'" (p. 54) In the centuries to come, when all those who knew Father Gstir and his goodness have died, no one will remember him. But all will see and wonder at his church or at the great ruins of his church – or so he hopes.

In the creation of Father Gstir, so in love with his native Bavarian village of Inzell and the transplanted Bavarian village of Shoneval in Ontario, Jane Urquhart demonstrates her exquisite gift for establishing setting and landscape. But she does more than that. In her portrait of Gstir, Urquhart foreshadows another man who will look upon desolation and envision a great monument. There is a fine and delicate balance in the novel between Father Gstir's church at the beginning and Walter Allward's monument at Vimy at the end. Each came into being as a result of one man's obsession and after more than a decade of struggle, and each will far outlast its creator. It is impossible not to think of Shelley's poem to the ruined statue in the desert and its inscription to the long-forgotten Ozymandias, once the "King of Kings."

Shelley imagines a traveller coming across a ruined statue in the desert, with nothing left except the legs, a shattered face lying nearby, and the inscription on the base:

"My name is Ozymandias, King of Kings,
Look upon my works, ye Mighty, and despair!"
Nothing beside remains. Round the decay
Of that colossal wreck, boundless and bare
The lone and level sands stretch far away.

Who now remembers Ozymandias or the sculptor of his monument? And, in a hint of what is to come, who can prevent the ravages of time on the created work itself?

But the novel is not only a reflection on the permanence or impermanence of created art and the forgetting of that art's creator; it is also a meditation on how lives damaged into fragments may be made whole, and the vehicle for that will be largely the family of Joseph Becker.

Becker had left Bavaria for Canada when he was twenty and was working as a miller when Father Gstir first spoke to him in Shoneval. But his first love was always woodcarving, and it was his joy to carve for Father

Gstir and for God. He would marry the girl who made Father Gstir's vestments, and, as he later tells his granddaughter Klara, "'It was a Corpus Christi procession in the backwoods . . . that brought together the chisel and the needle.'" (p. 24)

Joseph's son Dieter would not inherit his creative gifts, and all Joseph's hopes fell upon the shoulders of his grandson Tilman. Joseph could imagine no greater fulfilment in life than artistic creation, but Tilman never seemed interested in learning anything more than a few basic carving techniques in spite of his grandfather's best efforts.

Joseph had to content himself with his son's second child, Klara, "though it was really her brother, Tilman, that the old man had his eye on." (p. 38) Klara began her carving with toys, even a complete Noah's ark for her brother one Christmas. She then moved to the reproduction of saints, and finally to beginning a life-sized statue of a medieval abbess, a project that would take many years to complete, like Father Gstir's church or Walter Allward's Vimy Memorial. At the same time, she learned the art of tailoring from her mother, who stressed always the superiority of the tailor over the mere seamstress: "'You are constructing something with shape and weight and volume. A garment that is *tailored*.'" (p. 45) We are reminded of Father Gstir's observations on the importance of building something that will last. The theme of construction is one that pervades the novel at every level.

In her late adolescence, Klara experiences a rare contentment as her scissors cut into cloth or as her chisel bites into her grandfather's beloved basswood, but she never feels her mother's love. Helga taught her, but "without tenderness, as if she felt that her young daughter . . . ought to be provided with some business to get on with." (p. 33) All of Helga Becker's love, until she dies of cancer when Klara is twenty, is reserved for her son, Tilman.

Tilman had been conceived in 1892 in a unique moment of bloodlust that had followed Dieter Becker's first and only experience of hunting.

> After he threw the brace of birds on a wooden chair, the husband and wife stood face to face in the dwindling light, like silent enemies. Then they fell groaning to the floor beside the stove, where they struggled to extract this new terrible pleasure from the other. . . .

Within twenty-four hours all relations between the couple would
be enacted with the same courteous affection that had become a part
of their marriage. Dieter never hunted again. (p. 58)

It is a brilliant piece of foreshadowing of the madness that would over-
take the Western world in 1914, and it is fitting that Dieter and Helga
Becker's first child would not be like other children.

At school Tilman could not remain in his seat, and was eventually permitted to remain at home and roam the family farm. At six he begins
the first of his many adventures, running away from home to follow the
migrating birds and relying on the kindness of strangers for survival. His
grandfather recognizes the boy's uniqueness as a *wunderkind* afflicted by
wanderlust, a recognized phenomenon in Bavaria, or at least in Bavarian
storytelling. In one of the intervals at home between his "walks," as he
calls them, Tilman becomes more interested in his grandfather's carving,
not in the main subjects, usually saints, but rather in the backgrounds, in
the landscapes. These he will carve, becoming "a genius of distant
views." (p. 97) On his travels, Tilman is always drawn to the far away,
stopping only at what he perceives as the chaos of unfordable bodies of
water like Lake Erie. He always returns home, but after six years of his
frequent absences, his mother becomes terrified that he will leave forever
and "infuriated by the notion that it was she that Tilman was trying to
escape from." (p. 63) Helga has a reluctant Dieter harness and chain the
boy in the woodshed. After days of his howling and refusing to eat, it is
his sister, Klara, who brings him the hammer to pry away the large, bent
nails that hold his chain. It is an act of love on Klara's part, to give her
brother his freedom. It will bind them together more surely than the
chains that bound Tilman, and it will be no surprise when Tilman returns
to Klara thirty years later to begin the second great narrative movement
of the novel.

Tilman's immediate problem after his escape is to remove his harness
and the dragging iron tether. His rescue comes in the form of a female
tramp, Crazy Phoebe, who takes him to a junkyard whose owner cuts away
the chains. The sequence at the home of the junkman Ham Bone is one
of the most exquisite and moving of the novel. After attending to Tilman,
Ham Bone bathes the seemingly wretched old hag, and, as the grime is
washed away, Crazy Phoebe is revealed as a beautiful young woman. We

are told that "the scene that unfolded before Tilman was one he would never forget," and it is indeed unforgettable.

> Years later when he came at last to love someone, the memory of this night would fall like rain into his mind: the gentle tenderness, the sound of falling water. He would remember the way the young woman's buttocks and calves shone when the man had put water there, and the glistening snails' tracks on her belly that, as an adult, Tilman would realize meant that she had borne a child. He would remember the tears on the large man's face as he moved the cloth under her breasts and down the insides of her thighs. And he would remember her utter submissiveness after all her protestations. . . .
>
> "Will you come home, Phoebe?" he asked quietly. "You don't have to be crazy no more. We could take in the boy."
>
> Tilman stiffened, preparing, as always, for flight at the suggestion of confinement.
>
> But Phoebe refused. "I don't hold with homes," she said. "Homes is where sorrow is at. . . .
>
> "If I was to let you get at me," said Phoebe, "we'd only have another baby what would die."
>
> She began to weep.
>
> Ham Bone held her. "I won't get at you, Phoeb," he said. "I know you'd only go away again anyways." (pp. 183–84)

Years later Tilman would explain what had happened in ten perfectly chosen words: "A man who loved a woman cut my chain off." (p. 212)

If I had not already known that Jane Urquhart is a poet, the four or five pages of the Ham Bone episode would have made it clear to me. The whole story of a much-loved young woman who found refuge in insanity after the terrible loss of her child and whose husband's love is not enough to bring her comfort is made poignantly clear by only indirect allusions. It is the most perfect example of poetry as the distillation of experience. The reader can extrapolate from the few lines of exchange between Phoebe and her husband a story of loss and love and suffering that would more than fill a novel of its own.

It is not only a poetic masterpiece that would justify the novel if the novel had no other virtues – and it has many – it is also an important addition to the narrative, because it poses a problem central to the work. Is there damage so terrible that it may not be redeemed by love? We will remember Crazy Phoebe when we meet others who have passed through the fire of suffering.

After Tilman leaves Shoneval for the last time, Klara is left alone with her father, her grandfather, and her mother. Her mother, unloving as always, Klara will nurse dutifully through her years of cancer, but Klara's tranquillity and her creations in cloth and wood will be disturbed by an intrusion "some part of her considered . . . an act of vandalism." (p. 40) Another young villager, Eamon O'Sullivan, from the only Irish family in the Bavarian village, decides to pay court to her. They had met while skating: "Klara had turned suddenly and they had crashed together, had fallen, as if killed in combat. Then they had lain quite still on the ice, mysterious, and knowing something neither could speak about." (p. 35) There is a foreshadowing again in their meeting. "As if killed in combat" refers not only to the violence of the emotions they will arouse in each other, but also to the carnage to come.

Eamon O'Sullivan comes every evening to the Becker home, but never speaks other than in monosyllables and then only to the grandfather and the father, who dub him "Silent Irish." Klara prays every night for "'One word . . . one sentence.' She had never in her short life been this perplexed by anyone." (p. 36) The tension of the silent courtship is remarkable – "she could feel Eamon's gaze touch her like a warm hand between her shoulder blades" (p. 41) – and when Klara demands that he finally speak, I was dry-mouthed in anticipation of his answer. The brevity of his response – "'And what is it you would have me say? . . . What can I possibly say to you?'" (p. 42) – is typical of Jane Urquhart's poetic economy. It says everything about his feelings of unworthiness and the pain of his love, feelings a lesser writer than Urquhart would have needed extensive prose to convey. In his inarticulate torment, Eamon first clutches at Klara's arm and then leaves the Becker home. At this point, Urquhart adds great power to the scene by focusing on the minutest concrete detail, in contrast to the intangible but raging emotion of the previous lines:

The shaft of setting sun that had so troubled Klara's eyes was now on the chair where Eamon had been sitting. He had forgotten his jacket. Klara's arm remained near her stomach, where it had come to rest after Eamon released it. It looked like a foreign object to her, something that was not now and had never been connected to her body. She watched with some interest as colour gradually returned to the white marks his fingers had left on her skin. (p. 43)

After six weeks of absence, Eamon finds a reason to speak. He comes to Klara to order a fine red waistcoat and then, in confessing how he thinks of her, reveals to Klara the soul of a poet. As she measures him, Eamon punctuates her movements with declarations of love:

> "Do you know," he asked, his voice breaking slightly, "do you know that your hands are like doves? . . .
> "You," he said, "with your neck like a swan." This statement was delivered when Klara had both arms around his middle and her cheek near his beating heart. "You who'll have nothing to do with a man like me." . . .
> "I'll die of this," he told her. "These words about you running and running through my mind. . . .
> "And me remaining silent for months and months, tasting the humiliation of knowing that once I spoke you'd be gone from me like a startled bird. . . .
> "I'll die of this," he said, and kissed her on the mouth.
> Klara found that she was kissing him back and the surprise caused her throat to constrict. (pp. 79–80)

The images Eamon fashioned for Klara are made tangible when, typically hidden from view, he flies a kite for his beloved to see. "Klara found herself smiling as she realized that he must have used his mother's bedsheets or muslin curtains in an attempt to make the object look like a bird. A swan. A dove." (pp. 86–87)

Eamon gives Klara a book of his father's songs from Ireland, and, in the fragments Klara shares with the reader, there are dark forebodings of damage to the self and of death:

> *A black frost has withered my heart*
> *She has taken the light from the hills of Cloonaughlin*
> *And I and my life are apart.* (p. 109)
> . . .

The minstrel boy has gone to war, she had read earlier in the morning, *in the ranks of death you'll find him.* (p. 114)

But there is no thought of the future for the young couple in the perfection of the moment.

By July it seemed that every one of Klara's senses had opened to the light of the long, long days. The scent of freshly chiselled wood in the shop, or of cloth in the sunroom, the taste of salt on new potatoes, the coolness of a damp cloth on her neck in the morning. . . . All this gave her joy. But, shaken by the thrill of this boy's touch, she was vulnerable now to things that in the past she might have ignored. Anything at all, a sharp word from her father, the sight of a newborn calf, even a flower wilting on a stem, could bring tears to her eyes. (pp. 120–21)

Finally they make love, and it is the most beautiful of moments: "Klara cried out once, in pain, then felt herself sink into an unrecognizable ache of tenderness. She would remember this forever, this act they called sin, her body boneless, some new vine flowering in her veins." (p. 130)

When I met Ms. Urquhart at a literary festival in Montreal, I told her how moved I had been by the love scenes in *The Stone Carvers*, and she did not disagree with me when I said the novel had a warmth that I had never felt in her earlier novels. I cannot imagine anything more lovely than the exchanges between Crazy Phoebe and Ham Bone or the beauty of the union of Klara Becker and Eamon O'Sullivan.

But the outside world of great affairs intrudes, and, minutes after Eamon speaks to Klara of marriage, Klara's father tells them that war has been declared. Eamon, always in love with kites and birds and flight, feels compelled to join the conflict, hoping desperately that he will be allowed to fly. He alone in Shoneval, a community thankful it has escaped the hatreds of the Old World, goes off to Europe, and Klara, bitterly resentful of his leaving, refuses to marry him before he goes. She resents more than she can say the loss of his presence. She had found him so perfect.

Klara loved each detail of his face, the fringe of black eyelashes and the perfectly shaped eyebrows that some might say were wasted on a boy. The unblemished jewels of his green eyes, the fine pale skin lightly dusted by freckles, the small white scar on his temple, and his full, expressive mouth. She had leaned forward once to touch his lips lightly with her fingers as if they were unusual flowers she had discovered and wanted to remember the texture of. (p. 120)

Alone, Klara puts away all the clothes she had worn with Eamon and burns the picnic basket they had used together. Eamon had left her with the words "'I can only hope that you'll love me better when I get back,'" (p. 141) but Klara, adding that touch of the supernatural to ordinary events that Margaret Atwood remarked upon, walks through her silent house "lighting lamp after lamp in the midnight gloom. Then she extinguished these same lamps one after another." (p. 141) The moment must surely have been intended by Jane Urquhart to remind us of the prophetic words of Lord Grey in 1914: "The lamps are going out all over Europe; we shall not see them lit again in our lifetime."

When the news comes of Eamon's death, not as an airman but as a foot soldier, we are as unsurprised as we are by the outcome of Greek tragedy. Stoically, Klara says, "I'll not speak of this again," (p. 163) and gives up not only mention of Eamon but also her much-loved carving and her ongoing project of the wooden abbess. It is her grandfather Joseph who ends the first section of the novel on a note of hope:

> "Someday," Joseph said to his granddaughter, "someday something will happen and you will want to go back to the carving. You won't be able to prevent yourself; that's just the way it is. The world always somehow takes us back to the chisel. Something happens and we have to respond." (p. 167)

The event Joseph Becker foresees that will restore Klara to her senses and to her carving will not come for another twenty years. After three decades away, Klara's brother, Tilman, returns to the family farm at Shoneval.

Much happens to Tilman on his road to recovery from the wounds he suffered when his mother and father chained him up like an animal. After six years of wandering alone, Tilman falls in with a much older tramp, Nicolo Vigamonti, nicknamed Refuto because of his hilarious habit of speaking only in negatives. Refuto has chosen topsy-turvy speech because he has declared himself a non-person, burdened as he is by the guilt of having urged a brother to take a dangerous job that caused his death. The pain is real but so is the humour, and there is a delightful Dickensian eccentricity and charm in his conversations with Tilman. When Tilman mentions Refuto's arms and the strength they display in chopping wood, an indignant Refuto challenges him with "'What arms? Who says I got arms?'" (p. 200)

Tilman and Refuto criss-cross the whole of Canada, riding the rails, until Refuto summons the courage to return to face his people, a close-knit clan of Italian immigrants in Hamilton. Their loving embrace heals Refuto's wounds, and he resumes his craft of carving the wooden patterns used in the cottage industry of making iron stoves. Thus in the little history of Nicolo Vigamonti does Jane Urquhart state small the theme of her novel, the redemption of the damaged soul through love and art.

Refuto has a son, Giorgio, of Tilman's age, and through Giorgio, an apprentice to a tombstone-maker, Tilman learns the delights of working marble. Giorgio loves in particular the carving of the names of the deceased. His is a love affair with the alphabet. As he declares later, "'There is absolutely nothing like the carving of names. Nothing like committing to the stone this record of someone who is utterly lost.'" (p. 347)

After four years with Refuto and his son, Giorgio, in Hamilton, Tilman is again possessed by his wanderlust and goes off to fight in France, where he loses a leg at Vimy Ridge. The post-war period sees a crippled Tilman carving wooden legs for amputees, but as the demand is met, he is reduced to odd jobs and sleeping at missions. In 1930 he is reunited with Giorgio, who has also taken to the life of the open road. Mass production has made the handcrafted Vigamonti iron stoves obsolete, and the Depression has diminished the call for elaborate marble memorials. Jane Urquhart gives a fine lesson in the Canadian history of the period to those who care to follow carefully the story of this one Italian immigrant family. It is another instance of her love for "smaller histories from smaller archives."

When in 1934 Giorgio hears that carvers are needed for a Canadian memorial at Vimy, he goes to join the workers already there, all Italian and all steeped in the Italian tradition of marble carving. He urges Tilman to go with him, but Tilman has other plans. After an absence of thirty years, he has decided to return to the family farm, the place of his grievous hurt.

Klara takes her brother's return and his account of Giorgio going to Vimy as a sign that she must return to carving. Shoneval has always refused to erect a war memorial, and the lover whose name Klara never speaks has no monument to mark his passing. "'I want to do it now, Tilman,' Klara continued. 'I want to carve. We should go to that man Allward's monument, where your friend is, in France.'" (p. 248)

Disguised as a man, for Allward would be reluctant to employ a woman, Klara goes with her brother to the great unfinished project in Picardy. We know it will be at Vimy that all the narratives of the novel will reach their climax, but Jane Urquhart takes time out for a digression that made me laugh out loud.

On their arrival at Le Havre, Klara treats Tilman to his first-ever meal at a restaurant, and Tilman falls head-over-heels in love with *haute cuisine*. One mouthful of *Coquilles St-Jacques meunière* and another of *Jambon d'Alsace à la crème*, and Tilman has an immediate recovery from a week and a half of seasickness. He comes to the point where, having discovered restaurants, these "miraculous establishments," he is reluctant to continue their journey – "'How can you just walk away from that fish soup? We could have it again tonight.'" (p. 298)

At Vimy, Klara continues her role as a man, claiming damaged vocal chords to disguise her woman's voice. She is attracted to Giorgio and his manifest love of the whole of humanity – "No person was to him too young, too old, too withdrawn or effusive to be interesting" (p. 363) – but it is the monument itself that has her whole attention. When the white plaster models of the angels are hoisted up to the elevated studio, "she was rapt, certain she had seen the expression on an angel's face change." (p. 305)

One spring dawn, Klara wakens early to creep into the studio and carve Eamon O'Sullivan's features into the face of one of the torchbearers. Surprised by Allward, she falls. She is unmasked as a woman, but Allward's greater horror is that one of his allegorical figures should have an individual face. Allward sees the skill of the work, however, and he is moved by Klara's confession, "'There was a boy I knew. . . .'" (p. 339)

The historical Allward is a figure of whom we know very little, other than the record of his work, but Jane Urquhart has made the Allward of her novel a full and complex human being. He is persuaded of the importance of the monument as memories fade, and the responsibility he finds overwhelming.

Rarely now did women weep in their beds for a man whose face and body they had known in the teens of the century, or for a child the earth took back too soon. Allward began to feel like a vessel into which the world's diminishing sorrow was poured for safe-keeping, and the weight of it was heavy on his bones. (p. 351)

Allward has been driven for more than a decade. It took him years to find exactly the right marble, at a quarry in Yugoslavia, years of resisting protests from the Canadian government against the delay and the spiralling costs. It took two full years to build the access roads to the monument, years in which hundreds of Chinese labourers lost their lives to unexploded bombs. Allward has sacrificed others, but he has also sacrificed himself, and all this goes through his mind as he looks upon the work of the young woman, initially hired to be no more than a polisher and general factotum.

Allward understands the young woman's sorrow and her need for reconciliation with the past. He knows that all the emotion he had himself felt for Canada's fallen "was entering the monument itself, the huge urn he had designed to hold grief," (p. 377) and he allows the face to remain.

Klara will continue to work on the monument, though as a woman under Allward's protection and sleeping in his office.

Now she has to face her desire for Giorgio. After all the years spent in a non-life at Shoneval, she has difficulty in coming back to living, and Urquhart handles her misgivings brilliantly: "Now that he knew she was a woman she felt middle-aged and unattractive. She found herself trying to remember what her woman's body looked like, whether there was anything left there that a man like Giorgio might receive as a gift." (p. 345) But Giorgio, after many relationships and in the middle of his life, has also fallen in love, and he and Klara will find physical and spiritual union in those same dank tunnels at Vimy "out of which thousands of young men had rushed into the brimstone air." (p. 355)

For Klara, their love is a resurrection: "And then there was the delight in the discovery that a woman of her age could still succumb to the warmth of passion, could feel this smooth, manageable desire, allow it to enter her life." (p. 357)

Giorgio has heard the whole story of Eamon O'Sullivan from Tilman, and, in his generosity of spirit, discovering that Eamon's name has not yet been carved, takes Klara to execute the name in the marble. "Klara knew this would be the last time she touched Eamon, that when they finished carving his name all the confusion and regret of his absence would unravel, just as surely as if she had embraced him with forgiving arms." (p. 376) Thus does Klara finally achieve a reassembling of herself, more complete than she could ever have imagined.

Meanwhile, her brother has been moving along his own road to healing, to the point at which the cracked pot of the self is made whole again. Motivated by his new-found love of fine food, Tilman has used every period of rest at Vimy to walk and hitchhike to the nearby town of Arras, where he makes a friend of the huge chef at the Hôtel Picardie. Monsieur Recouvrir is a veteran of the Battle of Verdun and still picks shrapnel from his body, "fragments that now and then, like Tilman's own memories, worked themselves to the surface." (p. 325) As the time of wholeness approaches, Urquhart intensifies the imagery of fragmentation. In addition to Recouvrir's shrapnel and Tilman's memories, there are the shards of marble Tilman gives to Klara as souvenirs, and the pocket bibles, photographs, scraps of uniform, and stained letters still being uncovered each spring by the farmers' ploughs. (p. 347)

Tilman and Monsieur Recouvrir recognize in each other a fellow craftsman, and Tilman begins an informal apprenticeship in his friend's kitchens. On his first visit to Recouvrir's apartment, Tilman, who had always hated to be touched, the hatred a visible sign of his alienation, "realized he had not flinched when the plump arm had touched his shoulder." (p. 327) So begins a delicate courtship that culminates in full physical union. It is perhaps the most beautiful of the many beautiful sentences of the novel when Tilman and Monsieur Recouvrir – what a perfect name, "recover," – first make love and "two damaged, fragmented middle-aged men made each other fresh and beautiful and whole again." (p. 330)

With the completion of the Vimy monument, which seems to have assumed into itself all the sorrows of the participants, our characters go to continue their lives in Canada. Tilman and Monsieur Recouvrir open a restaurant together in Montreal, Le monument de l'archange, whose name is an acknowledgement of the first name of Father Gstir who began the whole story. Klara and Giorgio go to the Becker farm in Shoneval. They marry, and Tilman and Recouvrir attend the wedding. Tilman gives the whistle to Klara that Crazy Phoebe had given him so many years before. He says that, as he wandered, he used the whistle "'as a kind of summons . . . [hoping] that someone would come.'" "'No one ever came,'" he adds, but Recouvrir contradicts him: "'Someone answered when it was a long time. It is impossible, I know, but someone answered.'" (p. 385)

All the loose ends are tied together as neatly as in any of the nineteenth-century novels that Ms. Urquhart so admires, but the novel does not end well for everyone. Allward, back in Toronto, cannot let go of the Vimy Memorial: "Traces of its brooding presence entered every drawing he made." And he has a reputation that precedes him; "his memorials took too long, cost too much money." (p. 379) In the end he is reduced to taking quiet walks to visit his earlier works in the park in front of the provincial legislature. The Second World War would be agony for him, imagining all the time that his creation would be destroyed in the conflict and that the site at Vimy would again be a landscape of tangled bodies and "burning clots of brimstone rained down from a savage sky." The Vimy Memorial would emerge in 1945 unscathed, however, but its creator would fade into the past. "Even those Canadians who would later make the trip to France and who would admire the monument would rarely take the trouble to ask the sculptor's name." (p. 381)

It is a supreme irony that the creator of the monument that brought healing to so many should not have found an inner peace himself.

The novel began with builders and buildings – such as Father Gstir and his church and his master, King Ludwig II of Bavaria, who built fairy-tale castles on the peaks of mountains – and it continued with Joseph Becker, who built the great altar for Father Gstir's church, and Klara Becker, who finally completed her wooden abbess and gave her a face full of peace. We end the novel with Allward's great creation at Vimy, and, in the last paragraph, we are told that all the buildings, churches, castles, and monuments "disperse light and strength and consolation long after the noise of the battle has ended."

It is clear that no one remembers Walter Allward, and I think I am typical in remembering only fragments of the story of Ludwig – that he built castles, patronized Wagner, went mad, and drowned himself. Only the Beckers remember Father Gstir, and Klara and Tilman have no children to continue the oral tradition. But time is the enemy not only of humankind but also of humankind's creations. I read recently that the names on the Vimy Memorial are being erased by weather and water leeching from the stone. It will come to pass one day that, like Shelley's ruined statue and its inscription in the desert, both the monument and its intention will cease to have meaning. That which we are and that which we create will all come to dust, Father Gstir's optimism notwithstanding.

In a world of impermanence, all we can cling to, it seems to me, is love and the joy of creation. We know that both are ephemeral and that for some people they are not enough, even temporarily – love could not save Crazy Phoebe – but they really are all that we have, and Jane Urquhart has done us a great service in reminding us of that essential truth.

AUNT JULIA AND THE SCRIPT-WRITER

Mario Vargas Llosa
(New York: Avon, 1985)

Mario Vargas was born in Peru in 1936. His given names were Jorge Mario Pedro, and in the Spanish tradition his mother's maiden name, Llosa, was added to his father's family name. He was born into the 8 percent of Peru's population of twenty-three million who are proud to claim descent from the Spanish *conquistadores* of the sixteenth century. Of white European heritage, they rank socially and economically far above the 46 percent of the population who are of Inca or other South American Indian blood and above the *mestizos*, the 46 percent who are of mixed Spanish and South American Indian ancestry. At the very bottom of the social scale are the relatively few blacks, the descendants of slaves, usually immigrants to Peru from other South American countries.

There are strong elements of autobiography in *Aunt Julia and the Script-Writer*, close similarities between Mario the author and Marito (a diminutive of Mario) the protagonist of the novel. Both were living, with a million other people, in Lima in 1954, the year in which the novel is set. Both were subjects of the military dictator General Odría, who ruled Peru from 1948 to 1956. Both were students at the same time, although the author was enrolled in the prestigious military academy while his creation Marito is a student of law. Both the author and his creation find employment part-time as a news director at a small radio station. Both get married at the age of eighteen to a woman named Julia, a former aunt by marriage who is, at thirty-two, fourteen years older, and both the real Mario and the invented Marito go off to Paris to escape a disapproving family and to begin a writing career. Both author and creation will be divorced after eight years of marriage.

We should, however, beware of regarding this novel as a memoir. In one of his many essays, "Is Fiction the Art of Lying?" (1968), Vargas points out that all so-called truth is made up of contradictory testimony, manipulated historical data, unreliable witness, and faulty memory. This is even truer of fictionalized material where the author is in complete control. To achieve his aesthetic effect, he can add, omit, or distort. The reader cannot know the changes that have been wrought. The business of the novelist, Vargas suggests, is to present no more than the *appearance* of seamless truth. Truth is not an absolute in itself; it is only one of many tools in the hands of the writer and can be sacrificed, fully or partially, in the service of his fiction. The character and world of the novel need have no reference to any external entity, except inasmuch as that reference may make the internal world of the novel appear more believable to the reader.

With that caveat in mind, let me give a brief overview of Vargas's life and work to date. His sojourn in Europe after 1954 included not only his eight years with Aunt Julia, but a doctorate earned at the University of Madrid with a dissertation on Gabriel García Márquez and work at radio and TV stations in Paris. His first novel, *The Time of the Hero*, came out in 1963, after his divorce, and established his reputation as a writer. A parody of life in a Peruvian military academy, it contained both autobiographical elements and an examination of *machismo*, that very Spanish-American emphasis on the heroic role that men of Vargas's culture are called upon to play in life.

In the nine novels that have followed, Vargas has often experimented with a multiple narrative viewpoint, changing the narrative voice frequently and without warning. Most of the novels demand the reader's full attention in order that he or she may establish who is speaking at any given moment. Almost all the novels present a panoramic chronicle of Peruvian society, deriving their strength from the fullness with which a large and diverse cast is portrayed. Vargas has a wonderful eye for detail, but the reader has to concentrate in order to keep control of the whole. This concentration is especially necessary in what Vargas has often claimed as his favourite novel, *The War of the End of the World* (1981), his only novel set outside Peru. The novel is set during a real revolt by Brazilian workers against the cruelty of the central government at the end of the nineteenth century. The story is told from myriad viewpoints and, in the end, it is the reader who must write the story, piecing it together from all the lies, the inventions, the myths, the realities, the unreliable testimony. Vargas used the technique again in *The Real Life of Alejandro Mayta* (1984), in which the reader has to sort through an immense amount of contradictory but fascinating and exquisitely delineated detail. By the time the reader finishes the novel, mentally rearranging it to make a coherent whole, he or she will have gone through a very interesting process of self-discovery. Why did the reader accept some of the evidence and reject other parts? What personal criteria and prejudices were brought to bear?

In fact, I chose to review *Aunt Julia and the Script-Writer* from among all of Vargas's works because I think it is the most accessible of his novels. Written in Spanish in 1977, the novel, like most of Vargas's creations, is set during the Odría military dictatorship. For most of Peru's history since it won its independence from Spain in 1835, the country has been governed by military autocrats. There have been only a few brief periods of civilian rule, notably the Prado administration during the Second World War. Peru seemed set to enjoy a new era of democracy in 1990, when the presidential election was won by Alberto Fujimori, the son of a Japanese immigrant, but he, too, succumbed to the temptations of power and soon suspended the constitution, dissolved Parliament, and began to rule by decree. Fujimori's opponent in the 1990 election was Mario Vargas. The writer's emphasis in his essays and novels on the importance of democracy, a free market, and individual liberty had won him a political as well as a literary reputation. He was regarded as a champion of cultural and intellectual freedom, but initially had no political ambition and refused the prime ministership of Peru when it was offered to him in the early eighties. Vargas saw the writer's function as "non-conformism and rebellion . . . protest, contradiction and criticism," a function he defined in his famous speech "Literature Is Fire" in Caracas in 1967, when he accepted the Rómulo Gallegos Prize for his second novel, *The Green House*. Vargas feared that, if he were co-opted into mainstream Peruvian politics, he would compromise his mission as a writer. He was, however, finally persuaded by his admirers to campaign for the presidency in 1990. After he lost, he very sensibly left Peru to live and write in Spain. Defeated rivals to would-be dictators in South America cannot look forward to a secure future with any great degree of confidence.

All of Vargas's novels share the same concerns: the differences between urban Spanish and rural Indian life; the effects of the dictatorships that have so bedevilled Peruvian history; the manifestations of that streak of cruelty brought to South America by the Spanish Inquisition of the sixteenth century; and the mix of sensuality and sexuality that seems particular to hot and Catholic countries together with the tension between that sensuality and the Catholic awareness of sin. He also has a profound interest in the effect of social institutions on individual identity. What, for example, does it mean to the individual to be born into a society so prone not only to dictatorship but also to rigidly defined sex roles?

How to do justice to both the seriousness of these concerns and the hilarity that pervades this truly funny novel? Let me begin by describing my reaction as I began to read the book.

We are told at the very beginning that this is a novel of memory, set "in those long-ago days" of the fifties, when General Odría was dictator in Peru. We met Mario (Marito), a member of Lima's Spanish-heritage upper class. While his parents are in the United States, Marito is looked after by his grandparents and a host of uncles and aunts, notably Uncle Lucho and Aunt Olga. He is eighteen, a law student, and the part-time news director of Radiopanamerica, a flea-bitten operation that broadcasts hourly news bulletins plagiarized from the newspapers. He has one assistant in the newsroom, Pascual, a superbly eccentric character who has an obsession with catastrophe. The moment Marito's back is turned, Pascual slips unbelievably horrendous news items into the program. One delicious set piece is fifteen minutes of broadcast time devoted to a pitched battle between lepers and gravediggers. Small matter that the battle took place in some remote village in India a number of years earlier. For Pascual, it is the stuff of contemporary life, and he reports the incident as if he were reporting live.

Radiopanamerica has a sister radio station called Radio Central, devoted mainly to soap operas, so dear to the heart of all South American audiences. The soap operas are imported from Cuba and are bought by the weight of the paper, seventy kilos at a time. All the soap operas are acted out by the same cast, headed by a cross-eyed dwarf and a woman with a pronounced moustache.

I enjoyed the first chapter very much, with its detailed account of life in upper-crust Lima and the daily doings of Marito and his family, and I loved the machinations at the radio station. Anxious to bypass its Cuban suppliers, the station hires Pedro Camacho, the Bolivian soap-opera script-writer himself. There is also the titillating hint of incest. Marito, involved as he is with his studies and his work at the radio station, finds the time to take his Aunt Julia to the cinema. The *Tia Julia* of the title, she is not Marito's blood relative but the thirty-two-year-old divorced sister of Uncle Lucho's wife, Olga. She is only going to the cinema with Marito to avoid the unwelcome attentions of an elderly suitor, but there is just the suggestion of a romance to come between the eighteen-year-old boy and his much older relative.

Properly involved with both narrative movements, I began Chapter 2. It centres on Dr. Alberto de Quinteros, a fashionable gynecologist with his own private clinic. I assumed that he is some relative of Marito's, an uncle perhaps, and I waited for the relationship to be made clear. Vargas's earlier novels had prepared me for a large cast of characters. His description was, I thought, a little banal, a little clichéd, "broad forehead, aquiline nose, penetrating gaze, the very soul of rectitude and goodness," (p. 18) but I was prepared to forgive the triteness of the sentence. After all, Vargas was being translated from the Spanish, and perhaps the translator had not done justice to the original.

At fifty, Dr. de Quinteros is perfect. Always fit and in good humour as a result of his daily workouts, he is looking forward to the marriage of his favourite niece, Elianita. She is as beautiful as he is handsome.

Only two points trouble the good doctor. Why is Elianita's brother, the equally gorgeous Richard, so downcast? And why did Elianita choose a groom as dim-witted as Red Antúnez?

Every detail of the wedding day is perfectly planned and superbly executed. Yet the bride is overcome, faints, and is examined by her uncle. He discovers that Elianita is three to four months pregnant and informs Red Antúnez of her condition. The bridegroom immediately goes into shock and it is clear that there has been no premarital sex between the engaged couple. In the garden, the doctor comes across a suicidal Richard who confesses to being the cause of his sister's pregnancy: "'I love her as a man loves a woman and I don't give a damn about all the rest, Uncle.'" (p. 37)

As the chapter ends, "a whirlwind of unanswered questions circled around and around" in the doctor's mind:

> Would Red Antúnez desert his reckless, foolhardy spouse that very night? Might he have done so already? Or would he say nothing, and giving proof of what might be either exceptional nobility or exceptional stupidity, stay with that deceitful girl whom he had so persistently pursued? Would there be a great public scandal, or would a chaste veil of dissimulation and pride trampled underfoot forever hide this tragedy of San Isidro? (p. 39)

I finished the chapter full of uncertainty. I thought I could distinguish a structural link between the second chapter and the first: the hint of a future incestuous relationship between Marito and Aunt Julia has its counterpart in the fully realized authentic incest between Elianita and Richard. But who on earth were these people, and what was their relationship to Marito? And why did Vargas the writer descend from the polished prose of the first chapter to the vulgar drama of the second, and, in particular, to the inflated hyperbole of the final rhetorical questions? I leaped to Chapter 3 for answers.

We are now back to Marito and Radiopanamerica, where Pedro Camacho works seventeen hours every day to produce eight to ten half-hour instalments of various soap operas. Short and fiftyish, the scriptwriter has some very bizarre idiosyncrasies. He hates Argentinians, introduces unflattering references to them in his scripts at every opportunity, and never, ever, reads the work of any other writer in case they might influence his style. We attribute his anti-Argentine prejudice, at least for the moment, to the fact that his soap operas have long been pirated by Argentinian radio stations without credit or the payment of royalties.

Vargas has spoken at length about Pedro Camacho:

> Pedro Camacho never existed. When I started to work for the radio in the early fifties, I knew a man who wrote radio serials for Radio Central in Lima. He was a real character who functioned as a kind of script machine: He wrote countless episodes with incredible ease, hardly taking the time to reread what he'd written. I was absolutely fascinated by him, maybe because he was the first professional writer I'd ever known. But what really amazed me was the vast world that

seemed to escape from him like an exhalation; and I became absolutely captivated by him when he began to do what Pedro Camacho does in the book. One day, the stories he wrote started overlapping and getting mixed up and the radio station received letters from the audience alerting them to certain irregularities like characters traveling from one story to the next. That's what gave me the idea for *Aunt Julia and the Script-Writer*. But obviously, the character in the novel goes through many transformations, he has little to do with his model, who never went crazy. I think he left the station [and] took a vacation. (Vargas interviewed by Ricardo A. Setti, *The Paris Review*, Vol. 32, No. 116, Fall 1990, pp. 46–72)

In Chapter 3 we are also introduced to further members of Marito's family and Lima's upper class, including Don Adolfo, Aunt Julia's unwanted suitor. It is well-known that his wife divorced him for his impotence, a condition caused by a pimp's knife attack while Don Adolfo was cavorting with a prostitute. He is now busy courting Aunt Julia, but she makes her position very clear in one of the very many comic speeches that decorate the novel. Speaking of both Don Adolfo's impotence and his advances towards her, she says, "'If I were certain he'd stay that way, I'd marry him for his dough. . . . But what if I cured him? Can't you just see that old gaffer trying to make up for lost time with me?'" (p. 47)

The narrative moves forward with Marito stealing two kisses from an astounded but not entirely displeased Aunt Julia.

Interesting, I think, but I am anxious to know what happened to Richard and Elianita.

The fourth chapter brings me even greater frustration. We are still in Lima – we are almost always in Lima – but the stage is occupied by a completely new character, police sergeant Lituma. He is described as "a man in the prime of life, his fifties . . . [with a] broad forehead, aquiline nose, penetrating gaze, the very soul of rectitude and goodness." (p. 60) The description struck me like a blow, and I turned back to the description of Dr. Alberto de Quinteros. Identical! For the first time I understood the structure of the novel. What I had read in Chapter 2 and was now reading in Chapter 4 were instalments of Pedro Camacho's soap operas. There will be two movements, soap-opera instalments alternating with the developing romance and its concomitant difficulties. What will become increasingly clear is that the soaps, set in all the different strata of Peruvian society, will provide the reader with insight into the whole of the society through which Marito and Aunt Julia will move. Chapter 4, the Sergeant Lituma episode, is especially illuminating. Lituma apprehends an inarticulate and mysteriously scarred black vagrant and is ordered by his superiors to take him to the beach, shoot him, and leave his body at the city dump. The prose of the chapter is spare and bleak, perfectly suited to the grimness of the subject. As Sergeant Lituma muses on what he is told to do, he repeats the rationale of his superiors: " '[I]f you let this character loose in the middle of the city, the only way he can survive is to steal. Or else he'll just die like a dog. We're really doing him a favor.' " (p. 81) This passage and the racist comments of the other policemen, who call the black man "a sambo," have the ring of truth, and I believe that we are witness to the possible fate of the very poor, especially the black very poor, throughout South America. What is even more horrifying is the response by the audience to this particular episode. The radio listeners accept that Sergeant Lituma's orders are normal. They see nothing untoward in what he is told to do: there is no moral outrage; the only interest is in what happens next. "Would he obey? Would the shot ring out? Would the dead body of the mysterious immigrant roll over onto the heap of unidentifiable rotting garbage? Or would his life be spared, would he flee, blindly, wildly, along the beaches beyond the city?" (p. 83)

There are other instalments as grim. In the alleged rape of a thirteen-year-old girl by a Jehovah's Witness, we are shown the extreme prejudice of a staunchly Catholic society against those who differ. In the story of the rodent exterminator Don Federico, who wages a lifelong war against the rats who ate his little sister, we meet the embodiment of misogyny in a society where man is king and machismo the norm. Over and over we come against the double standard that demands an experienced groom and a virgin bride.

But these fascinating soaps are not only a mirror of Peruvian life; they are brilliant little stories in themselves, often moving, often haunting, and always leavened with a humour deriving from the profound bigotry of their creator, Pedro Camacho. In one story centred on a miserly landlady of Argentinian descent we learn that "she has forced everyone staying at the *pensión* to adopt the Argentine habit – so widespread in the dwellings of that sister country – of flushing the toilet only once a day (she pulls the chain herself, just before going to bed)." (p. 208)

From his soap operas, we learn as much about Camacho himself as we do about Peru. On the one hand, we have the ubiquitous slums, the over-crowded jails, the wretched shantytowns of the Indians flocking to the outskirts of Lima; the pervasive amorality of the Odría dictatorship; and the conservative inertia of the upper class. On the other, we note that Vargas has created a writer who is the perfect example of a great natural talent without formal training. Camacho is capable of generating simple, compelling prose and dialogue, but it is interspersed with absurd hyper-bole and an evident love of long esoteric words, frequently invented by this gifted amateur who longs to impress his listeners. I looked in vain in my dictionary for "oligphrenic," "terratological," and "chremastic." All of Camacho's heroes are, like him, fifty or thereabouts, and all, unlike him, are built like Greek gods. Time and time again, the characters of his soap operas reiterate the claim that science has proved that only in his fifties does a man achieve his physical, sexual, and spiritual peak.

Camacho is a wonderful invention. Forced to produce so many hours of serials a day, six days every week, the little Bolivian begins to dress up as his characters to facilitate invention, but we can trace the progress of his mental collapse as he begins to lose control of his creations. Alberto de Quinteros the gynecologist begins to reappear variously as a cardiologist, a pediatrician, a priest, and a faith healer. Lituma becomes a captain, a cor-poral, once again a sergeant, and finally the mother superior of a convent. The illegitimate son of Richard and Elianita plays different roles in different serials, and children who die reappear full of life the following day. It is significant that this confusion does no harm to the radio ratings, up 20 percent, and the station's owners, Genaro father and son, even see the confusion as existentialist in a lovely jibe by Vargas at those who insist on seeing chaos as profundity.

Camacho tries desperately to regain control by killing off his charac-ters in multiple catastrophes: fires, earthquakes, and mass drownings. Some he even kills off twice. But the damage has been done. His frenzy of creativity has burned itself out, and he is a shell at the end of the novel. But we too are burned out. As we read, we try to keep track of what is hap-pening, and it is like trying to impose order on a tornado. At the end of the novel, or at least at the end of the soap-opera chapters, we are as exhausted and drained as the scriptwriter himself. But, in spite of all the cruelty and poverty, how we have laughed!

We have laughed at Camacho's inspirational talks to his cast at the beginning of every broadcast. We have laughed when an adoring Josefina, she of the moustache, declares that Camacho has sanctified the acting profession in his provision of dreams for the multitudes. We have laughed at Camacho's radio attacks on the proverbial virility of Argentine men, asserting that nearly all of them practise homosexuality, preferably in the passive form. And we have laughed at the Puddler, Camacho's sound-effects man, who ends every instalment wild-eyed and shaking.

Meanwhile, the relationship between Marito and Aunt Julia has developed. As a counterpoint to the near-hysteria of the Camacho chapters, the forbidden romance has kept the novel firmly anchored in reality, although in the final chapters the romantic narrative begins to slip its moorings. Marito and Julia have never gone further than kisses and caresses, but eventually they are discovered and Marito's parents are summoned back from the United States. What has been a delicate and hesitant courtship blossoms into a full-scale affair, and the couple elope. After trying unsuccessfully to get a number of comically incompetent and/or corrupt town mayors to marry them – in scenes highly reminiscent of Camacho's soap operas (so does one narrative infect the other) – they finally do consummate their love and manage to get married, in that order. Even after that, Julia is briefly exiled to Chile, but finally the family is reconciled to the *fait accompli*, and the happy couple go off to Paris, where Marito will become a writer.

But we know that he is still a prisoner of his background. Exile from Peru does not necessarily mean exile from the world of machismo in which he grew up. During their courtship, Marito felt unable to let Julia pick up a cheque, and he had to work at seven different part-time jobs to support their relationship. Julia, too, is a prisoner of the attitudes of the class into which she was born – her speech is peppered with racist comments on "dusky chiquitas" and "sambas" – and both Marito and Julia were nurtured in an extended family where kinship is everything. However, flawed as they are, their defiance of convention must elicit our applause as, in the penultimate chapter, they appear to leave Peru and the novel for another world and a new beginning.

And then we come to the final chapter, a chapter I, for one, wish that Vargas had not written.

It is now many years later, and Marito returns to Lima. A successful writer, he has been long divorced from Julia after eight years of marriage. He is taken by Pablito, once a gofer at the radio station and now a restaurateur, to meet his old friend Pascual, now the chief copy editor at a vulgar tabloid. In comes Pedro Camacho, a wreck of a man, reduced to picking up items of information at police stations and kept on at the tabloid by its owner only for the comic relief he provides. In the cruelty of the laughter, I thought I detected a part of that legacy that Vargas thinks has been in the Peruvian psyche since the Inquisition of its Spanish conquerors in the sixteenth century.

Camacho has no memory of Marito, who discovers that the one-time scriptwriter of raw genius is married to a striptease dancer, a bullying woman of Argentine origin. It appears that they have long been married, separated only during Camacho's heyday of radio success. Now we understand what caused that odd strain of bitterness during Camacho's glory days.

But I did not want to know that, and I wish that I had not been told. I wanted to remember Camacho as a creative giant whose world collapsed under the weight of his imagination. I wanted to remember him as a whole person, containing multitudes of contradiction and prejudices and brilliance. I did not want the quirks of a ruined man explained to me.

And so I felt about Marito, now married to his new wife, his cousin Patricia, so sensible, so practical, and so determined not to put up with any nonsense from her husband. What a contrast with the exotic, flamboyant, exuberant personality of Aunt Julia.

I wanted to remember the madly-in-love Marito and the magnificently insane Camacho of the penultimate chapter. I wanted tragedy, not the satiric vision of fallen heroes compromising with a fallen world. The wildness, the passion, the defiance that had so informed the bulk of the novel have all disappeared under the cold scrutiny of time and reason. I was exhilarated during the novel as I was swept along by the frenzy of Camacho's creation and the frenzy of Marito's youthful passion. I know that the final chapter is more sensible and more likely and more akin to life as it is, and that is why I find it so unbearably sad.

Those who wish to label Vargas often see him as a deconstructionist, seeking to break apart the traditional, linear structure that has dominated the novel for nearly three centuries. There is some truth in that as far as many of his novels are concerned. They are full of changing narrative viewpoints and are often without regard to chronological development.

But *Aunt Julia and the Script-Writer* is a novel in the grand, traditional sense. It has done its didactic duty in presenting us with a portrait of a world unfamiliar to most of us, a complete picture of all the levels of Peruvian society. Within that believable world, Vargas has moved complex and fascinating characters. In the exquisite detail of the created world and in the superbly drawn characters, he has done all that the traditional novelist seeks to do. It should come as a surprise to no one that he is one of the world's great authorities on the works of Flaubert. Vargas shares with the master the ability to create outrageous characters whose outcome the reader cares deeply about.

If only he had ended with mad Camacho in a chaotic universe and the two lovers in each other's arms, defying the world with their forbidden romance. But that would have been contrary to Vargas's often expressed belief in the circular and satiric nature of the human comedy. I know that he is right, but in my rereadings of the novel, I always omit the final chapter. For me it is better thus.

PUBLISHER'S ACKNOWLEDGEMENTS

Excerpts from *Alias Grace* by Margaret Atwood, copyright © 1996 by O.W. Toad Ltd. Reprinted by permission of McClelland & Stewart Ltd., *The Canadian Publishers*.

Excerpts from *The Hiding Place* (Key Porter Books Ltd., 2000), copyright © 2000 by Trezza Azzopardi. With permission of the author.

Excerpts from *Disgrace* by J.M. Coetzee, copyright © 1999 by J.M. Coetzee. Reprinted by permission of Martin Secker & Warburg.

Excerpts from *Cold Mountain* by Charles Frazier, copyright © 1997 by Charles Frazier. Reprinted by permission of Grove/Atlantic, Inc.

Excerpts from *The Dress Lodger* by Sheri Holman, copyright © 2000 by Sheri Holman. Reprinted by permission of Grove/Atlantic, Inc.

Excerpts from *The Remains of the Day* by Kazuo Ishiguro, copyright © 1989 by Kazuo Ishiguro. Reprinted by permission of Alfred A. Knopf, a division of Random House, Inc.

Excerpts from *A Gesture Life* by Chang-rae Lee, copyright © 1999 by Chang-rae Lee. Reprinted by permission of Riverhead Books, a division of Penguin Putnam, Inc.